BABAYLAN SING BACK

BABAYLAN SING BACK

Philippine Shamans and Voice, Gender, and Place

Grace Nono

SOUTHEAST ASIA PROGRAM PUBLICATIONS

AN IMPRINT OF CORNELL UNIVERSITY PRESS   ITHACA AND LONDON

Southeast Asia Program Publications Editorial Board
Mahinder Kingra (ex officio)
Thak Chaloemtiarana
Chiara Formichi
Tamara Loos
Andrew Willford

Copyright © 2021 by Grace Nono

All rights reserved. Except for brief quotations in a review, this book, or parts thereof, must not be reproduced in any form without permission in writing from the publisher. For information, address Cornell University Press, Sage House, 512 East State Street, Ithaca, New York 14850. Visit our website at cornellpress.cornell.edu.

First published 2021 by Cornell University Press

Library of Congress Cataloging-in-Publication Data

Names: Nono, Grace, author.
Title: Babaylan sing back : Philippine shamans and voice, gender, and place / Grace Nono.
Description: Ithaca [New York] : Southeast Asia Program Publications, an imprint of Cornell University Press, 2021. | Includes bibliographical references and index.
Identifiers: LCCN 2021007690 (print) | LCCN 2021007691 (ebook) | ISBN 9781501760082 (hardcover) | ISBN 9781501760099 (paperback) | ISBN 9781501760105 (epub) | ISBN 9781501760112 (pdf)
Subjects: LCSH: Shamanism—Philippines. | Shamans—Philippines. | Women shamans—Philippines. | Women healers—Philippines. | Women mystics—Philippines. | Rites and ceremonies—Philippines. | Oral tradition—Philippines.
Classification: LCC BF1622.P6 N66 2021 (print) | LCC BF1622.P6 (ebook) | DDC 133.4309599—dc23
LC record available at https://lccn.loc.gov/2021007690
LC ebook record available at https://lccn.loc.gov/2021007691

To all Natives

My dream is for us to keep what we have alive by uniting as a tribe and by uniting with other tribes.

—Mendung Sabal

Contents

Preface ix
Acknowledgements xi

Introduction 1

1. Who Sings? A Baylan's Embodied Voice and its Relations 14
2. Shifting Voices and Malleable Bodies 63
3. Song Travels: Mumbaki Mobility and the Relationality of Place 123

Afterword 177

Notes 179
Glossary 201
Bibliography 209
Index 231

Preface

It is the 500th-year anniversary of the first contact between the Natives of the Philippine islands and the colonizers. Several groups are staging lavish celebrations to commemorate the arrival of Christianity and civilization. Others decry the centuries of brutal conquest of Native lands, the carnage of Native bodies, and continuing attempts to erase Native lives, histories, and identities. Still others memorialize Native survival, resistance, and ongoing negotiations of relations of domination.

The anticolonial revolutions waged by the colonized during the nineteenth and early twentieth centuries led to the creation of politically independent nation-states. Not a few have contended, however, that political independence has given rise to social hierarchies that have preserved colonial power structures. Greater social status has been accorded to those who are fluent in Spanish and English, are fair-skinned and conform to patriarchal and heterosexual gender ideologies, own private property, have formal education, membership in dominant religions, and residence in urban and First World locations. Within the nation-state, the social inequalities of citizens have been normalized alongside the imagined, nonredistributive form of "legal civil and political equality" (Anibal Quijano, "Coloniality of Power and Eurocentrism in Latin America," *International Sociology* 15, no. 2 [2000]: 222, 230). Among those who have found themselves at the lower rungs of the intersectional structure of domination are the Native ritual specialists who have been variously constructed by those at the centers of power in ways that have not allowed them to be heard. This book foregrounds the embodied voices of a number of Philippine Native ritual specialists as they contest hegemonic claims about the babaylan, voice, sex and gender, and place, and assert Native contributions to advancing history.

Acknowledgments

It took a village to birth this book.

The Native Philippine ritual specialists and their collaborators and interpreters whose voices saturate the succeeding pages deserve utmost mention: Mendung Sabal (since 1998), Lordina "Undin" Potenciano (since 2005), Mamerto "Lagitan" Tindongan (since 2012), Robilyn Coguit (since 2005), Jolina "Bie" Gulae (since 2018), Gunintang Freay (since 2019), Jose Havana and Florencia Havana (since 2000), and Myrna Pula (since 1998). Also noteworthy are the scholars whose works are amply cited in this work: Fe Mangahas, Zeus Salazar, Mary John Mananzan, Leny Strobel, Carolyn Brewer, Ellen Koskoff, Manolete Mora, and José Buenconsejo. My professors at New York University's Department of Music (2009–2014), headed by Suzanne Cusick (adviser), together with David Samuels, Martin Daughtry, Deborah Kapchan, and Tomie Hahn, helped me write the foundational text for this work. Ann Braude and Catherine Brekus (2015–2016) of the Harvard Divinity School's Women's Studies in Religion Program allowed me precious time, space, and library resources to develop my manuscript for publication, while Michael Jackson of Harvard Divinity School gave me much encouragement. Yale University professors Tisa Wenger, Evren Savci, and Willie Jennings (2017–2018) provided further insights for this book, and thanks go to the Asian Cultural Council for supporting my stay at Yale. The Institute of Spirituality in Asia, the ANVIL Publishing and Fundacion Santiago, the Center for Babaylan Studies, and the Tao Foundation for Culture and Arts—all publishers of my earlier works cited here—and my editors through the years, Bobby Malay and Martin Cohen, all deserve special mention.

Jim Lance of Cornell University Press, Sarah Grossman of Cornell's Southeast Asia Program Publications, and Mary Gendron of Westchester Publishing Services all deserve credit for their support of this book's publication.

I lovingly dedicate this work to my parents, Igmedio and Ramona, and my daughter, Tao.

To the Creator, ancestors, and other guides for blessing this book, making it possible,

maraming salamat po.

INTRODUCTION

On March 27, 2019, a young Agusan-Manobo woman named Robilyn Coguit spoke at an event in Manila that was part of the International Women's Month celebrations. Wearing a beautiful red dress that she herself embroidered in red, black, white, and yellow—the colors of her tribe—Robilyn spoke in fluent Tagalog to officials and rank and file alike. She discussed her work as a *manunuyam* (traditional embroiderer) and as a ritual specialist-in-training descended from generations of "babaylan" lineage holders. Many in the audience were bewildered, whispering to each other their disbelief that they were face to face with a babaylan novice. Weren't these priestesses wiped out by the Spanish and American colonizers who gifted Filipinos with Christianity and civilization? Just a week before, an article came out in a popular magazine describing these ritual specialists in the past tense, associating them with precolonial herbalism and women's power but also curses and black magic, until "God won," driving these resistant "witches" to their end.[1] With her embodied voice, Robilyn demonstrated that the babaylan have not disappeared. They are as much of the living present as those who write about them. In strong terms Robilyn asserted the beneficent roles of Native ritual specialists, whose services as helpers and curers are crucial to the survival of whole communities, especially those underserved by public institutions. Addressing concerns about her location in the city, contrary to the far-flung ancestral lands where many urban, middle-class folks imagine the babaylan to be, she explained that ritual specialists can be wherever they are needed. Her countenance calm and confident, Robilyn gave the impression of being assured in her power, a leader, supporting popular images of the babaylan as protofeminists and symbols of gender equality. Unknown to her audiences, Robilyn was then suffering from gender-related abuse, her response to her predicament generally departing from hegemonic feminist prescriptions.[2]

Embedded in the narrative about Robilyn's encounter with urban, middle-class audiences are several discourses about the babaylan. First is of the babaylan as a precolonial priestess, witch, and sorcerer who resisted colonization and was eliminated by it. Second is of the babaylan as a symbol of woman's power and gender equality. Third is of far-flung ancestral lands as the appropriate places for babaylan survivals, where traditions have been carried out since time immemorial. Different as these constructions are, they converge in depicting the babaylan as either of the silent past or of the marginal present, with no ability to intervene in ongoing historical processes. In her capacity as a twenty-first-century babaylan-in-training, Robilyn used her embodied voice to participate in babaylan discourse-construction, asserting herself as a historical subject capable of contesting hegemonic constructions of the babaylan.

This book foregrounds the voices of a number of ritual specialists who represent important aspects of Native epistemology, historical agency, and authority. When the European colonizers arrived in the sixteenth century, they observed voice to be an "important tool of cultural reinforcement in the lives of indigenous peoples."[3] They wasted no time in transforming this voice into a site of colonial control.[4] Considered savage, the Native voice was disciplined, softened, sweetened, and diminished in value when compared to writing, which the colonizers claimed possessed greater legitimacy.[5] In the hands of the colonizers and local elites, written discourses about Native ritual specialists proliferated in ways that did not necessarily give the latter voice. In more recent times the term "voice" was reclaimed by feminists as a metaphor for textual authority, power, agency, autonomy, and expressive freedom, a welcome development to many.[6] When the metaphor became too pervasive, however, some contended that this led to the repression of voice's physicality and, I might add, of people who have primarily operated from the spoken and/or sung word.[7] But while some written discourses have tended to silence certain groups, oral discourses among the subjugated have been noted to stimulate creative responses against the forces of domination. In her book *Talking Back*, activist scholar bell hooks provided a frame of reference for "speaking as an equal to an authority figure."[8] *Babaylan Sing Back* draws from hooks, replacing "talk" with "sing" to signal many of the Native Philippine ritual specialists' roles as oral singers and speakers and to index their often undifferentiated acts of singing and speaking.[9]

Babaylan?

The term *babaylan* as well as *bailan, baylan, baliana, balyana, babalyan* have been cited in five centuries of Philippine historical, anthropological, medical, religious, gender and sexuality, and decolonial literature. These terms have been used by many scholars to refer to ritual specialists in the Visayan region in central Philippines, specifically, among the Antiqueno, Aklanon, Capiznon, Panay-Bukidnon, Ati, Waray, Cebuano, Boholano, Cuyunon, Tagbanua, Palawan, and Batak peoples. In other areas of the Philippine archipelago, ritual specialists have been called similar names. Among the Bukidnon and the Manobo, the *bailan* or *baylan* have been reported; among the Bagobo, the *mabalian*; among the Tagakaolo, Mansaka, and Subanon, the *balian*; among the Mandaya, the *ballyan*; among the Teduray, the *beliyan*; among the Livunganen-Arumanen Manobo, the *walian*; among the Negrito, the *balyan*; among the Pampango, the *mamallyan* or *memallyan*; among the Ilocano, the *baglan*; and among the Gaddang, the *mabayan*. These ritual specialist titles have been noted to resemble those of the Ngadju Dyak of Indonesia and the Dusun of Malaysia where the priestess-shamanesses are also known as *balian*. In Kelantan, Malaysia, a similar ritual specialist is called *belian bomor*. Among the Sea Dyak in Malaysia, the séance of the *manang* had been noted as *belian*, and the impotent sexless priest-shaman as *manang bali*. In the rest of the Philippine ethnolinguistic groups, ritual specialist titles have borne no resemblance to the term babaylan. Scholars have referred to the ritual specialist among the Blaan as the *almo-os*; among the Kulaman as the *loKes*; among the T'boli as the *tau m'ton bu* or *tau meton bu*; among the Maguindanao as the *patutunong*; among the Maranao as the *pamomolong* or *pundarpaan*; among the Tausug as the *mangungubat*; among the Samal as the *mangubat*; among the Mangyan as the *pandaniwan*; among the Pangasinan as the *managanito*; among the Bontoc as the *insup-ok* or *insupak*; among the Ibaloy as the *mambunong*; among the Ibanag as the *mangilu*; among the Ifugao as the *mumbaki*; among the Kalanguya as the *mabaki*; among the Ilongot as the *magnigput*; among the Tinggian as the *alopogan*; among the Isneg as the *dorarakit*; among the Gaddang as the *makamong*; among the Ivatan as the *machanitu*; among the Kalinga as the *mandadadawak* or *andadadawak*; among the Kankanay as the *mambunong* or *mang-gengey*; and among the Tagalog as the *catalonan*.[10]

Other differences have been observed among Native ritual specialists. Numerous accounts have reported these to be predominantly women, while others have depicted them as male or transgender.[11] The ages of ritual specialists have further varied, with many scholars asserting the babaylans' mature age due to the amount of time required to master vast knowledges. I have, however, met some ritual specialists who were barely in their twenties or thirties.[12] The class status of ritual specialists has also differed, with a number of scholars claiming that from a position of privilege during precolonial times, many if not most Native ritual specialists have since been thrust to the bottom of the social ladder.[13] What this claim does not consider is the discrepant social locations of different ritual specialists within the same ethnolinguistic groups. Finally, ritual specialists have differed based on their respective communities' responses to the histories of colonization, resulting in greater hybridization in some areas than others with Christianity, or Islam, and/or secular modernity.

The widely discrepant geographic, linguistic, and social locations of Native Philippine ritual specialists have rendered the notion of a unified babaylan identity untenable. The term babaylan in this introduction functions more as a shorthand for the widely heterogeneous institution of ritual specialization. It additionally exposes exclusions engendered by hegemonic babaylan constructions.[14]

A Brief and Partial History of Babaylan Discourses

The five centuries of babaylan discourses have seen many Native ritual specialists defined by languages not their own, judged according to standards not their own, deemed wanting of religious conversion, development expansion, and metaphoric and/or hyperreal representation by interests not necessarily their own. The following section explores three interlocking babaylan discourses that emerged from, on the one hand, Spanish and American colonists and some Philippine scholars, and on the other, from a number of Philippine and Philippine diasporic gender and decolonial scholars and activists.

Archaic Witches and Agents of Superstition in a Dying Order

Backed by the Doctrine of Discovery, a fictional legal principle that traced itself to the Dark Ages, popes in the fifteenth century authorized European kings to invade, capture, vanquish, enslave, and subjugate Native lands and peoples outside of Europe.[15] The brutalities that the agents of colonization carried out were compounded by acts of characterizing, classifying, comparing, and evaluating—often in disparaging ways—the indigenes they encountered.[16] At a time when Europe was witnessing hundreds of thousands of women—especially those from lower classes—being tortured, hanged, and burned on charges of witchcraft and sorcery, the Spanish colonizers likewise renamed the Native women ritual specialists they encountered according to images with which they were already familiar:

as *hechicera* (witch, sorceress, old hag), *diablesa* (she-devil), *sacerdotisa del infierno* (priestess of hell), and *bruja* (witch, old hag).[17] Carolyn Brewer argues that by changing the meanings of "baylan" and "catalonan," these signifiers were negated from colonial dictionaries.[18] When some of the women ritual specialists fled to the mountains to lead their people in resistance against the colonial *reduccion*, the Spanish mounted Inquisition-like campaigns against them, hunting them down, confiscating their ritual instruments, and putting them to death.[19] In 1587, friar Diego Aduarte boasted: "By the punishment of a few old women who acted as priestesses . . . the idolatry of the whole region was brought to an end."[20] In 1589, Juan de Placensia also reported: "May the honor and glory be God our Lord's, that among all the Tagalos not a trace of this is left . . . thanks to the preaching of the holy gospel, which has banished it."[21]

When the United States forcibly annexed the Philippine islands in the late nineteenth and early twentieth centuries—destroying hundreds of thousands of Native lives—it deployed colonial officials, missionaries, and anthropologists armed with Protestant and/or secularist ideas to areas that the Spanish colonizers could not earlier penetrate. This resulted in new findings about Native ritual specialists, who, contrary to Spanish claims, had survived. The Americans used a mix of racialized religious and secular slurs to construct the Native ritual specialists they encountered. Anthropologist Albert Ernest Jenks in 1905 wrote of a Bontoc Igorot *insupak* as having "few of the earmarks of a priest. He teaches no morals or ethics, no idea of future rewards or punishments."[22] In 1907 Captain George Bowers reported to the US War Department about the Negros Occidental's babaylan tradition as "not religion in the commonly accepted term, but that conglomeration of ignorance and superstition in which someone comes forward and by his cunning and deceit appoints himself as god, a pope, priest, or some other."[23] In 1946 anthropologist Roy Franklin Barton wrote of the practices of the Ifugao *mumbaki* (Ifugao ritual specialist) as

> a distorted reflection of the Ifugao himself. [I]t reflects his ignorance and not his knowledge, his slothfulness and not his industry, his wishful thinking and not his resourcefulness, his credulity and not his inventiveness, his helplessness and not his strength. Out of his weaknesses the Ifugao has created fantastic conceptions of refuge from a harsh reality and has made them his gods.[24]

The modern secular ideologies that undergirded the American portrayals of Native ritual specialists would persist in later treatments of the babaylan by a number of Philippine historians writing from the young nation's centers of power. These depicted the babaylan, babailanes, and catalonan either as precolonial women priests or as male priests who led religious revolts against the Spanish and

American colonizers and their Philippine elite collaborators.²⁵ Notwithstanding the valorization that the efforts of some male babaylans received, they would be condescended to by some Philippine writers as "instinctual mass actions with weak theoretical guide posts," indicating that the "old religion was dying away in the face of the new."²⁶ Seen as belonging to a vanishing order, the babaylan then ceased to appear in Philippine history's pages following babaylan Papa Isio's surrender to the American colonial government in 1907, suggesting that these ritual specialists had finally acquiesced to the modern national order in which they ought not exist. The discursive erasure of Native ritual specialists by Spanish and American colonial agents and by a number of Philippine historians would provide the conditions of possibility for other babaylan discourses to proliferate during the late twentieth and early twenty-first centuries.²⁷

Archaic Feminists and Symbols of Gender Egalitarianism

Writing from urban sites during the late twentieth and turn of the twenty-first centuries, a number of Philippine feminists began to write about the babaylan as powerful women during the precolonial times when gender relationships were egalitarian.²⁸ To counter colonial and nationalist historiographies' marginalization of the women babaylan and women in general, feminist historian Fe Mangahas depicts the babaylan as "protofeminists" and as sources of precolonial women's power for fighting against the colonial patriarchy that eventually crushed them. Out of the babaylan's demise, Mangahas writes, arose women revolutionaries and feminists in whom the babaylan's power survived, they who would become the new babaylan.²⁹ Feminist theologian Mary John Mananzan upholds the claim of gender egalitarianism during precolonial times.³⁰ In the face of historical sexism and violence against women, for which Mananzan holds colonial Christianity accountable, she constitutes the babaylan with the "power roles" of warrior, teacher, healer, visionary, and priestess. These roles and the title of the babaylan, Mananzan asserts, could be assumed by any empowered contemporary Filipino woman.³¹

A number of gender and sexuality studies scholars, and LGBTQ activists also began to invoke the precolonial bayoquin, bayoc, asog, or the effeminate male ritual specialists that the Spanish colonial chronicles reported.³² These scholars and activists assert precolonial gender pluralism and ritual transgenderism that they claim were suppressed during the Spanish colonial period, followed by the active stigmatization and pathologization of non-heteronormative subjectivities during the American occupation.³³ Like many feminists, several of these scholars and activists also began to ascribe the babaylan title to themselves.

The construction of the archaicized, nationalized, and valorized babaylan as symbol of power available for all to appropriate has proved to be a compelling rallying point for many urban and diasporic gender scholars and activists, themselves battling patriarchal and heteronormative neocolonial regimes. Numerous books and articles have been published and several conferences organized around the babaylan as symbol of power and resistance. Not everyone agrees with the premises of this construction, however. The denial of Native ritual specialists' embodied contemporaneity and the appropriation of the babaylan title by subjects of greater privilege are considered by some as seriously offensive. The subsumption of regional ritual specialist identities by the nationalized Visayan term babaylan promoted by mostly urban, middle-class gender scholars and activists demonstrates for some the complicity of feminism with colonialism.[34] Still others contend that claims of gender equality and women's superiority before the time of conquest—taken up by more affluent voices—are false, hindering the more "accurate depiction of women's subordinate status" even during precolonial times.[35] Critiques also surface against the tendency to look to the past for models of power.[36] Although a "necessary step to (anti-colonial) liberation," Ofelia Villero writes, the "dangers to this strategy are many, including nostalgia and romanticization" that have led to an "uncritical evaluation of power dynamics among the different classes and religious orientation of women involved in the retrieval."[37] Some Indigenous quarters also assert that citing a number of overtly resistant babaylan to represent all Native ritual specialists is historically inaccurate. Many Native ritual specialists have been defending their lands, people, and traditions in less overt ways.[38] In gender and sexuality scholarship, critiques have likewise surfaced over the invocation of the babaylan as a largely middle-class phenomenon that ought not to be imposed on working-class counterparts.[39] All these point to a glaring disconnect between discourses that have unproblematically associated the babaylan with power and resistance and those that have pointed to exclusions that such constructions have engendered.

Contemporary, Land-Based Figures of Anti-colonial Resistance

A slightly different view has framed the babaylan as contemporary subjects who have survived colonization but who are now bifurcated into two variants. One of its leading proponents, Leny Mendoza Strobel, writes:

> Today there are still primary Babaylans in indigenous communities in the Philippines where they have been performing their roles as they have done for thousands of years. Outside of these land-based communities

the [secondary] Babaylan is now often distinguished and donning a different dress and language; she walks among us like a shadow, revealing herself only to those whose souls cry out to her.[40]

In this construction, those referred to as "secondary" babaylan are mostly lowlander descendants who have been colonized the most, gaining greater social privilege through colonial and neocolonial tutelage. Many of them reside in urban and/or First World locations, where they themselves battle multiple forms of oppression, leading some to want to rediscover Native resources for empowerment and healing. By embarking on decolonization that Strobel describes as a "psychological process that enables the colonized to understand and overcome the depths of alienation and marginalization caused by the psychic and epistemic violence of colonization," which results in "healing leading to different forms of activism," people come to embody the babaylan spirit that is the "deep structure of Filipino subjectivity" available to all.[41] Reminiscent of feminist scholars, Strobel urges her readers to "desire to discover the Babaylan in you."[42] Writings like Strobel's have struck a chord among a number of Filipinos in the diaspora. Conferences and publications about the babaylan have attracted sizable crowds and readers.[43] While this movement has been lauded by many of its participants, the involvement of what has been framed as primary babaylan has been limited. Numerous reasons have been cited for this, including "communication differences and other logistical impediments."[44] So-called primary babaylans both in the homeland and in the diaspora have, thus, been little heard in these babaylan circles, their mostly working-class backgrounds inhibiting them from sharing the cultivated critical language of their secondary babaylan sisters of greater privilege, resulting in non-Native, middle-class voices dominating babaylan conversations.

The association of the Native ritual specialist with a psychological state—i.e., uncolonized, nonmodern—finds parallels in Western shaman discourses. In the 1960s, the shaman's mental state, referred to by psychologists as an altered state of consciousness, became to many Westerners the shaman's defining characteristic. As a mental state, shamanism became detachable from its sociohistorical (Siberian-Tungus) context and it could then be pursued by Westerners.[45] Some have critiqued this move for reducing shamanism to a psychological function and for disregarding social dynamics and power relations.[46] Other commentators have accused this discourse of romanticizing shamans as isolated spiritual beings when some of the shamans have equally mediated oppressive class and caste conditions.[47] The habit of likening shamans to healers and doctors has further been noted as a false analogy because shamans, unlike physicians, deal not so much with illness but with the "'preconditions' of affliction."[48] Some Native scholars and activists have particularly been vocal in their protests against the appropriation of the "shaman" title by wellness practitioners and, conversely, the term's imposition on all Native ritual specialists. "We don't just pluck names out of somewhere," Native American activist Betty Cooper states. "The Indian name comes from a very honored place . . . like a family carrying on its tradition through its name . . . those are treated with great respect and honor."[49] Another Native activist, Tony Incashola, remarks on the white fascination with Native ways: "I don't think you have to adopt a culture to show your respect."[50] Incashola recommends to seekers: "If you're interested in a culture, and you wanna know more about it, go to the source, go to the people, and the people will tell you as much as they are allowed to tell you, and you get to know the culture, then you start to respect, you'll understand if you respect it."[51]

To their credit, some of the proponents of the secondary babaylan discourse in the Philippine diaspora have engaged with several political issues including the Filipinos' participation in the settler colonialism of North America. A growing number are also involved in Indigenous advocacies in the homeland. Still others are becoming more aware of the power dynamics between them and those they have constructed as "primary" babaylan, where the latter provide them with the occasion to "remake" themselves while being relegated to marginal spaces, unable to dialogue on equal terms.[52] At the heart of the matter is the long-standing view of Indigenous Peoples as not only incarcerated in the pre-modern past but as detained in ancestral lands. The latter, without a doubt, is of great merit, but taken to an extreme, has been used to justify Native peoples' exclusions, silences, and erasures. Not a few scholars have contended that the construction of Natives as authentic only if they are in ancestral lands—"the only places appropriate for them"—has effectively incarcerated them in such places.[53]

All this raises questions about the construction of the babaylan as an empowerment discourse. Whose empowerment are we talking about when those who get to participate in its acquisition are, indeed, struggling against the powers of domination, yet at the same time, have enough privilege to write out the voices of others? There is a deep alienation and stark hierarchization between the mostly urban and diasporic middle-class secondary babaylan and the Native ritual specialists who are called many different names, run the gamut of social locations, and do not bifurcate the babaylan into primary and secondary variants. While efforts to bridge Native ritual specialists, on the one hand, and urban and diasporic scholars and activists, on the other, have taken place at various historical junctures, these could only go so far as long as Native ritual specialists and leaders themselves do not take the lead in conversations toward the breaking down of social hierarchies inaugurated by the histories of colonization.

Author's Location and History of the Text

I am not a babaylan. I am a scholar, singer, and cultural worker from Northeastern Mindanao, Southern Philippines. Three decades ago, I accidentally met a living ritual specialist. This led me to suspect a disconnect between written discources about the babaylan's extinction and living ritual specialists' oral discourses about themselves, launching me into a longstanding quest for answers. I spent a significant amount of time these last thirty years interacting with a number of Philippine ritual specialists in the Philippines, in the United States, and in Italy. In these engagements I have sought consent to learn from the ritual specialists themselves, their collaborators, and their spirits. Native expert interpreters have mediated these encounters as I have made full use of my multiple Philippine language competencies that have allowed me to communicate directly with the ritual specialists, many of whom are also multilingual. My relationships with the different ritual specialists have been multifaceted. In addition to ethnographic interviews and my attendance at some of their rituals, I have learned from some of them the performance of a number of oral prayer songs that nonritualist singers like myself are allowed to sing. I have given concerts and talks alongside some of my chant mentors, in addition to writing and publishing books about our encounters. Concomitant with these, I have spent over ten years participating in babaylan-inspired feminist and decolonial circles in the Philippines and in North America. This has allowed me to spearhead the organization of bridging encounters of Native ritual specialists with urban and diasporic scholars and activists in the last few years.

Plan of the Book

What follows are ethnographies that provide glimpses into the contemporary lives of a number of Native Philippine ritual specialists in Agusan del Sur, South Cotabato, Sarangani, Davao del Sur, and Ifugao (figure I.1). Structured around the theoretical themes of voice, sex and gender, and place, these ethnographies highlight the ritual specialists' embodied voices that contest dominant discourses in ways that assert Native epistemology, historical agency, and authority.

Chapter 1: "Who Sings? A Baylan's Embodied Voice and Its Relations" is an ethnography of full-fledged Agusan-Manobo woman baylan (ritual specialist) Lordina "Undin" Potenciano and young woman baylan novice Robilyn Coguit, with important contributions to the text by ex-baylan Agusan-Manobo pastor Jose Havana and his wife and fellow-pastor, Florencia. The chapter weaves the

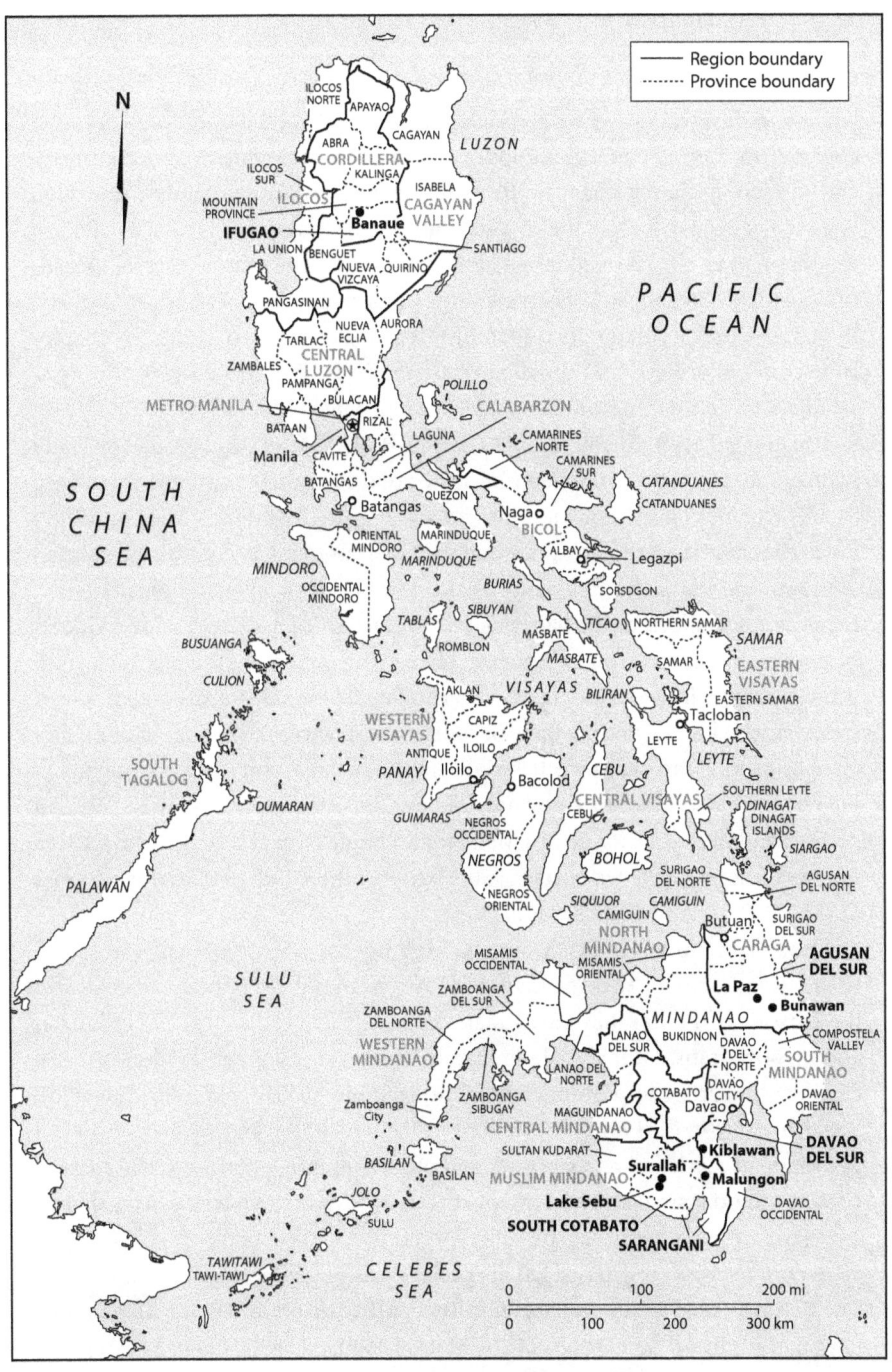

FIGURE I.1. Map of the Philippines, showing Agusan del Sur, South Cotabato, Sarangani, Davao del Sur, and Ifugao

Map by Bill Nelson.

baylan's and baylan novice's embodied voices with the Agusan-Manobo peoples' larger histories and variegated responses to colonization, missionization, internal colonialism, formal education, modern medicine, development, armed conflict, and human-spirit relations. By focusing on the baylan's ritual and nonritual voices in song and speech, the chapter contests the longstanding construction of the babaylan as incarcerated in the silent pasts, bringing to the fore ritual specialists' historical agency and Native theories of voice, listening, and translation. Researched and written over a span of fifteen years (2005 to 2020), the chapter is based on interviews and ritual participation in La Paz and Bunawan in Agusan del Sur, and in Quezon City and Tondo in Metro Manila.

Chapter 2: "Shifting Voices and Malleable Bodies" is an ethnography of T'boli woman tau m'ton bu (someone who sees, ritual specialist) and singer Mendung Sabal, with important contributions to the text by Mendung's cousin, Myrna Pula. The chapter introduces intersectional analysis to a T'boli epic song accused of promoting women's subjugation. It also complicates gender complementarity; feminist associations of the babaylan with women's high status; and individualist understandings of women's power. The second part of the chapter looks into the experiences of two contemporary Blaan female to male transgender nungaru (persons who know), putting these in conversation with currently circulating theories of gender and sexuality. Based on interviews and participation in gatherings in Lake Sebu, South Cotabato; Malungon, Sarangani; Bunawan, Agusan del Sur; and Quezon City, Metro Manila, the chapter was researched and written over a span of twenty-two years (1998–2020) for the T'boli part, and three years (2017–2020) for the Blaan section.

Chapter 3: "Song Travels: Mumbaki Mobility and the Relationality of Place" is an ethnography of two generations of Ifugao mumbaki (ritual specialists) in the persons of Philippines-based male mumbaki Bruno "Buwaya" Tindongan and his son, transnational male mumbaki Mamerto "Lagitan" Tindongan. The chapter also carries important contributions to the text by baki followers, allies, and detractors in the Philippines and in the United States, among them Lagitan's neo-shaman teachers and associates and other Filipino Americans. The chapter contests the discursive confinement of the babaylan in ancestral homelands, emphasizing a Native ritual specialist's multiple emplacements. It also complicates portrayals of land-based ritual specialists as uncolonized and nonmodern. The chapter draws on interviews and ritual participation in Banaue, Ifugao; Bunawan, Agusan del Sur; Quezon City, Metro Manila; Athens, Ohio; Los Angeles, California; Philadelphia, Pennsylvania; Queens, New York; Wallingford, Connecticut; and Ontario, Canada, spanning seven years (2013–2020).

At noted earlier, the book's title, *Babaylan Sing Back*, draws on bell hooks's "talk back" (1989).[54] It invokes the ability of the embodied voice in song and speech to assert Native aency that contest hegemonic discourses about ritual specialists, voice, sex and gender, and place. To "sing back" is not just to describe the world, it is to transform it.[55] It assumes participatory engagement, responsive agency, and relationship. That most Native ritual specialists are on call for the troubled, the sick, the oppressed, as they are to spirits with messages and instructions for them and for others, presupposes chains of responsive encounters, a continual singing back and forth, bringing enhancing gifts to those who participate and listen.

On the question of scholarly skepticism for ontological claims of spirit worlds perceptible only to Native ritual specialists and others like them, I will, in some instances, bracket assertions that are beyond my ability to verify or claim as having objective reality. Yet I do not accept the premise that the discourses of psychological projection and philosophical constitution, though valid to an extent, are bases for dismissing any evidential value to the experiences of those who report spirit participation in human affairs. This book joins others in maintaining that along with the demonization of Native ways by colonial and neocolonial agents, the scholarly habit of circumscribing "reality" according to Western anthropocentric and materialist suppositions has been equally responsible for silencing Native voices for centuries, causing the distortion and reduction of much of Indigenous experience that scholars have wished to understand in the first place.[56] While this book attends to the material and political intricacies of contemporary Native ritual specialist experiences, it will do so without sacrificing the descriptive, evocative, and nuanced accounts of spirit realms that are, to many ritual specialists, no less empirical and real than the silencing they have received from the colonizers and neocolonial elites.[57] This book's larger goal, therefore, is the decolonization of Native and non-Native social relations, dialogue, and reciprocal learning, in the service of the mutual survival of all. Like other ethnographic work, the findings of this book are time- and context-specific and may not apply to other cases.

1

WHO SINGS?
A Baylan's Embodied Voice and Its Relations

It is 1989. I am in the mountains at the boundary of Agusan del Sur, Davao del Norte, and Bukidnon. Fresh out of college, where I read books about the babaylan's demise, I am having an unexpected encounter with a living Native ritual specialist referred to by the Manobo as baylan. Keeping my bewilderment to myself, I come face to face with Laco, a tall, slender man with deep voice and dark eyes, his countenance more recessed than that of the convivial *datu* (chief) who warmly welcomes the group of literacy teachers I am traveling with.[1] An hour or so later, my companions and I head downhill to the next village where we will spend the evening. I, who, until then, have heard only Western and westernized songs from school, church, radio, and television, listen for the first time to an oral chant by a mother named Baunsoy whose lilting voice moves me deeply.

Traveling back to the lowlands I feel inspired but also confused and angry. Why have voices like Laco's and Baunsoy's been hidden from my generation and perhaps from generations past? What conspiracy is it that has been suppressing such voices from rising to our ears? I will spend the next decades finding ways to further listen to the voices of ritual specialists, many of whom are oral singers.

Sixteen years and several ritual specialist encounters later, I find myself at the edge of the back seat of a motorcycle, hugging my seventy-eight-year-old mother in front of me as we move along an old winding logging road toward the innermost parts of our home province, Agusan del Sur.[2] We try to keep our balance as the driver swerves or obstinately moves forward in response to the challenges posed by the slippery ditches and mud pools. Awaiting us at our destination is an event that many Filipinos like ourselves do not believe happens in the modern age: a *panumanan* (ritual) officiated by a *baylan* (Agusan-Manobo ritual specialist). Practices like these are widely thought to have perished during the Spanish and American colonial periods, a notion welcomed by those who see Indigenous pre-Christian and pre-Islamic practices—labeled paganism by the orthodoxies that have tried to eradicate or convert Native populations—as, at best, deficient and, at worst, a road to hell. Such a view is equally embraced by agents of the modern nation who have relegated such practices to the past or to the realm of ignorance and superstition. In contrast to these detractors are those who lament the alleged disappearance of these traditions, particularly the predominantly women priests who led them, who have become idealized as protofeminists and/or as land-based symbols of anticolonial resistance. Both camps generally agree that the woman my mother and I are about to meet either no longer exists or exists without a voice to make a difference.

My mother struggles to remain stable on the seat in front of me. I keep stopping her aged body from tilting as the fragile vehicle bumps and sways. Raised during the middle years of the American colonial period, when Indigenous ways were actively suppressed following campaigns by the Spanish, she, too, grew up unaware of the baylan. It is only a year after this trip when she finds out that there have been *mamuhatbuhat* ritual specialists among her aunts and uncles in Camiguin, and seven years after her death when the Kamiguin tribe itself, is declared ingidenous.

At sundown, we arrive in *barangay* Panagangan in the town of La Paz and are warmly welcomed by the baylan's brother in-law, Jose, and his wife Florencia. Both Jose and Florencia are Agusan-Manobo pastors of the local Free Methodist Church, and my mother's former students. We have come at their invitation after my inquiry if I may be allowed to listen to a baylan's voice in ritual to know how ritual participants listen to and understand this voice. Although opposed to baylan practice, pastors Jose and Florencia lend their secular expertise as Agusan-Manobo language experts to my study. I am to rely on them for the transcriptions and translations to *kuntoon* (modern) Manobo, Visayan (one of Mindanao's lingua francas), and English of the old Manobo utterances of the baylan and the *abyan* (the baylan's spirit companion, helper). Pastor Jose himself was once a baylan before he became a pastor so it was not too long ago when he, himself, sang what was believed to be the voice of his abyan. Also welcoming us upon our arrival is the baylan's niece, young woman Robilyn.

My mother and I meet the baylan. Her name is Lordina "Undin" Potenciano. Quietly observant, she seems to be both with us and not with us; present, yet in a world beside ours. Her composure—like those of other ritual specialists I have met—is not projected or displayed. Unlike the outwardly heroic depictions of the babaylan in books, films, television, and the Internet, here is a ritual specialist who gives concentrated care to arranging beads for ritual rather than to arranging blatant political resistance. Undin introduces herself to us through a *todom* (song).[3]

> Mgo uda paliman kad uda
> Padongog kad man mayonsad
> Pigdangkagan ko hipag dig
> Dawdangolan aw dodogi kay
> Aman aboy ka nu ti
> Limuk pinintu tiajun ni mgo
> Uda aw nolinugoy
> Aw natinayod on nighibayandug
> Tugaman ta no mangoyag no songlitan
> Makayogoy on no timpo din aw inggad
> Pad ilingon no mga uda inggad
> Pad ilingon nu igpanawsangkuab
> Ad kakuli insondad ad kapuy-
> ajat anoy ad
> Maniajun anoy on man manim-
> Bang to tugaman ku no pintu
> Inggad pad itingon nu igduyagid
> Ad kakuli insondad ad kapuyajat
> To kona kay no iyan on aw kona
> No iyan on narambaja to Ginuo
> Nog pamintod to kadigoy to ingodnon
> To domyog to yugnabanon no
> Tahomon ku nalinugoy
> A da man najon-od su inggad
> Pad ilingon nu inawa inawa
> Kay ogkamiling to inajun ku
> No potong no iyananda
> Man iyan iyananda man
> Ogtabang to dajawag ku no
> Potong no iyanda man iyan
> Iyan nanda man ogtabang to
> Dajawag ku no potong iyan nanda
> Man miglimbutung to kahungan ku no

Pintu kagona ku no linimuk
No aboy ka nud dinaan ko
Wada ogkayawangan di wada
Kalinugoy nasimuyag nasimuyag
On pagtini-ajunay noy no inggad
Pad ilingon nu ko kani mig-
timamanwa on to kanoy no kahungan
Migtumbilaan ku inanoy on nasim-
buyag koy on nigbaliwaan on buyan
Nigbayluhan on payagkajun no
Adu ka nu dinaan inawag
To buyan to kanig panimbanag
Silat si panagkajun igkapana-
Wodsawod ku si dadaya kug
Oyogon si yuha kug anugunon
To kagona ku no pintu aw dangat
On to kaway no ogtumbilangan
Su matuod man iyan aw
Kalinimuk nanda kahungan ta
Ko pintu nan da to kagona ta
No kinuyang kid ogmakagtey pang-
Idap buyawan sayapi
Nogkatapnoy na adu ka nu dinaan
d-adka nud mgo iyan
Ko iyan kow on mogpasibu iyan
Kow on mupuangod to kagona
Ku no pintu nakayogob kad
Tukib kad takokos on no limuk
Kabos on no pa-iyak adu ka
Nu dinaan aboy ka nud
Monsanga aw dodogi kay no
Bukyad bangkulis ka ko iyan
Kad mayonsag dig dangkagan no hipag
No dawdongulan no makatapnoy
To kanay no tumbilangan adu
Ka nud dinaan aboy ka
Nud mon sanga sambajon
To Magbabaja adu ka nud
Monsonga su inggad pad ilingon

Nu igduyagid ad kakuli igsondad
Ad to kapuyajat konad no
Aguwantahonon to kanay no kagona
Kanay nogtumbilangan su hintawo
Pad tog pangidap hintawo pad
Togpa makuli man
Naan to wada ti-ajun ta
To wadad on timbang ta no wadad
Mag pangidap wadad mag ogmakanga-a
Maginona nanda mag tumbilang
A to tuyugan no nalindog bayoy
No natangkajang iyan on
Magbayagadan ku ko kani kay
Kani kay abyan ku kani iyan
On man ogpaigu iyan da mag
Ajangatan ku man.

Hear now, my friend.
Now listen carefully.
My brother-in-law [Jose] requested for me, and really
I am requested a lot.
So you,
Lady [Grace], we have
not seen
each other before.
It is a very
rare time, even
as I am
now suffering from too many
difficulties and brought to much hardship.
No matter how
hard I have tried to work
as a woman
I still have a very difficult
time. I am destined for difficulties.
If not for
the Creator who controls
my life, who directs human beings,
who guides humanity,
I thought I would

die. And even
if you say that "this is your way"
this is really the way my life
is. My only
help is my friend,
the spirit.
My ultimate
helper
is my spirit friend. S/he is the
only one who protects me, such
a woman like me
and really
there is no other way except to
be separated from
my husband. Even
if you saw me
at home, in our life
at home, we have been slowly
drifting apart. It has been a month now
and more months have passed.
In times when the
moon is full, when the moon
shines full, I
shed my abundant tears.
I feel bad about it, I
don't want to cry like a woman.
Each time I reach home
I realize that I
am just a woman and
to a woman like me, it is
difficult to earn money, very
difficult to find gold or silver.
It is difficult to receive money,
to find what I expect.
It is for you to consider, it
depends on you to see my
condition as a woman, but
I am truly very poor.
Lady, even if you investigate
me, I am the poorest one.

> And really it is a great
> assurance that you are able to help me.
> You, my brother-in-law, can
> supply my needs, and can
> help me in my situation
> where I live.
> This is the
> plan of God.
> You see,
> I am now suffering from difficulties,
> hardships
> beyond compare in my life.
> At my home, no one
> will work to earn money, no one
> will take responsibility.
> It is really difficult to have no
> partner because no
> one will work and earn money, nobody!
> I just stay at home
> at the house where I stay
> at the house where I live
> where I expect help from
> my spirit friend,
> the one to find a way, the
> one I am always depending on for help.

In her tod-om, baylan Undin introduces herself as a woman destined for poverty and difficulty, with neither gold nor husband to support her. She appears to belittle her womanhood, associating it with domesticity, suffering, helplessness, and tears. She begs her brother-in-law, Jose, a pastor who is clearly against her baylan practice, and me, a stranger, for assistance. She also declares her full reliance on her abyan. This sung self-introduction paints a picture of a ritual specialist that departs significantly from the baylan's image as symbol of woman power and as leader of anticolonial resistance. While it is possible that other practitioners in other times and places may have served grand political roles alongside their ritualist vocation, Undin appears removed from this depiction. I verify Undin's disclosed circumstances with her niece, Robilyn, and they are confirmed. Reflecting further on Undin's words alongside José Buenconsejo's assertion that the sentiment of pity is common among Agusan-Manobo whenever

FIGURE 1.1. (From left) Ebeng Coguit, Jose Havana, Florencia Havana, Robilyn Coguit, Lita Pondog, and Undin Potenciano, La Paz, Agusan del Sur, 2005
Photo by Grace Nono.

they meet—the singing of tod-om providing a venue for expressing and communicating intimacy, hidden thoughts, and feelings—I form some preliminary considerations.[4] While Undin, by her own and by others' admission, may indeed be experiencing much hardship in her life, that may not necessarily mean that she is bereft of power. Her full confidence in her abyan and her ability to give voice to her thoughts and feelings through her tod-om allow her to negotiate her place in our encounter.

The Panumanan

Baylan Undin commences the panumanan as soon as nightfall descends on the hut by the hill where she, pastors Jose and Florencia, Undin's nephew, Sayson, Robilyn and her mother, Ebeng, the elder Lita, my mother, and I have gathered (figure 1.1).[5] It is a cool late October evening and the surroundings are abuzz with cicada songs. Undin carefully lays out betel quid preparations on a white porcelain plate, beside a glass of tuba (fermented coconut juice) and ornaments of red, black, white, and yellow glass beads strung together with tinkling brass bells, all of them dedicated to her abyan. She recites a *panawag-tawag* (invocation) in a half-whispering tone. This is followed by a brief wordless melodic passage in her mild-mannered *yagong* (voice). She then launches into a tod-om in the old

Manobo language as she pays respects to the spirit dwellers of the area and prays to Magbabaja (Creator) for protection.

Pastor Jose points out what some of the other ritual participants notice as a barely perceptible change in baylan Undin's yagong. I, too, observe Undin's breath tremble and her voice quaver, as it takes on a gruffer, brasher, more masculine tone that is also swifter at shelling out words. Jose whispers to me that at this point Undin's yagong is crossing over from tod-om, generated by Undin's voice alone, to *gudgod* (spirit song), sung by Undin's abyan rendered audible by Undin's voice. For the whole duration of the panumanan, the responsibility of *paghilwas*—the articulation of the spirit's old Manobo utterances, understood only by the older-generation Manobo, to kuntoon Manobo and Visayan for the benefit of the younger Manobo and Agusanon ritual participants—lays on Jose.[6] The abyan sings:

> Ku ko mayumpajag to tugam-an
> si Oknabanon ko dagnoy aw
> dagnoy ni Ojombuan nanambod
> konag tulin ko dasag konag
> yuganud no kadongog ka
> no magajun paliman ka mahitugu
> bayanduga ogyantujan
> tinuyan ogkabanibat?
> obos ogkanawnangon adu
> kan dinaan aboy kanud
> sambajon tuwali kinuyang
> ogkabanibat
> obos ogkanawnangon aboy
> kanud dinaan no makuli
> kay kahadat tog dadanginon
> kahadat togdang-oyan ki

> If only the name were clear, this is
> Oknabanon, the nickname
> is Ojombuan, a man
> who will not grow up, eternal child.
> Listen now. [*addressing the ritual participants*]
> Listen to my story.
> It is only now that we meet. [*referring to pastors Jose and Florencia, and Grace and her mother*]
> What is it that we must talk about?

> What shall we talk about now?
> I pity you all.
> What do we talk about?
> What shall we speak of?
> What is it that you would like to tell me?
> What is the difficulty?
> For it is troublesome to be called.
> Cumbersome to be asked to do something.

We, the ritual participants, notice baylan Undin take a pause, then breathe heavily. Again, she sings a wordless melodic passage, then picks up on the gudgod, this time, in a slower, heavier, more authoritative yagong in a lower register and a tune that is different from the one she has been singing a few seconds ago. The abyan continues to sing through her:

> Inggad pad ilingon nu
> matuud dayojagman indanon
> nokoy tog-ipongan binuyusanto
> Potong iyanda magbisaya
> Sangkuyugan to mayunta pamasiagadagadan

> Even though [it is cumbersome to be asked to do something]
> it is still important.
> Whatever problem our medium has, we must immediately help her.
> Whatever the matter is, we must join her.
> Wherever she goes, we must watch over her.
> Follow and agree.

Then we hear the abyan reprimand Undin's nephew, Sayson, who has been mocking the panumanan since it began. Sayson, like many other modernized Agusan-Manobo youth, doesn't believe in his ancestors' ways. He ridicules his own father for having an abyan, provoking the abyan to remark:

> Aboy ka nud inggad pad
> hintakay buwa, wadakay kayangan

> Stop your insolence![7] [*addressing Sayson*]
> Who among us here are not listening to what is being said?[8] [*the spirit speaks to the ritual participants*]

Since the panumanan is taking place not in Undin's house but in her cousin's, the abyan asks why it is not in a house that it is familiar with.

> To tuwali kay
> kagidin konaman no tuyugandin

> How come I am hearing the song from
> a different house?⁹

The abyan appears to provide its own answer:

> Di mano tuyugan no
> Nalindog, paliman ka

> Even if this is not our own house, one must still listen.
> Stand up and listen.

Pastor Jose, who up to this point has only been listening and articulating in other languages the abyan's old Manobo utterances, suddenly speaks in kuntoon Manobo, without a tune. He asks Undin's abyan about the future and what it holds for humans in the face of mounting problems, like illnesses.

> Aha ka kanami no mgo ingoino
> wada koy kataga to umaabut no
> panahun, su kaling ogpangusip koy
> to nokoy buwa to ogkadeygan-noy
> Su madogi on
> Seegdinogon noy, no mgo sakit
> No og-abut dinikanami, kaling
> Yagi, ogsugud koy og papanalipod
> No sikuyu ubag to mato-u
> Nog bantoy kanami, kaling
> Ogpamaliga koy

> Now you see us, humans.
> We don't know what will happen
> to us in the future. That is why we wish to
> inquire about what might happen to us.
> We hear of so many things.
> Diseases that are emerging,
> that come to us. That is why, friend,
> we are beginning to defend and protect ourselves
> and you are the ones to faithfully
> watch over us. That is why we are here
> to ask you for help.

Brashly, the spirit responds:

> Ajaw kad, uda, tajabukon ku
> gadey nu bonae, man no
> bisaya nu di makuli on
> kay yagi, hadat on kay
> mgo uda, kadigoy to ingodnon
> domyog toyognabanon di
> wadad man kasusukud, wadad
> man ogdawat to balaod to Ginuo
> kaling, kona kow
> oghuwali, igduyagid kow kakuli
> igsondad on kapuyajat to otawon
> to natompas to kani pasidihon
> on igyuwan on to lidok

> I will accept what you are
> saying and asking.
> But friend, it is a difficult matter, that which
> concerns humans,
> the life of
> people on earth.
> It is known that no one
> accepts the law of God anymore,
> that is why you shouldn't be surprised
> if you encounter hardships,
> if you suffer from crises. Humans
> of the world, you will be winnowed.
> You will be thrown into the lake of fire.

Now speaking in a softer voice similar to baylan Undin's lucid yagong, the spirit adds:

> Anoy man sei binuyusan noy
> di dodogion bunsaya
> dodogi ot-igkasodyot ku, wadad man
> sakuyu din nokani
> katotopong pad

> Even our medium
> commits many mistakes.[10]
> There is much to be angry about her.[11]

> Her own children have no understanding of tradition (and) they despise her.
> They (also) disagree among themselves.

Jose presses further in his kuntoon Manobo:

> Iyan-on iyan, kan duma no
> igkapanawag iyu, su ahakat
> kan kinabuhi noy makasasayaon
> na, og-amonuhon
> noy buwa, pagtubos to kinabuhi noy
> gawas ko iyu nomgo diwata sikuyu
> iyan ogtabang kanami

> That is why we call on
> you because you see our life.
> Our life is sinful.
> What should we do then to save
> our lives, if you who are our
> guardian spirits
> are reluctant to help us?

To this, the abyan responds, again singing brashly:

> Aw matuod man, odang
> Aman, kanay, takokos on no
> Umli ko kobos on no dajawag
> No kinuyang ad ogpasalig
> Kagonat to ingodnow domyag
> To yognabanon su tambog
> A da to bunsaya to tilapad
> No kakuyu ku no makuli on
> No sikan da, nogsibog ad kanda
> Og-angkonod ad

> That is true.
> But I am not capable
> as spirit. I do not have
> power. I can no longer give assurances
> to humans because
> I myself am a sinner, and all
> my companions too. It is difficult for them.

And now this is the only thing
I can say. I will return
to my home now.

We, the ritual participants, hear a loud heaving sound from baylan Undin, as though she is drowning. Jose tells us that this is *henghong*, signifying the abyan's release from the baylan's body. Before the spirit can fully depart, Jose hurriedly says:

Ajaw kow naag dali-dali pag-uli
su aha ka, meduon pad igpaahanoy
no masakiton, ajaw kow naa
ogdali-dali, aha ka, bag-u koy
kikita, na angod meduon masakit
duon no masakit to kobong
ahaa now, kon dow nokoy to ogkadeygan?

Please do not be in a hurry to go home.
We want you to examine
this sick person [Sayson]. You see,
we just saw each other now.
There is pain in his
leg. What will
happen to him?

Jose's question is followed by a brief pause, as though the abyan is determining what to sing next. The abyan then launches into a wordless melodic passage, then proceeds in a mellow voice similar to baylan Undin's lucid yagong:

Kani ku nogbontoya ko kani
Migdasun on diya to Maibuyan
Buwa, ni Makahagtong madugtana-kad
No potong to kani imaon
Buyawan takilidon aman
Kogkayanos on, madugtana ka di
Awdi kad ogyangan, dikanog
Linugoy, buyawan, pangutana kad
Ko dagasun on to banwa, no
Makahagtong, banwa no Maibuyan

I will examine the matter through this peso coin.[12]
Let me check Maibuyan,[13]
the place of Makahagtong.[14]

[Then brashly, the abyan sings:]

> Stick to my forehead now.¹⁵ [*addressing the peso coin*]
> If you fall, it means that the patient will die.
> But if you stick, he will live.
> Do not tarry.¹⁶
> Find out what will happen.
> It is on its way there now
> to the house of Maibuyan.

A few moments later, the abyan sings again in a mellow voice, bringing forth news to the ritual participants:

> Noy-aman su nabontey kun
> iyanman to gikanan to sajawigan
> ogsigikananman to inanitan iyan
> kabonteyku, iyanman ogkasod-ong ku
> igsangkujuganman
> igkapasigurohi tigdui to dajunas
> no potong di da magkayanos
> di matagkabontaeman na kagikan
> to dajawag kagikanman to Umli
> aboy ka, no dinaan sikandag
> angkonad-ad aboy kad no dinaan
> su matag mayangan koy
> matag madinogyaon inggadpad
> ilingon nu magajun matagsajahiton nu
> no kani ogsangkujuganman
> to Inajow, matag impamalinsugu
> man ni tundajokonman
> yumay din aduman dinaan
> balwasanman no potong yumopad
> balilingaonman

> I understand it now.
> It began as a transgression.¹⁷ [*Sayson's transgression*]
> The illness came from his father's abyan, the Inajow.¹⁸
> This is what I see.
> If only the young man's father were here to accompany him.
> Just make sure not to anger the Inajow further
> so that the illness will not worsen.¹⁹ [*addressing Sayson*]
> But do not worry.

I will speak to the inflicter now
otherwise, it could still add to your suffering.
I accept on its behalf your plea for forgiveness
for if we delay, this illness could worsen and not be healed.
You must stop being insolent and begin to show respect to the abyan.
The truth is, there are only very few of us who can advise you about this.
And if you tarry, other spirits could join in inflicting more illness on you.[20]
For the Inajow has already invited others to contribute to your suffering.
Make sure to ask forgiveness from the one you offended.
You must also ask forgiveness from your father.
Perform a ritual with chicken as payment/offering for the return of your soul,
an exchange.[21]

Addressing the inflicter, the abyan then says:

> Ni kani ipasibog-on namatae

> Stay away now, you that inflicted the illness.

Addressing the ritual participants, the abyan instructs:

> No ipaangkonod-on namatae
> su kona man nogkamiling
> ku wadag pamatae na
> tumbilang to inanitan no ogling-kongod
> to sajawigan

> Tell the sick person's father [who owns the abyan] to tell his spirit helper to take back the illness
> and to return his son's soul.[22] [*addressing the ritual participants*]
> For there would have been no illness had it not been inflicted by that spirit.
> If nothing inflicts, there is no illness.
> The illness was gathered from the marsh.

In closing, the abyan says:

> Magajun no panlimpas, kona
> jambiton din dajawag
> to mgo dajunas din.

> What had been said is good.
> Gather all the abyan now.
> Call the patient's mother, father, and relatives [to witness that it was his father's abyan that inflicted his illness].

At this point, we, the ritual participants, again hear Undin's henghong as she slowly emerges from the gudgod.

In the conversation that follows, Manobo pastor Florencia—despite her religion's judgment that all abyan are evil—could not help but acknowledge the Indigenous distinction between good and bad abyan, as witnessed in baylan Undin's gudgod. The good abyan are those who assist humans without asking for anything in return. Undin's abyan, Florencia says, is known to do such things. The bad abyan, on the other hand, are those that inflict illness or demand steep payments for any assistance they give. Florencia adds, however, that even good abyan can inflict illnesses if they find it reasonable to do so, as the case was with the abyan of Sayson's father who struck the young man because it felt disrespected by him.

Undin's niece Robilyn notes the different kinds of abyan, each with its own character. There are abyan committed to helping, turning their mediums into baylan like Undin whose abyan is finding ways to heal Sayson's leg. Other abyan are expert musicians who transform their befriended into gifted performers. There are artists who guide their medium into making beautiful things, like the embroideries that Robilyn's mother creates. There are also fierce *tegbusaw* that are considered assets in war, but in times of peace are considered harmful because they kill for minor mistakes. Representing a whole range of personalities, the abyan are no different from humans, Robilyn explains. Failure to understand this has led many observers to demonize them all.[23]

I was no longer in La Paz when Sayson's family performed the *limpas buya*, the fulfillment of the promise to perform offerings in exchange for Sayson's full healing. When I next heard from Robilyn, she told me that young man Sayson could walk again, suggesting the success of baylan Undin's abyan in negotiating for Sayson's recovery.

History and the Agusan-Manobo Baylan

The following section traces the Agusan-Manobo baylan's social location and history of diminishing influence over the past five centuries. The Agusan-Manobo people had been referred to as one of the "aboriginal non-negrotoid populations of Mindanao."[24] They are related to other Manobos spread out across the island who speak between nineteen and twenty-one Manobo languages.[25] Agusan in the

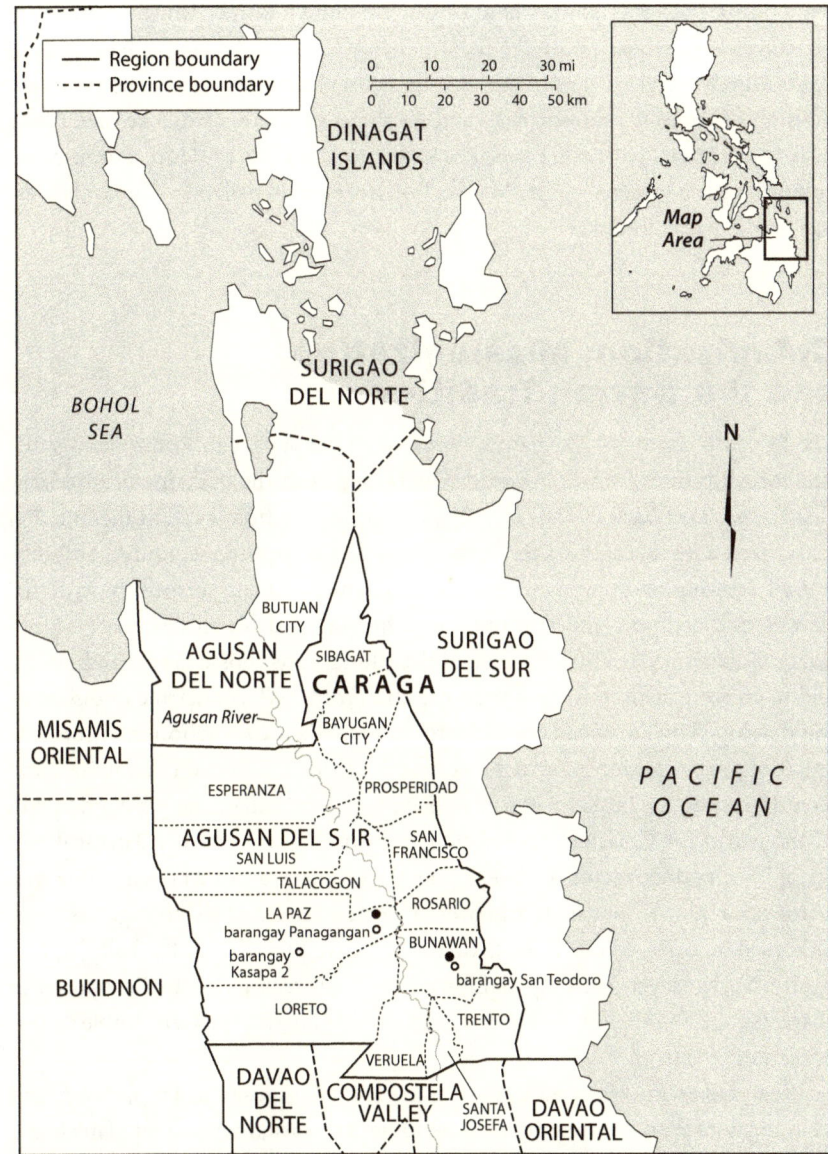

FIGURE 1.2. Map of Agusan del Sur, showing La Paz and Bunawan

Map by Bill Nelson.

Caraga region is the Agusan-Manobo peoples' ancestral land (figure 1.2). It is a valley bordered by mountain ranges and traversed by the Agusan River.[26] Agusan del Sur today is made up of one city and thirteen municipalities. Among these are La Paz, Undin's hometown, itself composed of fifteen barangays, including the mountainous Kasapa II, where Undin lives, and lowland Panagangan, where her cousin—in whose house the panumanan was held—resides. Adjacent to La Paz is Bunawan, where part of this chapter takes place. Long before the 1967 subdivision of Agusan into northern and southern parts, the province had a long history of contact with other peoples. Archeological finds evidence a robust precolonial trade between Agusan, Manila, Borneo, Siam (Thailand), China, and perhaps India via Indonesia.[27]

Colonization, Missionization, and the Baylan Tradition

The fifteenth century—like earlier times—saw the papacy in Rome claim spiritual lordship over the whole world. Operating from the doctrine of discovery that traced itself back to the Dark Ages, popes issued bulls such as the one that authorized a European king to "invade, search out, capture, vanquish, and subdue all Saracens and pagans whatsoever . . . to reduce their persons to perpetual slavery, and to apply and appropriate to himself and his successors the kingdoms, dukedoms, counties, principalities, dominions, possessions, and goods, and to convert them to his and their use and profit."[28] The doctrine of discovery was developed by European countries to "control their own actions and conflicts regarding exploration, trade and colonization in non-European countries," and would become the basis for the 1494 Treaty of Tordesillas, the papal "division of the world for Christian exploration and domination between Portugal and Spain."[29] The doctrine of discovery granted property and sovereign rights to a European country that first "discovered" a new land and its contiguous areas unknown to Europe. It justified taking over Native property and refusing to recognize Native sovereignty by claiming Natives were inferior to Europeans in character and in religion so that civilization and Christianity were ample "compensation" for them.[30]

When the Spanish landed in Butuan in northern Agusan in 1565, they found a barangay or clan community associated with a coastal settlement. This had a thriving commercial center, a datu (chief) who led his people in war and in the settlement of disputes according to the customary laws and oral history. The barangay in Butuan traded with foreign lands so that junks regularly brought in Chinese porcelain jars and iron tips for swords and spears in exchange for Butuan's gold, wax, civet, cinnamon, and slaves (whether these last were chattel slaves captured in war or people reduced to bondage for failing to pay a debt deserves further study).[31] Seeing that the Butuanons and Caragans in general were fierce and warlike, Miguel López de Legazpi requested King Philip II of Spain for more soldiers and arms to pacify the Natives. He also asked for more men to settle the land and more money for materials to "increase your royal income and add to the universal good of your kingdoms."[32] Thus began the *encomienda* system that awarded Spanish adventurers with the Native Agusanons' land, forced tributes in rice and gold, exclusive business dealings, tax exemptions, and the enslavement of moors.[33] Still, the Spanish *encomenderos* found it difficult to subjugate the Natives, so, they requested missionaries to come and help in the task of pacification.[34] In 1596, the Jesuits arrived to teach letters and religion.[35]

Beyond coastal Butuan, the Jesuits ventured into upper Agusan, land of the Manobos, who were led by the datu and baylan, and protected by the *bagani* (warriors) known for their personal exploits and prescribed norms of conduct, duty and privilege required for leadership.[36] The Jesuits relocated what they saw to be "scattered jungle residents" in *reducciones* (settlements) to control the Natives more effectively.[37] One reducción was Linao, an area that now covers Bunawan, La Paz, and Talacogon.[38] When the Jesuits were expelled in 1622, Linao was maintained by the Recoletos who encouraged Cebuanos and Boholanos from the Visayan islands to resettle in Agusan.[39] With the Jesuits' return in the 1870s came the establishment of more reducciónes including one in La Paz.[40] With these settlements came baptism, as well as instruction on the Judeo-Christian creation story, the Trinity, original sin, repentance, and redemption.[41] Not only did the reducción seek to demolish Indigenous religious traditions labeled by the Spanish as paganism, it destroyed the Native social structure by introducing the idea of a nuclear family that would own private property. This went against the clan system and the shared use of mountains and rivers where the Natives hunted and fished, outside the grounds where their houses were built.[42] The reducciónes further transformed the datus into *capitanos* or *tenientes*, reducing their powers and their constituents or dependents.[43] The upper Agusan-Manobo's response to the reducciónes was immediate. Soon after their establishment, "there was hardly any area in Agusan that had not risen in open rebellion, resulting in the abandonment of the new settlements."[44] Fierce fighting also broke out between the colonized or Christianized Manobos and those who wished to remain free and uncolonized.[45] The Spanish had to abandon some reducciónes, while reporting that some "Christianized" Manobos had maintained their Indigenous practices.

Following the Philippine Revolution that crushed the Spanish forces and ended over three centuries of colonial rule, the United States betrayed the Filipino leaders by refusing to acknowledge the Republic of the Philippines forged by the blood of Filipino heroes. Nor did it recognize the uncolonized Moro sultanates and the Indigenous communities with their communal lands. Instead, it forcibly annexed the Philippine islands during the 1898 Treaty of Paris. One of the first things that the American colonizers did was divide the Filipinos into "civilized" (Christian, colonized) groups and "wild" (non-Christian, uncolonized) tribes. According to Mindanao historian Rudy Buhay Rodil, "by the simple act of official labeling, the American colonial government transformed the symbolic glory of retaining... freedom into a stigma and a marked disadvantage. These labels later made their appearance in very important laws like those affecting ownership and distribution of land and the disposition of natural resources."[46] One such law was the Land Registration Act No. 496 of 1902 that required the registration of lands occupied by private persons or corporations, an idea that was alien to the Natives who could not read and who saw their lands as communal.[47] When settlers, private logging and mining companies, and government development projects began to take over ancestral domains, many of the Agusan-Manobo and other Native peoples found themselves "squatters in their own lands."[48]

The American colonial regime (1898–1946) provided opportunities for large numbers of Protestant missionaries to enter the islands.[49] Reminiscent of European kings who divided the world among themselves, Presbyterian, Baptist, and Methodist leaders met in New York City in 1898 to discuss how they would evangelize Filipinos. They came up with a comity agreement that divided up the different areas into different ministries to avoid conflicts among themselves and their converts.[50] Fired by the desire to educate what they saw as culturally backward Natives in the way of the truth instead of "hear(ing) how God had already been speaking in and through them," many of these Protestant missionaries applied strategies similar to those of the Spanish Catholics: learning Native languages, customs, traditions, behavior, feuds, enemies, and allies, all in the interest of eradicating Native ways and converting "pagans" to Christianity.[51]

In the early 1950s, Free Methodism was introduced to Agusan by missionaries Walter and Gertrude Groesbeck, who established a palm-roofed chapel in Bunawan before moving their headquarters to Butuan in 1953.[52] It was around that time, according to pastors Florencia and Jose, that Groesbeck came to La Paz to try to convert Agusan-Manobo Supreme Datu (chief) and baylan Tagleong, Jose's brother-in-law and Robilyn's grandfather. Florencia claims that Groesbeck succeeded in convincing Tagleong to "believe in God."[53] Groesbeck was followed by a long line of American missionaries, a number of them linguists, who initiated the Summer Institute of Linguistics' Bible translation project with which Florencia and Jose were involved.[54] The centuries of religious, linguistic, and academic instruction paid off with many Agusan-Manobo like Jose abandoning their baylan ways.[55] If he and Florencia have been willing to serve as guides for researchers like myself interested in learning about the baylan, it was made possible only by their cognitive separation of their religious functions as missionaries from their cultural tasks as Agusan-Manobo language experts. From a strictly missionary perspective, however, they consider the baylan's panumanan and gudgod as demonic practices to be extirpated. The only times Manobo songs are permissible are when they are rid of connections to the baylan and the abyan and if they accommodate Christian or secular themes. Despite the histories of suppression of baylan voices and ways, however, a number of studies have shown the continued patronage of baylan services even by some Christianized Manobos.[56]

Settlers, Dominant Natives, and the Baylan

In addition to the colonial disruption of Indigenous structures and functions, the Agusan-Manobo have had to face the influx of Christianized settlers from more colonized areas in Luzon, Visayas, and Mindanao.[57] Some of these were schoolteachers like my mother, from northern Mindanao, who would formally educate generations of Agusan-Manobo. Those who were formally educated, like Jose and Florencia, have since lived in lowland town centers where they have been able to participate in local systems of governance, a positive development for them. It has been reported, however, that some educated Manobo have discriminated against their kin—like baylan Undin—who have remained in the mountains where they are seen to persist in their "heathen and uncivilized" ways.[58]

Language, Music, and the Baylan's Voice

With the emphasis on literacy and proficiency in the colonial language of English, the national language of Filipino, and the settlers' language of Visayan came the diminished use of the Agusan-Manobo's Indigenous language, particularly the old Manobo of the baylan's ritual songs. In 2016 the Philippine Department of Education began to push for mother-tongue-based learning, but implementation has been riddled with problems, including the lack of Indigenous materials, in some cases resulting in the continued dominance of non-Indigenous languages. Some Manobo professionals like Florencia have taken the initiative to teach schoolchildren Christianized Manobo songs that make use of kuntoon Manobo, which is a mix of Manobo, Higaonon, Bukidnon, Subanon, Bagobo, Mandaya, Visayan, and Tagalog.[59] They have, however, steered clear of anything related to the baylan. They have also approached teaching in ways that have significantly departed from the oral/aural methods of singers like Undin. Of her pedagogy, Florencia said:

> Since we are now writing down the songs, I stick to the same words and tunes, instead of the old way where each performance was extemporaneous and the singer always introduced variations. I employ text transcription and Western music notation as aids to quick learning. The intention is to teach the songs to schoolchildren so everything has to be documented [written down].[60]

The advantage of fixing oral performances as notes and words on a page as what Florencia has done is that Native songs can now be disseminated to people who are literate, literacy being so highly prized in the modern nation. There are, however, numerous disadvantages to this innovation. First, it freezes singular renditions of what are otherwise dynamic and variegated performances, altering their relationships to time, and stifling the creative improvisation that is at the heart of oral performances. Second, it abstracts vocal performances from the bodies of singers like baylan Undin, who become delegitimated as music experts. Third, it objectifies, disembeds, and decontextualizes vocal expressions from their larger human contexts such as the panumanan that is rich with social and historical meanings.[61] Fourth, it standardizes oral performances according to the Western parameters of pitch, rhythm, and form.[62] The latter departs from what the Philippine ethnomusicologist Ramon Santos has observed among many Philippine Indigenous traditions where musical excellence and aesthetic satisfaction is "not determined by exact intonation and other quantitative factors deemed significant in Western music. . . . Rather, esthetic pleasure is derived from individual timbres, tonal resonance, improvisation, poetic depth, and the relationship of the musical elements with other elements of the artistic activity."[63]

The impact of colonial and neocolonial education, according to Robilyn, is such that Manobo voice performances may now be heard only in far-flung areas like Undin's barangay, or during special occasions when the elders organize *usiba* (entertainment) in the form of song contests, or when a baylan is called upon to perform a ritual for the benefit of a sick person who has no means of going to the hospital. In lowland barangays where educated Natives and settlers reign, and where videoke, radio, and now, YouTube dominate the soundscape most nights and days, one may no longer expect to hear the tod-om, let alone the gudgod that have come to be associated by many with the Agusan-Manobo's uncivilized and heathen past. "People are ashamed to sing and listen to these songs," Robilyn claims.

Modern Medicine and the Baylan

The facilities and personnel officially authorized to respond to La Paz's healthcare needs belong to the government-run rural health unit, comprising a municipal health center, barangay health stations, and the La Paz District hospital mostly manned by a doctor, a dentist, four nurses, and other staff.[64] Such paltry resources and the inadequacy of the rural health unit to effectively service the growing population have been officially acknowledged.[65] On the other hand, Native baylan like Undin are elided in official reports in their capacity as healthcare providers. Neither are the diagnostic procedures, illness taxonomies, etiologies, and healing modalities like the panumanan that the baylan are known for. In the 2013 census of La Paz there is one reference to *hilot* (healers through blood vessel, nerve, and musculoskeletal manipulation), some of whom are baylan, but only in relation to their need for extensive (formal) training.[66] The reports show little signs of implementing the national government's 1997 Traditional and Alternative Medicine Act that pushes for the integration of traditional and complementary or alternative medicine. The World Health Organization and the United Nations Children's Fund have recommended officially utilizing Indigenous practices to "extend primary health care currently beyond the reach of national health budgets" and to address issues of cultural specificity.[67]

The elision of the baylan in official reports may not, however, always reflect what actually happens on the ground. In an early study of the Manobo pathway of curative resorts, the anthropologist Linda Montillo-Burton observes that the Manobo she engaged with consulted—at the onset of illness—traditional healers like the Manobo baylan or the Visayan settler healer who also utilized Native methods. When they did not achieve a cure, the Manobo consulted medical practitioners. When they also failed, the Manobo—in the final resort—returned to the baylan. Montillo-Burton explains that the Manobo's decision to first consult traditional healers was largely influenced by their ethnicity, that is, their being Manobo, despite their having had some formal education. By consulting the baylan, they hoped for not only treatment but also advice related to their condition, that is, the etiology or cause of illness. Based on what they found out, decisions were made on who to consult next. A second reason why many Manobo consulted traditional healers first was their meager income, which prevented them from seeing doctors who charged prohibitive fees. In contrast, most Manobo baylan and Visayan curers did not charge anything. A third reason why Manobo chose to see traditional healers first was because the healers usually lived among them and were accessible, unlike the hospital and clinic that required vehicular travel, making it less possible for the sick to be transported immediately.[68]

After seeing a baylan, according to Montillo-Burton, Manobo often consulted a medical doctor for a second opinion, especially when the baylan's diagnosis indicated that the condition was not caused by supernatural forces. The decision to consult a medical doctor was often influenced by the severity of the condition or because the sick person appeared to be beyond the help of a traditional healer. In such cases, the sick person was usually brought to the hospital despite the lack of money and other constraints. In the final resort for seeking a cure, however, the Manobo likely returned to their Indigenous healers. In contrast, the non-Manobo usually consulted the doctor first, and if that failed, they sought other doctors.[69]

The reputation of the baylan for efficacious healing has been acknowledged even by some educated Manobos like Florencia, who recalled: "When Jose was a baylan, he never consulted a doctor. The abyan was always there to help."[70] When Jose gave up his baylanhood to become a Free Methodist pastor, however, things changed. Not only did he stop communicating with his abyan, he and Florencia, together with other missionaries, organized medical missions in La Paz's far-flung barangays to convince people to consult the doctor instead of the baylan for most of their medical needs. Of these missions, Florencia said:

> Our church group served as volunteer social workers in Undin's village. We were assisted by missionaries as well as by one physician, Dr. Trosio. Our objective was to convince people of the benefits of seeing a doctor, of getting hospitalized, of believing in Western medicine. This was to counter the people's practice of consulting the abyan each and every time they fell ill with fever, or cholera. What our church did was to pay the people's hospital bills, sometimes, up to 3,000, or 4,000, or 7,000 pesos. We wanted everyone to understand that there are natural causes to sicknesses that are best addressed by doctors, as opposed to illnesses that are caused by spirits and cured by them through the baylan. But there were also cases that Dr. Trosio, who was a Muslim, referred back to us because he knew that these were best approached the traditional way. This doctor understood the work of spirits. The result of our drive was that people began to realize that the doctor was also an expert at curing, that perhaps the reason why many have died in the past was because they did not believe in the doctor's treatment. Our efforts succeeded in convincing people that they need not call on the abyan each time they got sick, for not all illnesses are inflicted and cured by the spirits. We ourselves recognize the abyan's contributions to healing the sick. But we also wanted people to not close their minds, and to equally recognize the doctor's abilities. With the help of missionaries, we did this education campaign for several years.[71]

A direct consequence of efforts like Florencia's and Jose's is that fewer people now consult the baylan at the onset of illnesses. Robilyn reports that people nowadays prefer to see the doctor or to be rushed to the municipal hospital in La Paz, the municipal hospital in the neighboring town of Loreto, or the provincial hospital in Patin-ay.

The Manobo peoples' increasing abandonment of ancestral ways because of medical institutions, churches, and schools, according to Undin, contributed to the straining of relationships between humans and the abyan, and to the diminishing of the latter's powers. "The abyan are different now," Undin laments. "Unlike the olden days when there was no need to see a doctor because the abyan would readily come to heal the sick and was effective so that even without pills and capsules, one found relief, they may still help now but are no longer as powerful."[72]

Florencia attributes what seems to be the diminishment of the powers of the abyan to the many obstacles that now beset them. She said:

> Long ago, the abyan had no competition or rival for the people's devotion. But now there is religion, as well as pills and capsules to relieve the sick. As a result, not too many people invoke the abyan now. While all the abyan wanted was to assist humans in peace, there are too many forces against them now.[73]

To this, Undin added, "Many (abyan) have departed, crying, leaving the human world behind for a place far away."[74] Pastor Florencia pointed out that the biggest change has been that "many of the followers of the abyan have come to embrace Christianity because the spirit of God is also real. People have begun to attend churches, listen to sermons, read the Bible, and sing Christian songs."[75] These are the very same people, Undin observed, "who have cursed the spirits, shaming them, insulting them, casting them away. That is why only a few of them continue to be around," she says. Her abyan has remained only because she has stayed devoted to it (figure 1.3).[76]

Becoming a Baylan

Recalling her path to baylanhood, Undin said:

> When I was a little girl, I lived with my grandmother who was the highest baylan during her time. She was powerful and could dance on water. When she grew old and weak, I took care of her. I asked, "What will we do when you are gone? We'll have no one to call on to help us, to answer

FIGURE 1.3. Baylan Undin Potenciano during her panumanan, La Paz, Agusan del Sur, 2005

Photo by Grace Nono.

our questions." My grandmother replied, "It will be better for you when I am gone. Whenever you have a question or difficulty, just call on me and I will help you." Sometime after my grandmother died, I fell ill for about a year. There was no clear diagnosis of my illness. I just felt weak and had no appetite for food. Then one day, I was made aware of a woman who was having a difficult pregnancy. As I slept that night, my grandmother appeared in a dream rousing me from my sleep because it was time for the woman to give birth. I stood up and became the one to deliver the child even if I didn't know anything about such things. As it turned out, it was my grandmother's abyan who guided me throughout the process. My grandmother appeared to me again and said, "From this point on, you will fulfill certain obligations. You will dance in the house where you will offer a pig. You will also dance and offer another pig on the water where there are other abyan." Following her instructions, I regained my health and began to serve as an abyanan (someone who has an abyan) and a baylan. My grandmother's abyan became my own abyan who came to me to instruct me about different things. I fulfilled my obligations during the designated times. It is our tradition, for instance, to regularly hold the kahimunan (big annual rituals with offerings, todom singing, ritual dancing, and feasting) to renew our vows and to express our devotion to the abyan.[77]

Related to her role as maternal nurse, Undin was also a *mananambe* to *kajo-kajo/bagnot-bagnot* (herbalist), and a *hilot* (healer through blood vessel, nerve, and musculoskeletal manipulation). Undin stressed that in a place like La Paz where there is only one hospital, which happens to be far from where many people live—even if it were near it could not address all conditions—the baylan is very important indeed.[78]

Florencia emphasized that "Of all diwateros or people entered into by the abyan, the baylan is the most respected, for there are diwateros who could do nothing but call on the spirits. To be a baylan is to be so much more. It is to have a full-time job. It is to be an expert at helping and healing people, including other baylan."[79] Thus, Undin noted, "If anyone calls on me, or needs my assistance, I must go and help that person no matter what time it is, even if it is late at night. And if I am asked for anything, I must give even the little that I have."[80] A baylan may also be *marajow nug sambag tu utow*, someone who gives counsel, at least to members of one's own family.[81] A baylan may further be an *ognangon* (prophet) or someone who foretells the future, but "it is the abyan that speaks," Robilyn said.[82] Of the different baylan she knows, Robilyn observed them to be mostly "kind, truthful, merciful, helpful, even to strangers."[83] Undin pointed out, however, that "there are also baylan who have ill intents or are jealous and destructive. The baylan are just like other human beings," she said.[84] Florencia summarized why she thought Undin was called to baylanhood:

> First, she inherited the practice from her own grandmother. Second, when the abyan searches for a medium, it chooses someone who is faithful and devoted to fulfilling the obligations to spirits. Third, the abyan selects someone who has a good yagong, and a good speaker and singer. The abyan will never select someone out of tune.[85]

The Relational Voice

Immediately following the panumanan officiated by Undin, I knew that while I could partially make sense of Undin's yagong based on Jose's retelling in languages I was familiar with, I did not necessarily share the elderly Manobo ritual participants' modes of listening shaped by years of ritual participation and specific human-spirit relations. I was outside this community of listeners. Although I was born and raised in Agusan, and recently learned of mamuhatbuhat ritual specialists among my maternal relations in Camiguin, north of Agusan, I was not socialized in Native rituals, having been raised in a more colonized setting where traditions like these were effectively suppressed. In an effort to better understand how Undin's yagong was generated, heard, and understood, I caucused with some of my fellow panumanan participants.

Yagong, according to Robilyn, is a term that the Manobo of La Paz generally use to refer to the human voice as this arises from the speaker's or singer's body, the mouth, especially, and the mind. Yagong is generally differentiated from *tanog* (sound), a term often used to describe the sound of animals, things, and spirits. The yagong-tanog distinction, however, is blurred for those who are able to decipher both the sonic and the referential meanings of tanog and the yagong. For them, yagong becomes equally appropriate to refer to the sound of, say, mating chickens. Conversely, when a human's yagong merges with the tanog of an abyan, the resulting utterance may be referred to as either tanog or yagong.

A *yagonganon*, Robilyn added, is a person who can sing different genres of song, among them the tod-om and the gudgod.[86] Undin is one such person. Tod-om as sung by a yagonganon is delivered extemporaneously, just like everyday speech, to introduce oneself, to describe the setting, to ask permission, or to give thanks, often provoking a response. Gudgod, on the other hand, is the voice of the abyan made audible by the baylan's voice, delivered extemporaneously just like speech in the context of ritual, as the abyan searches for and discovers answers to questions pertaining to illness, the future, or any other concern presented by the ritual participants. Of her story as a singer, Undin recalls first singing *kinaraan* or old-time Visayan settlers' songs. This was long before she sang the tod-om and before she became a baylan. All this changed, she said, when the abyan began to come to her each time the moon was full and the night was bright and she would find herself unable to sleep. These were the times, she remembers, when "The abyan would enter my heart and enable me to sing."[87]

I arranged for Jose and Florencia to listen with me to my recording of her gudgod with Undin's permission. As someone who had been a baylan and who was familiar with the experience of being sung through by the abyan, Jose explained:

The moment the abyan descends on the baylan, not one of the baylan's words can come out. She will no longer have her own ideas. And yet, she remains awake, seated, seeing and hearing with eyes and ears that pierce through things, as though watching television. The baylan's eyes, like a searchlight, can see beyond the screen, into the bright beyond.[88]

Reflecting on Jose's statements that suggest the disablement of Undin's words and ideas during the gudgod when her mind and comprehension were taken over by her abyan, I wondered whether Undin's yagong, the sound of her material body, remained somehow audible. Did the abyan's yagong in the context of gudgod totally eclipse Undin's voice? In my own hearing, Undin's voice continued to be recognizable. It remained a participant in the internal comingling of voices. My observation concurs with Buenconsejo's findings about the Agusan-Manobo voice in song:

> The ambiguous nature of voice in song (is such that) although personal song (*ted-em ne persunal*) is the voice of the person and stems from the singer's breath (*ginhawa*), it can, in performance, almost always merge with the external voice of the singer's spirit helper or simply her or his double (*kadengan-dengan*). This observation is of paramount importance because it means that voice in Manobo song constitutes a medial subjectivity, neither an entirely atomistic self, nor simply other. Singers breach the boundaries of sameness and alterity and envoice a subject whose *ginhawa* blends with that of the singer's external spirit-double. Song performance therefore makes contact with the invisible realms lying within and without a person. Personal song articulates what is inside the mind (*ginhawa*) and flowers into a singable "speech" (*dandanen*) resembling that of spirit voice. The affinity between what is inside and what is outside, a mimesis, resembles song's messages, which are about movements of living/dead in the cosmos.[89]

Undin distinguishes at least two ways in which the abyan relates to her at different points of the gudgod, with implications on her yagong. *Pig-aha dinpuli* (being watched by spirit), she explains, "is when the abyan does not enter me but simply focuses on me, e.g. to guide me on what to sing or say." In pig-aha dinpuli, therefore, Undin retains much of the material quality of her yagong, not to mention her own words and ideas. *Pigyunaan* (being entered into by spirit), on the other hand, Undin explains, "signifies full entry of the abyan into my heart, causing me to tremble." Yuna comes close to what had been described as possession trance: the "displacement of one soul with another."[90] Indeed, when Undin is *pigyunaan*, her yagong becomes dominated and upstaged by the tanog of her abyan. Yet it is not totally silenced. One should also understand that pig-aha dinpuli and pigyunaan are not mutually exclusive. Close to Marina Roseman's notion of "continuum of density and tangibility" between a spirit in motion and a spirit at rest, pig-aha dinpuli indicates the least dense and tangible abyan in relative motion while still able to exert influence on Undin's voice and mind.[91] Pigyunaan, on the other hand, indexes the densest state of the abyan in relative rest while momentarily inhabiting Undin's mind and thickening her voice.[92]

Such degrees of mingling between baylan and abyan, human and nonhuman voices, go against dominant understandings of the voice as individual, as arising from a body like no other, an idea that has a long history in the West. The Roman rhetorician Quintilian (35–100 AD) wrote: "Every human being possesses a distinctive voice of his own, which is as easily distinguishable by the ear as are facial characteristics by the eye."[93] Two millennia later, Roland Barthes made the canonical assertion that the voice is "something which is directly the cantor's body, brought to your ears in one and the same movement from deep down in the cavities, the muscles, the membranes, the cartilages. . . . The 'grain' is that: the materiality of the body speaking its mother tongue."[94] Among those who have recently reasserted the voice's embodied singularity are Adriana Cavarero, who writes, "The voice . . . is always different from all other voices, even if the words are the same, as often happens in the case of a song."[95] Cavarero cites Italo Calvino as attributing such difference to the body: "'A Voice means this: there is a living person, throat, chest, feelings, who sends into the air this voice, different from all other voices. . . . A voice involves the throat, saliva.' When the human voice vibrates, there is someone in flesh and bone who emits it."[96] Mladen Dolar argues, "[One] way to be aware of the voice is through its individuality. We can almost unfailingly identify a person by the voice, the particular timbre, resonance, pitch, cadence, melody, the peculiar way of pronouncing certain sounds. The voice is like a fingerprint, instantly recognizable and identifiable."[97]

There hasn't always been a consensus in the West, however, about voice arising from a singular material source, the utterer's body. Historicizing European conceptions of the body and the voice, Steven Connor writes that in the late classical and medieval periods, "the body was conceived, not so much as an object, or the home and expression of a personality, as a dynamism. Conceived in this way, the human body was seen as vulnerable to invasion by other forces and agencies. . . . The insides and the outsides of things are not so powerfully distinguished as they are in later conceptions; insides and outsides change places, and produce each other reciprocally."[98] The body's permeability is further alluded to by Gary Tomlinson in his study of the opera in late Renaissance Europe, when song and voice articulated a human subjectivity that was "one with the hidden regions of the world."⁹⁹ "The boundary between the two realms (material and immaterial) is so permeable as almost to be no boundary at all."¹⁰⁰ The conception of the body as permeable, according to Connor, became steadily eroded, particularly during the seventeenth and eighteenth centuries, to one of "the body as an object in a coherent and fixed field."¹⁰¹ The notion of a singular, distinct voice issuing from an individual body set against its environment, distinguishable from all other voices, persisted from early sources to its conceptual dominance in modernity, with interludes or subcurrents of competing conceptions of a more permeable voice.

In twenty-first-century Philippines, the isomorphism of the singular voice with the equally singular body has come to be the norm among the more colonized and modernized populations including the dominant Agusan-Manobo class. But to a hinterland baylan like Undin, the gudgod presents a condition of voice that is not only as a singularity but a relationship. To my fellow ritual participants, Undin's yagong in gudgod was not hers alone but also her abyan's. This relational voice proceeds from the knowledge that voice is both necessarily singular—the singer's body—and plural, constituted by the voices that one engages with at each moment of articulation. While this relational voice is not necessarily incompatible with the singular voice, relationality does tend to sonically "thicken" it in varying consistencies. As yagong in gudgod is inflected by the voice of spirit thickening the timbre native to the medium's body so the baylan's *paminog* (listening) during gudgod is not hers alone but the result of her sharing her abyan's auditory faculties. "The baylan perceives all of the sounds that her abyan hears," pastor Jose explained of Undin's audition in gudgod.

The ontology of voice and listening that emerges in the gudgod is one of relationality. The baylan's voice is not atomistic sonic material but is mediated through specific and contextual acts of singing, speaking, and listening by different kinds of bodies in ongoing interaction and transformation.¹⁰² Voice—including that of the non-baylan—arises neither from an isolated individual nor from an abstract social but in the ongoing interactions, transmissions, and receptions of internal and external voices. Every voice is already a relationship, an identity that is both complex and moving. The relational voice as an aspect of the relational person is an integrity that rests on the inevitability of interconnection.

There are indications that the intermingling of the baylan and abyan persists beyond considerations of voice and listening. Robilyn cites her grandfather, Agusan-Manobo Supreme Datu (chief) and baylan Tagleong as having had the ability to smell and feel his abyan keenly especially during full moons. Nor is it only the baylan and *diwatahan* (other people who have abyan) who sense the abyan in heightened ways. The abyan themselves are said to have very keen perceptions, particularly of the baylan they assist. Pastor Jose said of Undin:

> Now that she is a baylan, it is no longer necessary for her to call on her abyan in order for it to come to her. Each time she sounds her yagong, her abyan will hear it, and it is imperative that it comes to her. It's like a telephone connection [in which someone from a different place and/or time gains immediate sonic presence]. That is how it is to be a baylan or diwatero [another term for diwatahan] and one should not be surprised about it. Even if the tod-om or lisag [drum and gong ensemble] do not issue from the baylan, whenever these are sounded, they become heard loud and clear in the firmament, awakening the spirits that are familiar with them. It is the same thing when one plays the guitar and offers liquor and eggs or lights candles—how the dagatnon [from the sea, Visayan settlers] healers invoke their spirits—then it is the dagatnon spirits that will come. Even if the tanog and yagong originate from a recording, these have the same effect of attracting the spirits' attention. One time we played our recordings of the tod-om and the lisag to our fellow-Manobos, and their abyan came, thinking that they had been called.[103]

Of abyan ontology, pastor Jose explained further:

> Every abyan has an individual body that is not seen and is so light, it can travel with the wind and penetrate through walls as well as human body parts. It is a body that takes on a gender and an age that help determine the quality of its yagong and its bodily comportment during the gudgod. But it is a body that neither gets born, nor grows old, nor dies. While each abyan's body has an original form, i.e. resembling a human, it is able to shape-shift into a chicken, or a dove, or a snake. And while an abyan has an original voice, it has the ability to change that voice into that of a child, or an elderly person, or a man, or a woman, regardless of who the medium is. Whereas the abyan's body is not seen to physically ingest food, it is known to eat through olfactory sensing. The abyan's body could not be seen, heard, nor touched, except by those, who, themselves, have abyan.

Undin referred to the abyan as *tawo* or person. "The abyan looks like us but could not be seen," she said. These abyan, however, can be heard by the non-abyanan during the gudgod. The abyan, Jose claimed, "enters the baylan or diwatahan from the crown of the latter's head, and exits through the mouth, sonically marked by the henghong."

Contested Listenings

The many years that Pastor Jose spent as a baylan familiarized him with the abyan's old Manobo language. His formal education and interactions, on the other hand, prepared him to translate such archaic language to kuntoon Manobo, as well as to Visayan and English, for the sake of the younger generation Manobo, other Agusanons, researchers, and missionaries. Trained by the Summer Institute of Linguistics, Jose and Florencia believed in the possibility of the faithful translation of a source text, a view that can be traced to the centuries of Bible translation.[104] One may note that in Undin's gudgod, the abyan's old Manobo was the source language orally explained by Jose and Florencia to the other ritual participants in the intervening languages of kuntoon Manobo and Visayan. When Jose and Florencia listened to my recording of the gudgod, they transcribed [wrote down] the abyan's utterances in old Manobo, then translated these in the receptor language of English.

I invited Undin to join Jose and Florencia in listening to the gudgod's recording. Sensing her shyness in the presence of Christian pastors who were related to her yet disapproved of her continuing baylan practice, I decided to hold a separate session with her and Robilyn. Although Undin was not literate—in contrast to Jose's and Florencia's high-level literacy and multilingual fluency—I considered her, a yagonganon, to be a Manobo language expert herself, having mastered old Manobo oral performances and their Indigenous meanings.[105] In the process of listening to my recording, first with Jose and Florencia and then with Undin and Robilyn, I came across important discrepancies in the paminog or listening and paghilwas or articulation in another language of parts of the gudgod as arrived at by the two sets of listeners.

One of these discrepancies has to do with Jose's attribution of all gudgod utterances to the voice of "spirit," that is, Undin's abyan. When Undin listened to the recording, however, she offered a more nuanced account by identifying three abyan that her yagong made audible; the word "spirit" is inadequate for communicating all unseen beings most of whom have a name, classification, function, and personality. The abyan who sang in a loud, gruff, brash, masculine yagong, who grumbled over the cumbersomeness of being called, was Oknabanon, a male spirit who was the custodian of Undin's tod-om. A *teabobong* or spirit that resides in the *kabobonganan* (mountains), Oknabanon was invited only when there were important matters to be resolved requiring spirit intervention. A second abyan who was heard in the gudgod, according to Undin—the one who sang in a heavy, slow, low-register, and authoritative voice, who told Oknabanon to come and help whenever called by their medium, and who rebuked Sayson for not listening to the ritual proceedings—was Mikdong (literally, old person). Mikdong was Undin's departed grandmother, a famous baylan during her time. Like other Manobo departed, Mikdong, upon her death, moved to Maibuyan, the city of the dead, while regularly visiting the world of the living as an *umagad* (soul of the Manobo departed). Mikdong was the abyan who first descended onto Undin, turning the then young woman into a baylan successor. A third abyan who was heard in the gudgod was Tapnajanon, a woman healer spirit, who, like Oknabanon, was a teabobong. Tapnajanon was the one who sang in a mellow woman's yagong not much different from Undin's lucid voice, who complained about Undin's faults; encouraged Sayson to seek forgiveness for his offence; and urged the inflicter to withdraw the illness. Tapnajanon, according to Undin, has been the spirit behind her healing and child delivery. A fourth abyan that was not heard in Undin's gudgod but was sung about and sung to was the Inajow, the abyan of Sayson's father that inflicted the young man with illness as punishment for his disrespect. The Inajow is the custodian of the wind, rain, thunder, and lightning, and resides in Inugtuhan, a place between heaven and earth below the dwelling of Magbabaja. The Inajow is known to beneficently grant rain, but also to burn whoever provokes its anger.[106]

Each voice that Undin heard from the tod-om recording came from a different class of Manobo abyan representing a specific region of the Manobo universe. Such a voice converged with the other abyan voices and with Undin's yagong in the act of gudgod. Each abyan that was heard had a specialization: Oknabanon was a singer; Tapnajanon, a healer; Mikdong, Undin's main spirit helper and gatekeeper; and the Inajow, the custodian of the wind, rain, thunder, and lightning. Each of them had a history, at least in relation to Undin: Mikdong was her grandmother; and Oknabanon, Tapnajanon, and the Inajow were Mikdong's abyan until she passed on to become an abyan herself. Finally, each of these abyan had a gendered personality that was made audible by Undin's yagong.

While Jose's and Florencia's attribution of all utterances to "spirit" was technically correct, it made for a severely impoverished appreciation and understanding of the gudgod. I offer two possible explanations for why this happened. First, Jose and Florencia were unfamiliar with Undin's specific abyan, whom they "met" for the first time during Undin's panumanan that they attended. It would be unreasonable, therefore, to expect the two to come up with more nuanced listening. Jose may have been a baylan who sang the gudgod in the past but he was then listening to the voice of his own abyan, not Undin's. A second possible explanation may be Jose's and Florencia's tendency to attend, first and foremost, to linguistic utterances. By focusing on the words of the abyan, which can be visually represented as texts for the purpose of translation to English, and not on the quality of the sounds and the silences between the sounds, it was not difficult for Jose and Florencia to miss out on the various sonic transformations that took place within Undin's voice indicating the comings and goings of the different abyan speakers and singers. The shift of attention from the dynamic sounds that issue from the performer's body to the extractable and fixable texts derived from such sounds has led to a mode of listening more aligned with those of Bible translators, older-generation anthropologists, and many literate elites.

As for Undin's attention to the relationships between the linguistic and extralinguistic features of the voices of her abyan—their gendered timbres, pitches, tempos, manners of articulation, methods of persuasion, and feelings—it allowed her not only to decipher the referential meanings of the words uttered by her abyan but also to identify the voices that were familiar to her from the start, even as these voices merged with her own.[107] Undin's mode of listening intersects with the renewed attention to the "sonic material of articulation."[108] Provoked by the hegemony of linguistically motivated approaches to music description and analysis of sound and the voice—and of the mind over the body—protests have been raised against music's reduction to language. Although appearing to be "a simpler formal system to describe with logical rules . . . meaning in music is notoriously more complex to formally characterize when compared to the semantic structures of language."[109]

In addition to the discrepant ways of listening to the gudgod's voices by Jose and Florencia, on the one hand, and by Undin and Robilyn, on the other, the two sets of listeners differed in their paghilwas of some of the old Manobo utterances of the abyan. On several occasions, Jose's and Florencia's translations were given decidedly Christian meanings that were absent from Undin's. During Jose's conversation with Oknabanon about "the future of humans," for example, he translated Oknabanon's response as: "You will be winnowed . . . thrown into the lake of fire." The "lake of fire" is a Christian image taken from the bible's Book of Revelation. It signifies the second death or separation from God following physical death, spelling eternal damnation for the dead judged to have led wicked or non-Christian lives. When Undin offered to interpret Oknabanon's response, her take was slightly different: "Like rice grains you will be winnowed; the good ones will be chosen to stay, the rest thrown away." There was no mention of the "lake of fire" that is not part of her understanding of what transpires after death. Jose, himself, as an ex-baylan, once explained that the umagad go to Maibuyan, the city of the dead, a place where there is no judgment. Another discrepancy was found in Jose's and Florencia's paghilwas of Oknabanon's response to Jose's other question: "What should we do then to save our lives, if you who are our guardian spirits are reluctant to help us?" Oknabanon's response, as translated by Jose, was: "That is true. But I am not capable as spirit. I do not have power. I can no longer give assurances to humans because I myself am a sinner, and all my companions too. It is difficult for them. And now this is the only thing I can say. I will return to my home now." In both Jose's question and his translation of Oknabanon's response, he used the word "sin," which in Christianity is the state of humankind until saved by God's grace. He and Florencia further interpreted Oknabanon's response as an admission of the spirit's powerlessness and acceptance of Christianity's judgment of all abyan including himself as "sinful," that is, deserving of condemnation. In comparison, Undin's understanding of Oknabanon's words was: "That is true. For we whom you call have become weakened and lowly. I can no longer give assurances on the future of humans who always commit mistakes, which is why you are going through many difficulties. That is all. I will return to my home now." Here, Oknabanon admits to being weakened and thrust low in the order of things, but attributes the hardships of human beings, not to the sins of the abyan, but to the mistakes of humans.

It is tempting to dismiss Jose's and Florencia's paghilwas as faulty and Undin's as more accurate, but there may be more to this than meets the eye. It is worth noting that Undin was not listening to a recording of her words and ideas but to those of the abyan, even as these were carried by her material voice. She therefore was partially removed from the gudgod's source utterances, as were Jose and Florencia. In addition, and in consideration of the vast cultural and linguistic differences between the old Manobo spirit language and English—notwithstanding the intervening languages of kuntoon Manobo and Visayan—untranslatability may be paramount here. Aspects of the spirits' song may have expectedly resisted capture within the system of conventional human meanings. In such light, neither Jose's and Florencia's nor Undin's and Robilyn's paghilwas of the old Manobo utterances of the abyan can be presumed to fully and faithfully reproduce the spirit helpers' meanings. Not only is complete faithfulness in this situation theoretically and practically impossible, the faithful reproduction of source texts is little known as a norm among many oralists like Undin. In an oral context, paghilwas constitutes more a creative retelling in another language, one that may involve narrating, elaborating, interpreting, commenting, equating, quoting, deleting, arranging, explaining, and other narrative strategies to render the source text accessible.[110] This may explain Jose's and Florencia's elaboration of the gudgod's texts to include "sin" and "lake of fire," concepts that have become part of their religious ideology as Christianized Agusan-Manobo. That may not be all, however. Following years of missionary training, Manobo pastors Jose and Florencia may have already judged the abyan as a lying demon condemned to sin and to the lake of fire, even before they heard it sing.[111] Like many other missionaries, they saw the abyan as "demonic" and "evil," conflating these with the "legions of spirits that rebelled against God together with Lucifer, and who have since become fallen angels."[112] Even if they had stayed faithful to the spirit helpers' words, they may still have been motivated to provide a translation which would expose and refute what they, as missionaries, believed to be the false religion of the baylan and abyan. Such ideological motivation that undergirds their translation work has historical precedents.[113] Vicente Rafael traces such "standard missionary practice" to the colonial times when Spanish friars erroneously equated Indigenous respect for ancestral and nature spirits with the pre-Christian past and with the Christian notion of idolatry unknown to Natives then.[114]

Despite her missionary bias, Florencia as Agusan-Manobo herself, complicates the abyan's total demonization by stating in theological terms: "I feel that because God, Himself, created these beings and endowed them with talent and goodness in the beginning, qualities which God did not take away, they continue to have the capacity to do good. They are therefore of a mixed nature, of good and bad. They can do good because of the essence of goodness already in them that God did not take away."[115] Outside of theological considerations, social factors may also have accounted for the differences in Jose's and Florencia's paghilwas compared to Undin's and Robilyn's. That Undin was an uneducated, illiterate, poor woman from the mountains who sang in old Manobo may have further contributed to the impulse of educated Christian Manobos to wield discursive power over her and her oral gudgod.

The different interpretations of parts of the gudgod as arrived at through the paminog of Jose and Florencia, and of Undin and Robilyn, support what some scholars have asserted about listening as a site of ambiguity, multiplicity and contestation.[116] Deborah Kapchan stressed listening's performativity, as opposed to the view of listening as "passive perception."[117] Listening "does something in the world, engaging imagination, evoking memory but also creating meaning."[118] Jose and Florencia listened to the gudgod and translated its texts into English in ways that transposed dominant values into the language of the subordinated.[119] Undin and Robilyn, on the other hand, also listened and interpreted the utterances of the abyan according to how they perceived the world in ways that contested the pastors' understandings, demonstrating that translation is a site of creative negotiation.[120] The different interpretations generated by the two sets of listeners illustrate the changing norms of listening and voice generation among the Agusan-Manobo, with members of the dominant Manobo class leaning more toward text-centered communication strategies following centuries of colonial rule, public school education, missionary Bible translation, and neocolonial capitalist conditions.[121] While necessary for coping in today's world, text-centered communication strategies like writing have been observed to be limited and fallible instruments "in the service of acoustic memory."[122] If modern communication strategies that place a premium on literate and textual analysis have not been able to fully silence oral performances like the gudgod and their utterers' Native interpretations suggests the tenacity of the baylan's voice and listening practices.

These attend to the relationships between the linguistic and extralinguistic aspects of language, sounds and the silences, allowing the plural voices within the baylan's voice to emerge and be heard. Further attested to is the adaptability of the baylan's listening practices that allows sounds to be partially inscribed as texts in ways that could not, however, fully capture them.[123]

Healing: A Practical Benefit of Relational Voice and Listening

Returning to Undin's panumanan, one notes that the commitment of the different classes of abyan (Oknabanon, Mikdong, Tapnajanon, Inajow) to come together in Undin's yagong, and of the different Manobo ritual participants (Jose, Florencia, Undin, Robilyn)—regardless of their social and ideological differences—to listen to human and nonhuman relations, determined whether young Sayson's condition could be traced to its cause and healed. Illness in many rural Philippine communities, writes F. Landa Jocano, "cannot be understood mainly on pathological grounds. Illness is (often) due to conflicts between the self and its environment."[124] Should maladjustments and problems occur, "certain culturally valid medication is required to rectify the error. This is one reason why prayers and rituals—often surrounded by a substantial body of beliefs, knowledge and practices—are effective therapeutic instruments. In this way, harmonious relations are restored and the self is reintegrated into the community."[125] Health, therefore, is achieved by maintaining mutually beneficent relationships that entail reciprocal gifts of food, song, and respect, as witnessed in Undin's panumanan. Such relational understandings of health, illness, and healing have equally been noted in other parts of southeast Asia, where ill health, writes Carol Laderman and Penny Esterik, "may be thought of as originating in inharmonious or inappropriate behavior on the part of the patient's relatives and neighbors, as well as due to his own lapses."[126] Healing in this case may be "accomplished by reopening blocked communications between human beings, and between humans and spirits."[127]

Through Undin's gudgod—an embodied technology that made it possible for ritual participants to listen to spirit voices as they searched for answers to questions—Sayson's illness was traced to the young man's disrespect to his father and to his father's abyan that had been rendered sinful and shameful by the colonizers, missionaries, agents of the modern nation, dominant Manobo classes, and modernized youth. As a diagnostic tool, gudgod's findings would be rejected by those who trace illness exclusively to physical and psychological causes and by those who relegate such practices to the realm of superstition, multiple personality disorder, and illusion.[128] Limpas buya will not be acknowledged as an appropriate part of the treatment by those who invalidate whatever lies outside the established modes of biomedical intervention. Sayson's recovery may also be dismissed as a case of the placebo effect, an interpretation that renders it unreal and illegitimate.[129] Finally, Undin the baylan will not be recognized as a legitimate healthcare practitioner but as an ignorant, superstitious, heathen woman who should be subjected to discipline and extensive training or banished permanently to the silent margins. Ritual interventions and the spirit possession they often entail are rarely taken for what people who practice such tradition say they are, Steven Friedson writes.[130] And yet they persist, perhaps because of their efficacy.

Rich Land, Poor Communities

In the years that followed baylan Undin's 2005 panumanan for her nephew, Sayson, the municipality of La Paz, the province of Agusan del Sur, and the region of Caraga made the national news on three separate but interrelated accounts. The first featured Caraga's rich natural resources. Not only has the region's forests provided 70 percent of the Philippines' lumber needs, Caraga is known to have the Philippines' largest mineral deposits.[131] According to the Department of Environment and Natural Resources' Mines and Geosciences Bureau, Caraga contains the country's biggest iron ore, nickel, and gold deposits, with large reserves of copper, chromite, and coal.[132] All this has earned Caraga the title of mining capital of the Philippines, ranking first in the world's iron ore deposits, third in gold, fourth in copper, fifth in nickel, and sixth in chromite.[133] The second set of news headlines have reported the intense poverty in some of these areas, with the municipality of La Paz having ranked one of the Philippines' twenty poorest municipalities.[134] Agusan del Sur itself has been one of the twenty poorest provinces, and was the poorest in the years 2006 and 2009.[135] The third cause for Agusan del Sur's and Caraga's notability is the violence in these areas that has hit Indigenous populations the worst.[136] Three groups have been identified as responsible for the armed crisis: the government military known to recruit Indigenous Peoples to its ranks and thought by many to protect big business interests; the New Peoples' Army—the armed wing of the Communist Party of the Philippines—also known to recruit Indigenous Peoples to advance its revolution; and paramilitary groups sometimes suspected to have both the government military and big businesses behind them. The question is, where are the Agusan-Manobo baylan and abyan in all this? What relationship do they have to the wealth, the poverty, and the violent contests for power over Indigenous lands and bodies? Do the baylan, abyan, and their voices have any relevance at all to any of these?

Many if not most Agusan-Manobo baylan live in dire poverty, at least according to measurements of wealth based on monetary income, material goods, formal education, and employment. Many reside in dirt-floor thatched houses with no electricity, no indoor plumbing or other modern amenities. Unrecognized as a sector, the majority have no access to social services or institutional support. Whatever cash incomes and donations they receive are irregular and often fall below poverty levels. By most standards, many Agusan-Manobo baylan are among the poorest of the poor. But what about the vast riches that lie beneath the ground they stand on? Are they at least aware of these? How can they not be aware after almost a century of logging and mining that have afforded many Agusan-Manobo short-term employment but also longstanding environmental damage and dispossession. One sacred mountain in La Paz where eagles perch and where *diwatas* (general term for spirits) are believed to dwell has been frequented by picture-taking and sample-drawing foreign investors, Robilyn noted. "They have found gold there," she said. And yet "these investors' machinery has often broken down, or their workers have met accidents because the abyan are against these encroachments. They want the sacred mountain protected because once mining comes in, the mountain will be destroyed. They will lose their dwellings, and the people will suffer too," she added. In consonance with the wishes of the abyan, many baylan—contrary to the stance of some Agusan-Manobo political leaders—have not supported the desecration of their Native lands that are rich to them, first and foremost, because they are the spirit helpers' dwellings.

Unofficial reports have indicated that some of the male baylan have been conscripted by the various armed groups to attend to their wounded combatants. Many baylan, after all, are known for their healing abilities. But despite the mandate of many abhan that the baylan assist whoever is in need, regardless of ideology, class, gender, ethnicity, race, and religion, some of the male baylan have accordingly been suspected of siding with specific groups.

Baylan women like Undin, on the other hand, like many other poor Agusan-Manobo women, are rarely listened to these days. Their voices seem to be drowned out by modern entertainment, religious bashing, and artillery fire. Some of them ask: Who can we turn to? Who might guide us through these difficult times? Outside groups may lend a helping hand but the most that they can offer, depending on their intentions, are food aids, emergency medicines, temporary shelters, and the often false hope of progress once big business settles in. Similar to this is the promise of a classless society once the revolution that first claims their precious lives is won. The various groups that have paraded solutions to people's problems have tended to proceed in a top-down fashion without much consideration for how many ritual specialists understand their situations. Many baylan like Undin lament the Agusan-Manobo people's increasing divisions on the grounds of religion, ideology, and class, and their diminished interest in ancestral ways.

This was the context of the intertribal gathering that took place in Bunawan in 2015. The gathering was organized by a few indigenous professionals and some urban and diasporic, middle-class, babaylan-inspired scholars, artists, priests, healers, and activists who wanted to reconnect with the fabled babaylan. Ten Native ritual specialists from around the Philippines participated, including three from Agusan del Sur, Undin being one of them. The intention was to facilitate mutual listening that privileged Native voices and perspectives. Being part of the organizing group, little did I know that the call to listen would be relevant not only to the urbanites and diasporans but also to the Agusan-Manobo participants.

Learning to Listen Again

It is near daybreak in La Paz. The air is crisp from the evening rains. Undin boards a truck to Bunawan together with her fellow baylan Julia, as well as Robilyn, Robilyn's mother Ebeng, Robilyn's sister and her two children, and five male Agusan-Manobo traditional housebuilders led by Robilyn's uncle—Aylo Tawede, a Baptist pastor.[137] Also aboard the truck are *anislag* wood for house posts and carvings, *tuyay* and *kawayan buyo* for trusses, rattan for tying, and anahaw leaves for roofing that Aylo and his team would use to build a *tinandasan* (Manobo traditional house) to be used during the gathering. After several hours of travel, the group arrives in Bunawan, drenched from the relentless rains and famished. They sit down for a meal of hot fish soup, then nap under warm blankets. Once rested, the housebuilders begin to sketch the tinandasan's outlines on the clayish soil. They and their kin are part of the gathering's Agusan hosts and have come to Bunawan a week ahead of the other participants to allow time for the preparations.

Over the next two days, I find out that the tinandasan had not been built for many years because of its association with uncivilized forest habitation and with Agusan-Manobo rituals that many Christian missionaries have tried to put an end to. In addition, I find out that the women baylan (Undin and Julia) and the male housebuilders (led by Aylo) have not been speaking to each other. Rather, Aylo and his companions have refused to have anything to do with the baylan women, because they, the Manobo housebuilders, have embraced Christianity that to them is the only true way. Finally, young woman Robilyn, the group's coordinator, who was, herself, raised Baptist while being exposed to baylan traditions and cultural revitalization work, is caught in the middle, facing the daunting task of mediating between the two factions.

On the third day of the tinandasan's construction, I observe that no house-building ritual—supposedly mounted before the construction begins—has taken place. I ask Robilyn why this is the case. She speaks to the housebuilders and find out that they who feel entitled over their work see no reason for a Native (non-Christian) ritual to take place. On the other hand, Undin, whose views do not seem to matter to the housebuilders, has kept urging that ritual implements be purchased so that the ritual can transpire. This forces Robilyn to confront both the women baylan and the male housebuilders in the hope that the two would reach a decision acceptable to all. After an evening of discussion, Robilyn tells me that the two groups have reached a compromise. They will hold a ritual but one that will not summon the abyan to the site, unlike Undin's panumanan for Sayson a decade ago. Before noon that same day, I see Undin and Julia light candles and arrange raw eggs, coins, and betel quids on porcelain platters that they lay down with a bottle of liquor on the ground facing the tinandasan construction. Against the din of trucks and motorcycles and the tinkling of bells from the baylan women's head and neck ornaments, Undin and Julia each sing a tod-om to pay their respects to the dwellers of the land, and to seek blessings and protection from Magbabaja and the abyan for the tinandasan and the people who would gather there. While this is taking place, I see the housebuilders at a distance, hearing only faint sounds from the two baylan women. A week later, the scholars, artists, priests, healers, and the environmental, gender, and peace activists arrive. I observe Aylo and the other housebuilders becoming curious that the guests are listening with respect to the songs and stories presented by the various ritual specialists. Slowly, they become interested in the gathering's proceedings (see figure 1.4). As soon as Aylo realizes that there are four Catholic priests in attendance, he becomes emboldened to share a Christian prayer in his Agusan-Manobo language. At this point, he and the other housebuilders also seem to treat the baylan women better, even accommodating some of Undin's suggestions for the tinandasan's design.

During the final day of the gathering that coincides with the tinandasan's completion, Undin performs a final ritual alongside the other ritual specialists in attendance. She slaughters a chicken then pours libations on the ground before sharing the cup with others. Drums and gongs are beaten, and pastor Aylo and his fellow housebuilders joyfully

FIGURE 1.4. Pastor Aylo Tawede, baylan Julia Tawede, and Robilyn Coguit during the gathering of ritual specialists, Bunawan, Agusan del Sur, 2015

Photo by Antonio Jamora.

share tod-om and *sajow* (dances) that they have inherited from their own elders. It is a thanksgiving celebration for both the tinandasan's completion and the successful gathering.

Robilyn's group remained one more day in Bunawan after the gathering. Before departing, Robilyn took me aside to tell me what had happened to them the night before. Her mother, siblings and uncles, according to her, all cried to each other over what took place during the final ritual. For as soon as the drums and gongs were sounded, they felt as though their ancestors came back to them. This followed years, decades, perhaps even centuries of prohibition against the performance of their rituals, the building of their houses, the singing of their songs. Their ancestors, they said, were overjoyed and overcome with longing for the voices, sounds, sights, and smells of their descendants engaging in ancestral ways. While this was but a small celebration, it seemed to have awakened some dormant memories and relations, planting seeds of renewal.

What also struck Robilyn and her family members was their realization that it is possible to be Christians while maintaining their cherished Agusan-Manobo identities, both being necessary for their survival. While Undin and Julia, by their ancestral mandate, are expected to remain baylan and, by the same token, pastor Aylo and his fellow housebuilders will continue to be Baptists, what has changed is that the two factions have begun to listen to each other again. From a condition of alienation and power hierarchies based on religion, gender, and class, they have been reminded of their shared humanity as Agusan-Manobo. As for Robilyn, who inhabits the plural voices of the group, she at her young age was able to skillfully facilitate communication and relational listening between pastor and baylan, male and female, ancestor and offspring. None of this took place so they could all arrive at a singular and homogeneous Agusan-Manobo voice. Differences are expected to remain. But the cultivation of the relational voice and listening is itself a sowing of seeds for the healing of Manobo lands, spirits, and human communities.

A Baylan in Training

I first met Robilyn in Bunawan in 2004 or 2005. She was probably seventeen years old then. The last time I saw her, she had become an accomplished embroiderer who attests to the aesthetic and healing properties of her designs that she claims are revealed by an abyan (spirit helper) through dreams. In the summer of 2017, while she was living in Manila, I visited her home in the big city.

> It is a blisteringly hot afternoon as I make my way through a narrow alley in the vicinity of the port of Tondo, Manila. The houses crowd each other enveloped by the whiff of undigested waste from the belly of the sea, while large trucks load and unload cargo, and vendors peddle knickknacks from China. It is not a scene one would necessarily associate with a baylan in training. But perhaps neither are Agusan's mountains, which have been deforested, the gold in them gutted out. As soon as Robilyn sees me on the street, she ushers me into a dimly lit, two-floor space that she, her two boys, and non-Manobo husband lease. On the wall I see a picture of the Christian Holy Family and a chart of occidental fruits: persimmon, peaches, and grapes that I assume she wants her boys to know about. There is a big television set and stereo system. I feel proud of Robilyn for having a place she can call home. As a fellow Agusanon, I know how difficult it is to be in a position to rent decent lodging in the city. Robilyn first moved to Manila in 2011 to escape the violence in La Paz and to be with her husband, who had been working as a truck driver. Once she gave birth to two sons, she decided to stay on to be near the schools. "The school in my barangay in La Paz is too far from where we live," she says, "and even if my children attended it, the classes would only be held once a week because of the lack of teach-

ers. I do not want to destroy my children's dreams of becoming educated." Living in Manila has afforded Robilyn access to embroidery orders that are her primary sources of income. These have allowed her to occasionally send money back home.

Two years before this visit, Robilyn told me that she had begun training as a *babaiyon* (woman leader) under the tutelage of abyan grandfathers. Whereas there have always been numerous women baylan in the past and in the present, she says, only few have also been babaiyon. What she hopes to become, after the example of her own great grandmother, is both a babaiyon and a baylan.[138] Of her training she says:

> For a long time, the abyan did nothing to help our tribe because there was no one they could approach, no one they could draw courage from. (You see) the abyan need humans to do their work in the world. Having no material existence, their powers are useless unless coursed through the abilities of humans. But because most Agusan-Manobo have abandoned their abyan, there has been no way for the spirits to intervene. When the abyan saw that I was searching for answers to the *kaguluhan* (turmoil) in our communities, they felt encouraged and grateful. They came to me and expressed their wish for us to help each other.

Robilyn further notes that whereas in the past and present, most leaders or settlers of conflicts have been male (datu), they, the abyan told her, "have tended to be too aggressive, so that each time they spoke, people got killed. These male leaders did not know how to resolve conflicts through peaceable means. That is why the abyan would like to try to have a woman leader this time, someone who can help solve problems before these get big," she says.

Unlike Undin, who is a yagonganon, Robilyn has neither musical talent nor a singing abyan. She also has not undergone much trance possession. It is by Robilyn's insistence that her abyan do not possess her, out of her fear of losing control and becoming embarrassment in public situations. She and her abyan thus communicate directly through conversation and through pig-aha dinpuli, that is, when the abyan are close enough to guide her on what to say. "I hear and see them," she says. "They stand and sit around me but are not heard by others except by those who also have abyan."

Robilyn's constant communication with her abyan, she says, has allowed her to assist her family in La Paz, even when she is in Manila. "Either my abyan tell me what's going on or they enable me to see and hear my family there. Witnessing my siblings ask for help moves me to find ways to assist them with money or with prayers and rituals to help solve their problems about the land, about our mother's health, and about conflicts among relatives and tribes. With my abyan grandfathers' guidance, I perform rituals in Manila for the benefit of my family in La Paz," she says.

Knowing about Robilyn's religious background as a Baptist, I ask if she continues to go to church. She says yes. She now, however, only attends Catholic services, having observed Catholics to be more tolerant of Indigenous ways [at least since the Second Vatican Council)]. But she has also observed the Baptist Church to be slowly changing with its recent accommodation of the Native drum and gong ensemble, dances, and chants that have been made to carry Christian themes. I ask if the abyan agree with her going to church and she says: "Since I have been going to church since I was a child, that is, before I began to train as a ritual specialist, I have insisted that the spirits understand that this is my way and they cannot force me to put an end to it. So I go to church. I pray. I also perform rituals."

Robilyn then shares with me what seems to be her project of renegotiating her power relations with the spirits in ways that reflect some Christian ideas. "Above all," she says, "is God." Below God, the abyan are "like angels that have powers to guide and assist humans." Robilyn observed her baylan mother and abyanan father undergo extreme difficulties because "all they could do was cater to the extreme demands of their abyan" who claimed the lives of four of their children as payment for their offences, leading them to relinquish their abyan to become Baptists. Robilyn has vowed to change this *patakaran* (policy). She says: "Whereas my parents followed whatever it was that their abyan ordered them to do, I now insist that I, as a human being, will be the one followed by the spirits. From the very beginning of our relationship, I drew up an agreement stating that I will be the one in control, not the other way around. And whenever I find myself having to deal with an abyan who asks me to do something I do not agree with, I articulate my disagreement and do not follow its bidding," she says. Robilyn has also made sure to increase her own human capacities and resources so as not to depend on the powers of the abyan all the time. "I do not want to rely on the spirits for everything," she says, "especially not with the affairs of my family because I do not want them to interfere." She explains that "one must be careful about asking favors from the abyan because for every favor they give—even if they claim to not require payment—there will be a price to pay. Then whatever they ask of you, you will have to deliver." So Robilyn goes to church to gain added strength and courage in the knowledge that even if the abyan are not around, she is not without power "because God is with me." Robilyn's experience of religion is thus relational, inclusive of the different aspects of the Agusan-Manobo identity.

Robilyn emphasizes, however, that contrary to the blanket demonization of Indigenous spirits by many religions, there are good abyan. She stresses that it is also the character of the person who carries the abyan that largely determines how the abyan will act. Even if the abyan tends to do bad if the person who carries it does good, it, too, will do good, she says. Conversely, even if the abyan tends to do good if the person who carries it does bad, it, too, will do bad. She cites the example of her grandfather Datu Tagleong, who became a baylan when good and helpful abyan began to dwell in him. But this happened because he, himself, was already a good and helpful person who looked after the welfare of others before his own. Because of his own goodness and helpfulness, his abyan acted similarly. Later on, however, according to Robilyn, Datu Tagleong utilized the powers of his abyan for both good and bad purposes. In the end, this backfired on him. Similarly, Undin, according to Robilyn, was punished by the abyan for cursing her own cousin. This happened because Undin's children, Robilyn claims, have been fully dependent on their mother and her abyan, so that each time they needed something, they ordered their mother and her abyan to act accordingly. By using the abyans' powers for harmful ends, Undin incurred retribution from the abyan and fell ill. She died in late 2019, two years after pastor Jose's passing.

Framing the Baylan

One may frame the experiences of ex-baylan Jose, baylan Undin, and baylan trainee Robilyn as three Agusan-Manobo responses to colonization, missionization, and modernity in the late twentieth and early twenty-first centuries. Jose may be said to have taken the one extreme of assimilation to the neocolonial missionary order and the supersession of Agusan-Manobo ritual traditions in favor of the new, "superior" religion. This further entailed the acquisition of literacy and textual approaches to communication. Undin, on the other hand, may be said to represent the other extreme of staunch faithfulness to the baylan vocation, including being subject to severe punishments according to the strictures of baylanhood. Finally, Robilyn's position may be seen as a negotiation between the baylan and Christian traditions, and Native and Western-style modernities. The one problem with this scheme is it can misconstrue the three as representing distinct evolutionary stages with, say, pastor Jose as the most advanced of the three. In many communities, however, these three responses "exist together, sometimes in the same persons."[139] Another problem with this framing is the tendency to see baylan Undin as representing a pure, uncolonized state when, in fact, many of her actions were already negotiations with neocolonial realities. Her ritual to address Sayson's illness was caused by the young man's modern condescension to his father's ways. Her conceding to perform a ritual without the attendance of her abyan resulted from the need to appease the Christian Manobo housebuilders. It may also be argued that what seems to be her denigration of her own womanhood was influenced by colonial gender ideologies. Undin, therefore, was no less a historical subject than Jose or Robilyn. As for baylan-in-training Robilyn, her insistence to adhere to both baylan ways and Christianity—much to the consternation of Christian and decolonizer purists, alike—and her resolve to disrupt the baylan and abyan hierarchy display sterling agency.

With their embodied voices in song and speech as shown in this chapter, baylan Undin, baylan trainee Robilyn, and ex-baylan Jose demonstrated their resilience, not their victimization; their intelligence, not their ignorance; their resourcefulness, not their helplessness; and their conviction to advance a history that acknowledges the contributions of Native ritual specialists and other Native subjects.

2
SHIFTING VOICES AND MALLEABLE BODIES

There are many modes of human-spirit interaction. To listen to Mendung Sabal sing is to apprehend a spirited voice of lucid artistry. Unlike Undin's yagong in the gudgod that was generated by the internal comingling of Undin's material voice and those of her variously gendered abyan, Mendung's *lihol* (voice in T'boli) in *lingon* (song in T'boli) resulted from her alert mimesis of the voice of her woman *tau munung* (tutelary spirit helper in T'boli). Singing to a rapt audience of both T'boli and non-T'boli—the power of her lihol unrelenting and evincing inexhaustible sources audible to her alone—Mendung told the story of the beloved T'boli epic hero Tudbulul. Giving voice to the epic's variously gendered characters while closely following her tau munung's sonic trace, Mendung alternated between forceful, swinging tones, generally associated by T'boli listeners with the voices of *kem logi* (men), and calculated, exacting, highly embellished tones mostly considered to be those of *kem libun* (women). Through these vocal shifts, Mendung's lihol unintendedly collapsed the gender binary into a continuum of sonic relations, disturbing their inherited hierarchy, while remaining the voice of a *libun* (woman).

This chapter about the gender shifts in the voice of a *tau m'ton bu* (a T'boli person who sees, a ritual specialist, diagnostician, curer) named Mendung Sabal continues the thread of the embodied voice as relational sound. It also brings to the fore considerations of intersectionality that complicate hegemonic constructions of the babaylan as symbols of woman power and gender equality, and of complementary gender ideologies as necessarily egalitarian. The final section rectifies the silence of female to male transgender ritual specialists in the five hundred years of babaylan literature by introducing two *Blaan nungaru* (persons who know, spirited people), Gunintang Freay and Bie Gulae, whose understandings of their malleable bodies do not necessarily conform to dominant sex and gender frameworks.

Mendung Sabal

Mendung Sabal was a stunning T'boli woman of regal countenance. Dressed in colorfully embroidered T'boli garb and decked with elaborate brass and bead ornaments, she was a woman tau m'ton bu. Her home was Lake Sebu and Surallah in South Cotabato where the southwest coast and the Cotabato cordillera ranges merge, and where the three lakes significant to the T'boli people: Sebu, Siluton, and Lahit, rest (figure 2.1).[1]

As a tau m'ton bu, Mendung performed the multiple roles of *tau demsu* (ritual specialist or sacrificer) who offered food and plants to the spirits of the water, soil, and stone; *tau k'na* (dreamer) who dreamed to trace the etiology of illnesses and to locate plant medicines and lost souls; and *tau mulung* (curer) whose medicine was reputed to be "quicker than lighting." In addition to these roles, Mendung was a respected *libun kemukum* (woman settler of conflicts) who mediated cases, especially those that involved kem libun, with the help of her tau munung. Mendung was also a multi-instrumentalist, who played the *s'magi* (gongs), *hegelong* (lute), and *sludoy* (zither). She was a *tau mewel* (weaver), a *tau mesif* (embroiderer), and a *tau temool lemilet* (bead ornament maker).[2] Last but not least, Mendung was a renowned and celebrated *tau lemingon/temutul* (singer-storyteller), who sang for audiences in her home province of South Cotabato as well as in other parts of the Philippines and overseas.[3] Mendung's song performance was made part of a recording anthology of T'boli music produced by the Australian ethnomusicologist Manolete Mora.[4] A recording of her solo songs and instrumental performances was also published by my own organization.[5] At least three books and several ethnomusicological articles by Philippine and foreign scholars have discussed her life and work.[6] Mendung's process of transmitting T'boli songs to a young T'boli woman was further featured on the Discovery Channel. Finally, Mendung was given a national lifetime achievement award by the Coalition of Services of the Elderly for her many years of service as a champion of Indigenous traditions.[7] Mendung's astounding achievements as a Native libun suggest T'boli society as one that honors, supports, and cultivates the talents and powers of women.

In a 2008 conversation that I had with Mendung and her cousin Myrna Pula, Mendung recounted the three initiations that she underwent to prepare her for the tau m'ton bu vocation. When she was a little girl, she said, a boil grew on her lips and became infected. A *tau d'mangaw* (diagnostician by means of finger-span

FIGURE 2.1. Map of South Cotabato, showing Surallah and Lake Sebu; Sarangani, showing Malungon; Davao del Sur, showing Kiblawan

Map by Bill Nelson.

measurements) traced her malady to *benahung*, a condition caused by yearnings of the soul. Mendung's family sponsored the *d'sol be tonok* and *mo ninum* rituals that led to her recovery. Years later, as a young woman who was starting to sing in public, Mendung had a dream. In that dream a libun put a black ant's egg inside her mouth, giving her the good voice that she had after that, a voice that she used to sing about the spirits. This was her second initiation. The third one took place sometime during her marriage to Datu Sabal. She was bitten by a snake and lay dead for two nights and three days, during which she remembers being tested with many questions. By answering these questions correctly, she was given back her life.[8] Upon waking, Mendung began to sing about the spirits and creation, as well as to heal. This final initiation was the hardest trial for Mendung. By overcoming it, according to Myrna, Mendung was endowed with great healing power.[9]

The Gendered T'boli Universe

There are eight layers of sky, according to the older-generation T'boli. These are Longit Sedong, Longit Teyon, Longit Setang, Longit Lohon, Longit Lemfayon, Longit Kulon, Longit Helong, and Longit Son, all of them inhabited by gendered spirits. Below these eight layers of sky is *talak k'mawang*, home to supreme deities Bulon La Mogow (Moon goddess) and Kadaw La Sambad (Sun god) and their offspring, D'wata, the T'boli supreme creator. Talak k'mawang is also inhabited by the *tau t'fing*, D'wata's messengers, who once walked the earth but have ascended to the higher region. Among the tau t'fing are Loos Klagan (a masculine spirit healer), La Fun (a feminine spirit healer), Boi Henwu (a feminine ancestor who ascended the first), Lemugut Mangay (the masculine owner of living things), Kludan (the masculine keeper of Lake Sebu), and Tudbulul (a masculine epic hero). Mendung adds to the list of tau t'fing her tau munung, three of whom are feminine: Lentinum—the custodian of her songs—Manangguy, and Selimbuy; and two, masculine: Senatun and Keyufuy. Below talak k'mawang is *talak mohin* (the oceans, the place of salty waters), and *talak tonok* (the earth). Talak tonok, according to Mendung, overlaps with Lemlunay, a place that is felt but not seen. Lemlunay is a place of justice, fairness, harmony, peace among peoples, abundant food supply, contentment, freedom from illness, gongs, music, and celebration. Talak mohin and talak tonok, according to Myrna, are inhabited by the *tau ton* (visible persons) and the *tau la ton* (invisible persons). Among the tau ton are humans, plants, and animals, while among the tau la ton are the *fun*, the custodians of lands and waters. Each of these visible and invisible persons is gendered as libun, logi, or *boyos* (both feminine and masculine). The Fun libun—the feminine invisible custodians—include Fun El (the custodian of lakes), Fun Elmelel (of rivers), Fun

Mohin (of oceans), Fun Hikong (of waterfalls), Fun Tebul (of wells), Fun Ginton (of metals), Fun Deskulo (of head diseases), Fun Lekef (of colds), Fun Leem (of blindness), Fun Gofos (of cotton), Fun Lembentu (of bamboo groves), Fun Seket Kedekuy and Seket Kedelum (of perfumed grasses), and Fun Kedung Mabung (of the abaca). The Fun logi—the masculine invisible custodians—include the Fun Bulul (the custodian of the mountain), Fun Koyu (of trees), Fun Lenos (of the wind), Fun Linol (of earthquakes), Fun Kulon (of rain), Fun Letek (of thunder), Fun Blanga (of stones and rocks), Fun Temelus (of wild beasts), Fun T'dulok (of death), Fun Kekel (of fevers), and Fun Blekes (of skin diseases). Finally, the boyos or the custodians with both masculine and feminine genders include the Fun Lingon (custodian of songs), and Fun Kumuga (of eye infections).[10] One observes from Mendung's and Myrna's accounts of the T'boli pantheon, an almost equal representation of kem libun and kem logi, as well as the presence of the boyos, the multigendered deities. This seemingly nonhierarchical and pluralist gender ideology, coupled with Mendung's high status as a T'boli woman tau m'ton bu, *kemukum* (settler of conflicts), and tau lemingon/temutul, gives the impression of gender complementarity, equality, and plurality among the T'boli, and the high status of women ritual specialists, supporting claims made by some Philippine and Western scholars.[11]

Women Babaylan as Protofeminists and Sources of Philippine Women's Power

Starting in the 1980s, if not earlier, a number of Philippine feminist scholars and activists began to cite Spanish colonial reports of what today would be considered indicators of the high status of women during the time of the conquest.[12] The historian Fe Mangahas asserts that precolonial women enjoyed a "relatively equal, if not superior, status with men" in a "social world that produce[d] women with leadership qualities equal to the men."[13] Women then could become economic managers, pact holders, and babaylan priestesses, notes the feminist theologian Mary John Mananzan.[14] They could become chieftains, own property, name their children, divorce their partners, further writes Myrna Feliciano.[15] The women babaylan, according to the historian Zeus Salazar, were the "central personalities in ancient Philippine society in the fields of culture, religion and medicine and all kinds of theoretical knowledge about the phenomenon of nature." They took charge of the religious ritual, the mythology of the town, the medicine, and all the music, stories, and poems.[16] Carolyn Brewer theorizes that the women babaylan were so powerful they were emulated by the "male shaman (who) dressed and 'performed' as a woman."[17]

To further advance the claim of women's high status during the precolonial and early colonial times, a number of feminist scholars have cited Spanish reports of women babaylan who led fierce resistance against the colonizers, making it difficult for the latter to gain full control of the land and people.[18] Such resistance, according to these accounts, provoked the Spanish colonizers to subdue these women through shaming, demonizing, and military execution, with one woman ritual specialist impaled on a bamboo pole before being fed to the crocodiles.[19] Seeing themselves attacked, some of these women ritual specialists fled to the mountains, where they could carry on with their practices in relative freedom.[20] Others converted to the colonizers' religion while secretly practicing their rituals.[21] Still others assumed the role of *beatas* (blessed women helpers of male priests), who became the precursors of present-day Philippine Christian religious congregations of women.[22] The "deliberate assault on the functions of the *babaylan*" by the Spanish, Milagros Guerrero writes, had one enduring consequence: "the all too real diminution of the status of women in colonial Philippines."[23]

The portrayal of the precolonial and early colonial women babaylan as oppositional to patriarchal colonization configured them as protofeminists. Fe Mangahas contends that "Women's power in the Philippines is rooted and traceable to the *babaylan*."[24] Mangahas theorizes that long before the use of the words *femenina*, *feminista*, or *feminism* in the Philippine islands, "there was the word babaylanismo—a form of women's consciousness indigenous to the Philippines."[25] Babaylanismo, Mangahas explains, was premised on the assumption that since precolonial times women led powerful lives as babaylan priestesses who heroically rose up against the patriarchal colonial order to defend ancestral ways.[26]

Mangahas claims that whereas the women babaylan were annihilated, assimilated, or compromised by the colonial order, the power of Philippine women was not fully lost.[27] The babaylans' power lived on among later-generation Filipino women, particularly those who joined the revolution against Spain and those who fought for women's suffrage during the American colonial period—a time, according to Cristina Blanc-Szanton, when the "strength and independence of Filipino women . . . [were] recognized and valued."[28] During the postindependence era, reports Maria Luisa Camagay, Philippine women from the lower classes themselves rose to power by joining the ranks of rebels during the Japanese occupation, the American imperial rule, and the Marcos dictatorship.[29]

The discourse of the babaylan as the site of precolonial women's potency and as the source of contemporary women's power has spurred decades of vibrant scholarship and activism in the fields of feminist and gender studies, decolonial studies, and related disciplines. Many present-day women professionals, mostly from urban and/or diasporic middle-class backgrounds, have been attracted to the image of the babaylan and have ascribed the babaylan title to themselves. They have formed organizations named after the babaylan that advocate for women's rights and decolonization. These developments have inspired many in the face of ongoing violence and discrimination against women, immigrants, and other minorities, in domestic and work places, in the homeland and in the diaspora.

Scholars like Zeus Salazar, however, observe the alienation between what he calls the "*babaylan* of the elite and the *babaylan* of the real Filipino [who] still sit with their backs against each other."[30] Salazar warns that the "Babaylan tradition could be co-opted by new-age type spirituality-seeking affluent, middle class Filipinas whose end goal is individual spiritual enlightenment."[31] Ofelia Villero further points out the dangers of nostalgia, romanticizing of the past, and the "uncritical evaluation of power dynamics among the different classes and religious orientations of women involved in the retrieval [of ancient models of power]."[32] Still others have raised the often unacknowledged relationship between feminism and colonialism, the idea that white and/or elite women ought to be emulated by their little brown sisters in order for the latter to save themselves.[33] Related to this is the violence that takes place when the nationalized and rationalized constructions of the babaylan are imposed on other classes and ethnicities in ways that strip local practitioners of their culturally specific languages, experiences, and perspectives, often dismissed by modern elites as unnecessary if not inappropriate for the modern nation. There is further the hegemonic association of the babaylan with overt forms of "resistance," which often requires social privilege that is precisely what had been denied to many Native ritual specialists. It is insensitive if not irresponsible for commentators from locations of power to demand such resistance from Native ritual specialists who are already in the trenches of day-to-day struggle and the defense of ancestral ways. Some Indigenous observers have pointed out that to use a few overtly resistant babaylan to represent all others is historically inaccurate and detached from the realities that many Native ritual specialists face, those of saving lives and building peace. Finally, not a few have pointed out the problem of extracting the babaylan title as though it were a commodity to be acquired without first going through Indigenous channels and protocols, the forging of sacred trusts built on sustained reciprocal relationships with ritual specialists, ancestral and nature spirits, human and nonhuman communities. To abstract the title from the process and relationships just because one is attracted to images of Indigenous women that converge with feminist models or because one has the privilege to do so is facile and demonstrates a lack of respect for Native ritual specialists and their communities.

Some of these critiques have encouraged a number of self-ascribed babaylan to refer to themselves instead as "babaylan-inspired."[34] Others have taken strides to meet and engage with living Native ritual specialists, revising their positions along the way. There are those, however, who continue to show little interest in engaging with poor Indigenous babaylan with whom they have little in common. The framing of the babaylan as protofeminist and as a symbol of womanpower has been an inspiring development for many Philippine women and women of Philippine descent, but is of little relevance to many Native ritual specialists who are still consigned to the margins, surviving only as valorized symbols and spirits to be embodied by their modern elite sisters.

Women's High Status and Gender Complementarity in Southeast Asia

Intersecting with Philippine feminist claims of the relatively egalitarian gender relations in the islands during precolonial times, a number of Western observers have reported the high status of women in contemporary southeast Asia where they claim nonhierarchical gender complementarity pervades.[35] Shelley Errington writes that

> In a good part of island Southeast Asia, the part I call the Centrist archipelago . . . male and female are viewed as basically the same sort of beings, that is, ones whose souls and functioning are very similar or are parallel. . . . Gender differences tend to be downplayed in ritual, economics, and dress; kinship terminology and practice tend to be bilateral; and male and female are viewed as complementary or even identical beings [substitution-prone] in many respects.[36]

Errington's observations support earlier assertions that link forager, horticultural, and pastoralist societies with complementary and relatively egalitarian gender relations and matrilineal families. Private property, social class, and Western technology in these societies are claimed to have not yet polarized relationships and the domestic and public spheres.[37] The godhead tends to be female or is either male or female and there is interpenetration between the domains of nature and culture, supernatural, natural, and human.[38] In contrast, societies influenced by the West, based on private property, and dependent on technology have been associated with patriarchal and patrilineal gender arrangements. Women in these societies are relegated to the household and other private spaces. They also lose control over property.[39] The godhead tends to be male; culture, nature, and the supernatural sharply distinguished; and spirits seen as chaotic, dangerous, and requiring control.[40] Some of these gender theories are based on earlier works by Karl Marx and Frederick Engels that saw gender stratification as the result of the introduction of private property and the development of capitalism.[41]

Manolete Mora argued that gender complementarity among the T'boli is deeply entrenched not only in the relationships between T'boli men and women but in dualistic cosmological themes and the pairing of T'boli musical instruments, voice pitches, and compositional components that are all "analogues of the complementary social roles" of the T'boli genders.[42] Of the gendered tropes that are performed by the T'boli in daily life, Mora cites the T'boli conceptual pairs of *megel* and *lemnoy*, or hardness and refinement; *lembang* and *lemnek*, or large/broad/male/public and small/tiny/detailed; and *utom* and *tang*, or figure and ground.[43] About lembang and lemnek, Mora quotes Mendung in 2008 (figure 2.2):

> It is easy to learn the gongs because you can pick it up easily, but the lute is difficult to learn. It is like the work of a woman, lemnek. It is true that the work of a woman is not heavy, not so painful, but it is very lemnek, just like the utom [composition] of the lute. The gongs are like the work of a man, like ploughing the fields and cutting trees. All of that is easy for men to do even though it is heavy. But it doesn't compare to the work of a woman, just like the lute. Ma Sembalod [Gloyan Kan] says, "that if I hear the sound of the gongs it brings to mind kimu lembang [big property]." But the lute is like nawa lemnek [refined emotion], it is like Ye Lo ["mother of Lo"]. She is always occupied with many fine things; she is like two lutes! The gongs are like the nawa [literally "breath," but it can also mean character, disposition, or emotion] of man, and how he feels for a woman. But if we think about the lute, it is like the nawa of a woman and her feelings for a man.[44]

Complicating gender binaries, Mora posits what he observed to be the mutual inclusiveness and interpenetration of masculine and feminine principles in T'boli life.[45] Each complementary pair could contain elements of its other, thus, "'male contains female, female contains male, inside contains outside, and outside, the inside, and lembang performance contains lemnek instruments, and so on."[46] So while T'boli music making does "reproduce patterns of gender difference" that undergird exchange and reciprocity and, in turn, define the T'boli moral order, it also provides "ways of countermining those differences."[47] Women participate in realms and activities otherwise dominated by men, and vice versa.[48]

Mendung's performance of the *Tudbulul*, a *lingon lembang* (epic song with numerous characters) marked by gendered vocal shifts, further instantiates the claim of inclusive complementarity in T'boli gender relationships. Mendung's cousin Myrna remarked that when listening to Mendung's *Tudbulul* performance, any T'boli with *hungol* (listening) similar to hers and Mendung's can distinguish

FIGURE 2.2. Mendung Sabal, Davao, 2005

Photo by Skippy Lumawag.

if a particular utterance is delivered by a libun (woman) or by a *logi* (man).[49] All that the listener has to do is pay attention to the *kuwahil*, that is, the manner in which a phrase is sonically delivered, regardless of the text or tune. There are two kinds of kuwahil, Myrna explained. The *kuwahil klolo* (swinging kuwahil) is delivered in a *mefeges* (forceful) and *lebotu* (round) voice denoting a logi performing an action or an adventure. In contrast, the *kuwahil bot*, characterized by more *sogu* (embellishments) and a more calculated and exact rendition so that the listener can tell exactly when the singer will stop, denotes the voice of a libun. One can hear the kuwahil shifts in Mendung's *Tudbulul* performance that suggest the interpenetration of masculine and feminine voices within the voice of a single performer who has her own gender identity, libun.

Thus far, we have observed intersecting claims about the gender ideologies of the T'boli, Filipinos, and Southeast Asians in general. These suggest that the T'boli woman tau m'ton bu, framed according to theories of the precolonial babaylan and contemporary Southeast Asian women enjoy high status and a mutually inclusive, nonhierarchical gender complementarity that extends to nonhuman domains.[50] Assertions contrary to these have met caveats against perceiving gender differences among non-Western peoples as "analogous to the unequal and hierarchical asymmetries that we perceive in 'our' own," and have been attributed to ethnographic bias.[51] On the other hand, none of these claims have been able to silence suspicions that gender relationships in these societies have been less idyllic, or at any rate more complex, than numerous scholars have suggested. Shelley Errington noted that "we may be missing issues germane to the topic when we glance casually the 'high status of women' in an area where the treatment of women seems relatively benign.'"[52] All these have led me to question whether gender complementarity—described here as difference and mutual completion as well as interchangeability—necessarily implies negligible stratification and relative egalitarianism.

The *Tudbulul* and T'boli Gender Relations

My acquaintance with Mendung and Myrna began in the late 1990s when our common friend the Australian ethnomusicologist Manolete Mora visited me in the Philippines and told me about the two T'boli women.[53] I did not know what Mora's intentions were for the introduction, but perhaps it had something to do with a song I had written, sung, and recorded in the early 1990s, "Lawang Sebu." It was inspired by an article about the histories of land grabbing in the T'boli ancestral domain and by a brief visit to Lake Sebu, where Mendung was born and where Myrna lives to this day.[54] The year following Mora's introduction, I met Mendung and Myrna in Davao City where they were working as resident weavers at a resort.[55] Mendung taught me some songs then. We also discussed producing a record of her song performances, one that would be made available in the Philippines.[56] In 2001, three years after that first meeting, I dreamed of Myrna telling me, "Mendung is now ready." The dream also showed the two of them traveling, not by boat or bus, but by airplane. I tried to understand what the dream meant. Because of our earlier discussions, I thought perhaps this meant that now was the time for Mendung to record her songs. I withdrew my remaining thousands of pesos from a bank account to buy airplane tickets for the two women. They came without hesitation and with much enthusiasm to record, annotate, transcribe, and translate into English—processes they have been used to doing after decades of work with various researchers—Mendung's songs, stories, and instrumental performances for a compact disc and booklet publication.[57] Mendung whispered to me that "it may have been her tau munung who disguised herself as Myrna in my dream, so that I may recognize her and understand her message."[58] One of the songs that Mendung was keen to record was her short version of the T'boli epic *Tudbulul*. Tudbulul, according to Myrna, is the name of the foremost T'boli *tau gena* (ancestor), a man whose strong will allowed him to overcome all trials, turning him into a model for T'boli humanity. "Tudbulul's story has the weight of the Bible among the T'boli," Myrna said. "His story carries the totality of T'boli beliefs, values, practices," including gender ideologies.[59] Gender ideologies, writes Ellen Koskoff, are frameworks for what constitute appropriate behaviors of women and men, often codified as religious, moral, or legal systems.[60] One example of a gender ideology is the "traditional belief in male supremacy found in many Western religious systems [Christianity, Judaism, Islam] [one that] promotes the idea that women are not suited for religious leadership. . . . Written texts [have] supported and validated this ideology, and it is only recently that such beliefs have been questioned by both men and women."[61] In addition to written texts, oral performances like the *Tudbulul* are excellent sources and codifications of gender ideologies.

Of the *Tudbulul* performance, Myrna explained that this "may only be done by a tau lemingon/temutul who has trained under a human teacher and/or a spirit guide, as the case was with Mendung." Of her voice performance, Mendung said:

> Before I start singing, I know nothing. I just sing the hewot (introductory call), then a light turns on in my head. I hear Lentinum my tau munung (tutelary spirit helper) sing, and I must follow her every word and tune or I will not know how to proceed. When the light turns off, I stop.[62]

Singing the *Tudbulul* often takes place at night as an important centerpiece of the mo ninum or grand healing and marriage renewal ceremony. It may also be sung to entertain guests in someone's house or village during wedding festivities and similar occasions. Performing the *Tudbulul* takes anywhere between ten and twenty-five hours, depending on the time allotted for its singing and the version that the singer comes up with. The singer may also chant an *ukol* (short) rendition for instructional purposes.[63] For her service, a singer may receive a *malong* (tubular cloth wrapper), or a gong, a brass belt, embroidery, or cash.

The *Tudbulul* is composed of eight episodes that represent Tudbulul's journey from life to death. The first episode, Semgulang Tutul (Semgulang is a variant of the name Tudbulul), is the story of Tudbulul's birth. The second episode, Semgulang Konul, is the story of Tudbulul drowning. The third, Semgulang Kemleng Mugul, tells of Semgulang cutting his wrist. Semgulang Benahung, the fourth episode, is the story of Semgulang falling ill because his soul yearned for marriage. Semgulang Metad, the fifth episode, has Tudbulul arranging his sisters' and other women's marriages. In Semgulang Mifit Libun, the sixth episode, Tudbulul beats up his wives out of jealousy. In Semgulang Tawan Sohul, the seventh episode, Semgulang goes insane. The final episode, Semgulang Nodung, is the story of Semgulang's wake.[64]

When Mendung recorded her ukol version of the *Tudbulul* in 2001, her performance was not motivated by any discussion of gender but by what she and/or her tau munung may have thought to be the multiple points of interest among her T'boli and non-T'boli, Filipino and non-Filipino audiences. With an inspired and resonant lihol that emanated not only from her mouth, throat, and chest, but from her whole spirited being, Mendung launched into a "Hedeeee ehe eeeee!" a *hewot* (vocable) to summon her tau munung, the custodian of her song, to come and lead her in singing. She then delivered the *Tudbulul*'s florid melismatic passages with great power and ease. She sang all eight episodes in less than ten minutes. The following are Myrna's T'boli transcriptions and English translations of that particular *Tudbulul* ukol performance by Mendung with annotations of selected episodes and references to longer Tudbulul versions that bear on discussions of gender.[65]

I. Semgulang Tutul
Hedeeee ehe eeeee
ni bud lingon benoluyu
ben lemwoti ne
lemwoti
mon Semgulang tutul
ben kewoten be ifuyen
gon helos wen kenhulung le
helos wen se tutule we
ben gutun be Tudbulul
ke hewa-en be ifuyen
ke nga-en du Kemokul
mon le Semgulang tutul
ani la lana boluyen

Hedeeee ehe eeeee
This is a song that I shall sing again.
Now I shall begin to tell the story of Semgulang.
Now I shall begin
this story of Semgulang.
Upon his birth from his mother's womb
all skills began.
Every skill has its own story
of emerging from Tudbulul.
Born to his mother
the son of Kemokul
this story of Semgulang is told
so that his name will not be forgotten.

II. Semgulang Konul

Hedeeeeeee ee ehe eeee e
ni lingonu be gewun
de mon le we Semgulang konul
e deng kelogi'n tu kun
we deng hetonen keta-un
ben kenga-en du ifuyen
Kemokul Lunay Sebung
boluy ye-en Lenkonul
we yo ben nga-en Tudbulul
yo deng tonen keta-un
we mon Semgulang konul

Hede e e e e eehe e e ee
This is my second song.
They say that he is the drowned Semgulang.
When he was a boy
he displayed himself and his ability.
He was born of his mother.
Kemokul Lunay Sebung was his father.
His mother's name was Lenkonul
whose son was Tudbulul.
This time he showed his manhood,
the said, drowned Semgulang.

In the *Tudbulul* ukol's first two episodes, Semgulang Tutul and Semgulang Konul as performed by Mendung, Tudbulul's mother, Lenkonul, is mentioned primarily in reference to her reproductive function, that is, for having birthed Semgulang. In a number of Western feminist writings, the role of mother, origin, and nurturer has been associated with nature and nonagentive generativity that men are claimed to desire, dread, and consequently devalue and suppress.[66] This may not necessarily apply to much of T'boli experience, Myrna says, where women like Lenkonul, Tudbulul's mother, as well as Mendung, a tau m'ton bu and celebrated singer, are regarded as women of power and agency. On the other hand, Myrna contends that Lenkonul was highly regarded primarily because she was the mother of the hero Tudbulul, and Mendung, in part, because she was the wife of Datu (chief) Sabal. Discussions of T'boli gender ideology, in other words, cannot be divorced from considerations of social class and/or women's associations with powerful men, with most poor T'boli mothers not sharing the same high esteem that Lenkonul and Mendung enjoyed.

III. Semgulang Kemleng Mugul
Hedeeeeee
ni lingonu be getelu'n
de mon yo udelen moluy
du ben mon le de tu-u kun
du ben benwu'n Lunay Mogul
du ben ben tek sotu
boluyen ben sonen we Tudbulul
we Semgulang Kemleng mugul
we ben gonon hetoyo kun
we lan k'daw ne do medung
do ben gotu matay hulu'n
we gotu le melob kimun
we deng melan be ke imulen

Hedeeeeee
The third song that I sing
this is how it was sung.
They said that
in the place, Lunay Mogul
there was only one worthy individual
and his name was Tudbulul.
Semgulang slashed his wrist.
The reason why he killed himself (or attempted to)
was because a drought had ravaged his place.
All the plants had died.

All his properties were burned.
Semgulang could not bear the loss and the suffering
so he slashed his wrist.

In Mendung's ukol version of Semgulang Kemleng Mugul, Tudbulul, a wealthy and powerful man, is said to be the only worthy individual in his place, Lunay Mogul. This portrayal annuls the worth of both women and men outside of his class.

IV. Semgulang Benahung

Hedeeee ehe eeeeee
benahung ne eee gon helos wen sebulung
ben mon Semgulang benahung kun
benahung kun be libun
lemwot meyehen Tudbulul
nen melan ne benulung ni
helos deng me gutunen
benahung go Mo ninum
be sebu gonon tembul

Hede e e e e e ehe ee e e e
Benahung [soul yearning]
is the reason why there is healing until now.
The next song is Semgulang Benahung.
His soul yearned for a woman.
Tudbulul had to marry such woman.
But first, he had to undergo healing.
Until now, this is practiced.
He had to undergo Mo ninum
which originated in Lake Sebu.

In Mendung's ukol version of Semgulang Benahung, Tudbulul's *benahung* (yearning of his soul) is portrayed as being remedied by the act of marrying a woman. In the longer version, the woman who Tudbulul marries was like him, a powerful and skillful leader of her own domain. In the epic, however, the woman ends up playing support to the male hero.

V. Semgulang Metad

Hedeeeeee
ni lingonu be gelimun
ne deng gelimun ne tu kun
sal beng do Tudbulul luyungen

ne mon le we Semgulang ne we tudu kun
de ee Semgulang metad libun
de mon yo udelen moluy do
go'm mon du helos nutunen
wen gel heyehen le libun do
tibas la dengen montung we
ben do heyehen ifuyen ni
helos me deng nutunen wen
semunggud sembakung we e
ben wen melay talu'n we e
heni keding libun we ben
nen ne melan tu kun we

Hedeeeeeee
My fifth song
already the fifth one
is about Tudbulul.
They say it's Semgulang,
Semgulang who traded women.
It is said that
this is the reason why until this day
men arrange marriages for women
even if the women are too young.
The father arranges the marriage of the daughter,
a practice that is handed down.
Men give gongs as bride prices.
They give horses as bride prices
in exchange for women's hair.
All this, a man must go through.

In Mendung's ukol version of Semgulang Metad, Tudbulul arranges the marriages of his nine sisters, Boi Lemhadung Talun, Boi Gofos, Boi Lembentu, Boi Seket, Boi Kedekuy, Boi Kedelum, Boi Kedung Mabung, K'naban, and Heniton, in exchange for gongs and horses. This episode normalizes the practice of men marrying off girls without their consent and measuring women's worth against material things. Although Tudbulul's sisters K'naban and Heniton performed strong leader and adviser roles in the longer *Tudbulul* versions, the attention given to them far from matched what was given to Tudbulul and the other men in the epic. In Mendung's short version, the logi's predicament for having to pay the bride price is highlighted. What is not mentioned is what the bride's family has to go through to pay the price of the groom.

VI. Semgulang Mifit Libun

Hedeeeee ini lingonu be gehitun de
monen yo du Tudbulul
ini do gonon tembul
Lemlunay gonon hedung
Semgulang mifit libun
mon yo udelen moluy it
nedohen Lunay Sebung
milo Benekel Lobun
milo kotun gewolu'n
gotu atu-en benwu'n
geloken mebot sekafun
bong wen lenibug kulun
timbow koli ne ditu'n
daugen kede kimun
getaban kede benwun
ni ne me helos nutunen

Hedeeeee
This is the sixth song.
It is said that Tudbulul,
he sprang up here.
He is from Lunay.
Semgulang beat up his wives.
This is what was said.
He abandoned Lunay Sebung
and went off to Benekel Lobun.
He went to the eighth layer of the clouds.
He gambled and bet his own place.
He invited everyone to make a bet.
All this was to express his anger.
When he arrived there
he won all the prizes and properties.
He won the entire domain.
Until now this is practiced.

One finds out from the epic's longer version of Semgulang Mifit Libun that the reason why Tudbulul was angry and beat up his wives was because, coming home from a long journey during which he carried on with his adventures and relationships with numerous other women, he found out that his wives had gone off with other men. Myrna clarified that these wives' marriages to Tudbulul were not their choice. They were arranged by their own fathers and brothers without their consent. In response to Tudbulul's abandonment, they rebelled, reporting him to the council that exposed his inadequacies. Tudbulul was made to pay a fine, which he paid to be reconciled with his wives. The successful uprising of the wives against Tudbulul can, to an extent, be interpreted as a sign of women's agency. This important reading, however, weakens when singers stress, above all, not these wives' cooperation and defiance but Tudbulul's triumphs in gambling as well as his winning all prizes. The effect of this has been that Tudbulul's heroics, and not his wives' show of strength, have had the stronger impact on T'boli gender relations.

VII. Semgulang Tawan Sohul
Hedeeeeeeeee ehe eeee mon yo udelen moluy du
ini sotu ken hulungu
sal boluyen Tudbulul
we Lemlunay gono tembul
we mon ni lingo ken hulungu
Semgulang Tawan Sohul
we ni helos me deng nemungen
mon gel wen henbuk bulungen
mon gel wen gel wen lengel ni tun
de ben deng me helos nutunen
Semgulang Tawan

Hedeeeeeeeee ehe eeee
This is what the storyteller says:
Here is my other song
about Tudbulul.
He sprang from Lemlunay.
This other song that I have
is about Semgulang going mad [because of sorcery].
Until now this is practiced.
This is why we say we must burn herbs when someone goes mad, when someone goes mad.
These practices have been handed down since.
This is about Semgulang going mad.

VIII. Semgulang Nodung
Hedeeeeeeeee Lemlunay go setifune
gono sunung

yo boluyen Tudbulul
we yo ben las be gewolu'n
Semgulang Kemleng Mugul
gonon hetoyo taun
deng gotu deng tenutulu
de ni las be gewolun
mon le Semgulang Nodung
ben newit le ket benwu'n
ben lulon mulek lungunen ni
helos me deng nutunen
laendu matay taune
ke la melan be kenahune
Lemlunay go setifune
Lemlunay tey lemobung.

Hedeeeeeeeeee
Lemlunay is where we gather and meet.
The hero's name is Tudbulul.
In this eighth story
Semgulang slashed his wrist,
the reason why he died.
I have said it,
this is the last, the eight story,
Semgulang Nodung.
He is brought to every place.
They carry the coffin back to his home.
It continues to be practiced
that no one dies without a coffin,
if not passing through a coffin.
Lemlunay is where we gather.
Lemlunay, so exuberant.

Myrna stresses that there are other powerful women characters in the longer versions of the *Tudbulul*. One is Lemfayon, who wanted to marry Tudbulul. When he did not reciprocate her affections, however, she got furious and let Tudbulul be swallowed by a python that almost killed him except that Lemfayon herself saved Tudbulul by taking him under the sea. Based on this description by Myrna, Lemfayon was portrayed as undeserving of Tudbulul's love, a villain who nonetheless preserves the life and worth of the male hero. Besides Lemfayon, there are also Tudbulul's youngest sisters, K'naban and Heniton, who saved their brother each time he got lost. There is also Solok Minum (the light of the wine-making celebration), the leader of Tudbulul's numerous wives, who advised her husband on various matters, but who, like the sisters, played a support role to the male hero. Finally, notes Myrna, there is Sendowon, a goddess, who Tudbulul's father, Kemokul, sought out when Tudbulul was just in his mother's womb. Kemokul needed to get from Sendowon a very expensive betel nut that he would chew so that Tudbulul would grow. Goddess Sendowon said, "I will give you what you want but if the baby turns out to be a boy, you must give him to me." When Tudbulul was born on the same day that Kemokul's sister gave birth to a baby girl, Kemokul presented his sister's female child to Sendowon. Tudbulul was offered to the mountain instead, to become one of its pillars. Sendowon discovered Kemokul's trick and found a way to get the boy Tudbulul, who grew up in her house in Mohin Lubun, the bellowing ocean. One day, a bird told Tudbulul to kill Sendowon and to take the wealth that she had reserved for him. Tudbulul planted an herb that killed Sendowon. He took her wealth, then escaped to a faraway place where his youngest sisters found him. Based on this description by Myrna, Sendowon was portrayed as a powerful woman who would also be tricked, robbed, and killed by the male hero Tudbulul.

These few references to some of the epic's main characters suggest gender complementarity, the pairing of functions, and parallel existences. Tudbulul and Kemokul play the roles of sons, husbands, and fathers, while Lenkonul, K'naban, Heniton, and the other women of the epic play the roles of mothers, sisters, and wives. Tudbulul, the wealthy and powerful hero, is the epic's central character even when he loses contests or is depressed and wants to kill himself, while the women are mostly depicted as caregivers, providers, advisers, second-rate leaders, and saviors. They are also unrequited lovers or lovers dependent on men, if not villains who the hero destroys in the end. While Tudbulul and his wives are all portrayed as having multiple partners, the women are additionally burdened with arranged marriages that they do not consent to, abandonment, and violence inflicted on them by their jealous husband. But while complementarity marks the gender relationships in the *Tudbulul*, a reading of negligible gender hierarchy and relative egalitarianism is untenable. As Ellen Koskoff puts it: "In any binary contrast, one side is inevitably privileged over the other. . . . Binary contrasts could not simply be understood as value-free, but as hierarchically arranged, their construction inherently driven by social power dynamics that sought to privilege those on top."[67] The most apparent gender ideology of the *Tudbulul*, therefore, is unequal complementarity. The epic constructs, legitimates, and reproduces socially and sexually normalized women and men whose relationships with each other are complementary but far from equal. The question is: Is it not unfair to judge the gender ideology of a centuries-old text from the standpoint of twenty-first-century cross-cultural feminism? Indeed, it is. Except that the *Tudbulul* continues to be performed and listened to to this day, so that its influence continues to impact contemporary T'boli gender relationships.

Mendung's Other Story

Mendung Sabal, the highly accomplished, celebrated, and renowned tau m'ton bu, libun kemukum, and tau lemingon/temutul, had another story to tell. Inspired by the themes of her short rendition of the *Tudbulul*, she began to recount her (other) *tutul kemo ke taum* (lifestory), one that was later retold in English by her cousin Myrna.

> I was very young when my mother, Singgay, died of beri-beri. My aunt who was the cousin of my father Bansawan was charged to care for me. Without a mother, I felt incomplete. My father remarried three times, leaving me with my aunt. But then my aunt died, too. My father and my mother's brother told me I should marry. They arranged for me to marry a man named Fara who lived across the lake. They married me off because they were interested in the dowries: the gongs and the horses that they wanted to obtain. The moment they got all these, however, they left me with my in-laws. There, I grew up while my husband worked in the coastal areas. He was so much older than I was and had already been married. His separation from his first wife was an insult to his parents so he had to marry me to recover his family's pride. If the first wife had not been replaced, it would have been degrading for them. But Fara and I did not live together because I was just a child, and maybe because he really did not have any love for me. Though our names were married, we were not. My in-laws were very oppressive and unkind. They only paid attention to me whenever they ordered me to do something: "Take care of our child! Or, plant palay in the field! Or, do some weeding!" But when I wasn't working, they didn't care for me at all. After years of living with my in-laws, Fara and I separated. I was maybe fourteen years old then. Half of the dowry was kept (by my father and my mother's brother) because it was the man's fault that I was not cared for. I went to live with my sister. But my relatives married me off again. I did not want to marry a second time but they had already negotiated this. They had already received the gifts and dowries from the man: horses, ornaments, gongs, without leaving anything for me. So I was forced to marry a second time to this man, Ukuk. He was working at the church mission and was getting paid 250 pesos per day, money that he spent on drinking and women.

So I worked on my own in order to survive. I wove mats. I planted root crops. Sometimes, Father Rex Mansmann asked me to sing for a fee.[68] I was married to Ukuk for more or less ten years and we had two children who I supported single-handedly. Ukuk came and went, sometimes leaving us for a month or so. I was angry with him because he did not give me any money to buy the things we needed at home. When my tau munung (helper spirit)—the one, who, in my dream put a black ant's egg in my mouth to give me my good voice—saw that my relationship with my husband was not good, she told me to get out of there. So I left Ukuk. I won the settlement case presided by Bali Kukus, a Muslim leader and judge/settler of cases. My family did not have to return the dowries because I had children to support and because I was not cared for during the marriage. I went to live with my sister again. Then this Datu Sabal dreamt that a spirit talked to him, saying, "You already have six wives (in addition to others who may have already been separated from him), but you must take Mendung to be the seventh so that there will be someone to take care of you in your old age." I believe that he, too, had a spirit helper who had already communicated with mine. Datu Sabal was a tribal chieftain who settled cases like murder. He helped people who were in need of money to pay for their fines. He donated horses and carabaos to those who needed dowries. His mother was a Boi, a princess by inheritance, and his parents had property. That was how he came to be a datu. And so Datu Sabal went to see my father to tell him about his dream, and to ask him where I was. He already knew me because one of his wives was my cousin. He also knew that I was a singer for he had hired me to sing in the past. Sabal was very insistent and told my father, "I will marry your daughter, whether you like it or not." I told my father not to allow the marriage to take place because of the huge age difference of maybe more than fifteen years that could lead to future problems like the return of dowries should there be a separation. But both of them were insistent. Datu Sabal proceeded to give my father dowries so that I could no longer refuse. Datu Sabal's two wives and two children also came to our house to fetch me. This practice of taking a woman to the house of the datu is called "nangay." They stayed at our house for two days because I refused to go with them and threatened to commit suicide. The two wives told me that if I returned the four horses and the carabao that my father had already received, I did not have to go with them. So I was forced to go, but my second husband did not allow me to bring our children to this other man's house. He took them away from me. I went to stay with Datu Sabal's other wives who were angry and jealous of me. Jealousy was considered normal, but sometimes, I really don't want to tell this story anymore because it makes me remember the pains I suffered in the past. I decided to live in a separate house and told Sabal that if he did not allow me to do so, I was certain that we would separate because of how his family treated me. Datu Sabal gave me permission because he was afraid to lose me. The whole time, the spirits were sympathetic with me. They pitied me because I lived like a carabao that was taken from place to place where it did not want to go, and yet it followed. Datu Sabal and I had three children, one girl and two boys. The spirits told me to be humble, not to resist, but to watch out for the future. Now I understand why they advised me so. As time went by, my fellow-wives softened towards me. I helped them through my healing, especially when their children got sick. I was already practicing healing then, and people gave me gifts like gongs, betel nut boxes, tubular clothing, traditional blouses, brass belts, cash whenever I healed them. My fellow-wives came to me whenever they had problems or troubles in life. I helped them financially, by giving them my horses and my belongings. I supported all fourteen children through school but never received support back from them, nor do they recognize what I have done for them. All the wives have their own separate houses now and they have dumped their husband on me because he is old. I take care of him. I cannot say "no," for that would be against D'wata's will. I will have to wait until he dies.[69]

Listening to Mendung's story, I was astounded by the close parallels between her tale and those of some of the women in the *Tudbulul*. Mendung, like them, was a child-bride exchanged for gongs, horses, and ornaments by the men of her family. She also had to share her powerful husband with many other wives.

Like Tudbulul's relationship with his wives, one can glean complementarity in Mendung's marriage to each of her three husbands. Her first husband did wage work in the coastal areas while she did unpaid work at her in-laws' house. Her second husband did wage work at the mission, while she planted root crops, wove mats, and raised her children singlehandedly. The wealthy and powerful Datu Sabal was a tribal chieftain while Mendung was a singer, ritual specialist, and, like Sabal, a settler of conflicts (there may be a degree of substitutionality here). All three husbands of Mendung performed public roles in different degrees, while from being an exclusively private player, Mendung slowly gained a public presence through her song performances in Lake Sebu and beyond. If Mendung was able to gain high status later in her life, it was not necessarily because she was a ritual specialist or because of a relatively egalitarian T'boli gender ideology. It was because of her marriage to the wealthy Datu Sabal, as well as her spirit helper's guidance that allowed her to cultivate her talents, leading to more independent sources of income and prestige. Complementarity in these cases had been undergirded by a resounding inequality. More recent literature exposed gender complementarity's complicity in keeping women subjugated in gender relations with men. The feminist theologian Michelle Gonzalez writes, citing several sources:

> Rosemary Radford Ruether argues that gender complementarity draws on . . . traditions of the "good feminine." Women are called to exemplify this good femininity associated with altruistic love and service to "others," that is, men and children, in a way that re-enforces women's passive, auxiliary relation to male agency. A complementary vision of the sexes, Ruther contends, is based on a limited, idealized, patriarchal notion of women's identity, one that serves only men. Susan Ross dismisses gender complementarity for its "highly questionable understandings of human biology and sociology; they also perpetuate a psychology of women as 'receptive' and men as 'active' that has tremendously destructive consequences for relationships between the sexes." . . . Margaret Farley points out that the vision of mutual love within gender complementarity is not one of full complementarity and equality. Instead, it is constructed based on hierarchical relationships such as parent and child, ruler and servant.[70]

But how does the pervasive framing of the babaylan as a precolonial power figure relate with the experiences of historical Native women ritual specialists like Mendung, whose voices have been mostly excluded from dominant discourses? There is really no more excuse for scholars and activists to continue to propagate the false narrative of the babaylans' historical demise. In addition, they must come to terms with the fact that "babaylanhood" does not necessarily translate into social power and high status, as evidenced by the stories of Undin in the previous chapter, Mendung before her marriage to Datu Sabal, and other women ritual specialists who do not share the relative privilege that Mendung enjoyed later in life. Mendung's cousin Myrna could not help but be provoked by all the claims of gender complementarity, negligible hierarchies, and relative egalitarianism among the T'boli and Southeast Asians in general. Formerly playing support to Mendung, Myrna now claims prime space for her tale.

Myrna's Story

If relative egalitarianism exists at all in T'boli society, Myrna contended, "it may only be among the wealthy. For the poor and ordinary T'boli, there is no such thing. It is built-in in T'boli society that kem logi and kem libun are treated unequally." Myrna details the gender ideology that has affected poor T'boli women, especially:

> When a T'boli child is born, discrimination on the grounds of sex begins. If the child is a logi, the relatives of the mother become charged with supporting the family with food and gifts. If the child is a libun, it is the relatives of the father who support the family. The reason for this is so that when the girl grows up and gets married, it is the father's family that will collect the bride price paid by the family of the groom that is double the value of the groom's price that it will pay. This bride's price is not given to the couple but is distributed among the family members who have contributed to the groom's price that is smaller in value compared to the bride's price that they will receive. Conversely, when a boy grows up and decides to marry, it is the mother's family that will be responsible for raising the money for the price of the bride, which is bigger than the groom's price that it will collect.
>
> When T'boli girls—at least in my generation—grow up, they are not exposed to the public but are confined in houses where they learn weaving, embroidery, beadwork and other skills that will fetch for them higher dowries. The virginity of a libun is prized because a datu will pay a much higher bride price for a virgin girl.
>
> When I was growing up, I fought very hard to go to school, even without my parents' financial support. This I did to ward off the men who wanted to marry me. I knew that the more I stayed at home, the more likely I would be made to marry prematurely. Still, my parents arranged for me to marry. The man had already been giving gifts to my father without my knowledge. I ran away for a month. I was against it all. When I came back, the man continued to chase me. The situation continued up to my parents' deaths. My relatives wanted to return the dowries to the man but he refused to accept them back. My relatives didn't force the issue anymore because I could get killed. When I graduated from high school, I had to marry the man against my wishes. We had two children. Later, he died from tumor in his lungs.
>
> The unequal relations between logi and libun continue in marriage as decreed by the Kitab Tau Seyehen or Customary Marriage Law. When kem logi and kem libun farm together, they, indeed, play complementary roles. That means the kem logi do the clearing, while the kem libun are responsible for the planting, the maintenance of the

farm, the harvesting, in addition to housekeeping and the raising and supporting of children! That the women do most of the work can be explained by the men's finickiness with work they accept, even if they are poor. This is because they see themselves in the image of the T'boli epic hero, Tudbulul, who did not have to toil, having magic powers to provide for all his families' and for his own needs. And when T'boli husbands find employment, they keep most of their earnings to themselves. They might buy rice but will spend the rest of their income on drinking. When their wives grow old, these husbands look for younger women. The first wife is forced to accept this, otherwise she and her husband will divorce, which means the first wife must return all the dowries. All these decisions are generally upheld by the predominantly male *tau kemukum* or traditional judges. But then the second wife has almost no rights over her husband's assets. So the second wife will work double time for her children. On the other hand, if a wife takes on another husband, she can be killed. Men are not afraid to return the smaller amount of the groom's price, especially if they are financially able. They can also refuse to accept the return of groom's prices so as to keep their wives in bondage. And when these men commit adultery and are mandated to pay *betad* (fine) to repair their relationships with their wives, they may not pay to keep the wives waiting.

The Kitab Tau Seyehen stipulates that a libun cannot do whatever she wants without the approval of her husband. This applies to all. It does not matter if you are a tau m'ton bu. Although tau m'ton bu women—compared to tau m'ton bu men—are generally favored by spirits and human clients alike because of their reputation for being more trustworthy, respectful, conscientious, accurate in their findings, gentle and effective in their care, just the same, they require their husbands' permission and approval of all their activities, limiting their mobility. And if they violate the marriage law, they may receive threats of violence, be forced to return dowries, or worse, be killed.

Even in death, a T'boli wife's bondage continues. When my husband died, I was expected to marry one of his married brothers. I pleaded that I would rather live alone with my children than fight with another logi's wife or wives for the logi's attention and meager resources. What I did, instead, was marry a Visayan man who was single. As a result, my T'boli in-laws demanded that I return all the dowries that my first husband gave, even though he was already dead. I fought hard and argued that I had children to support, and won.[71]

Other T'boli Women's (and Men's) Stories

Eighteen years after Mendung recounted to me her (other) tutul kemo ke taum, I revisited Lake Sebu. I wanted to find out if Mendung's and Myrna's claim of unequal gender complementarity was shared by other T'boli women and if there had been significant changes in the T'boli gender ideology in the last two decades. Myrna arranged for several T'boli kem libun and kem logi, most of them musicians, to gather in a clearing that overlooked the lake. They came to share their songs, instrumental music, food, and stories about their relationships with the opposite sex. Above the waters that rippled quietly under the mid-morning sun, Biho Fikan, a tau lemingon/temutul like Mendung, from Barangay Telubek, Lake Sebu, sang several episodes of the *Tudbulul* that she had learned from her own mother and brother. Biho's *gebela* or fair voice and skillful storytelling in the old T'boli language, incited laughter, raucous remarks, and animated sounds of approval among the women and men who came to listen. Her rendition was matched by the singing of Milin Manguwan and Danilo Kasaw, themselves *Tudbulul* singers, dancers, and instrumentalists. Other women shared lute and dance performances amid betel nut chewing, text messaging, and selfie taking, as trucks and motorcycles screeched in the background and karaoke loudspeakers blasted old American pop hits in the nearby street. Between the singing of *Tudbulul* episodes, the listeners shared lighthearted reflections on the epic's themes against their experiences of relationships between T'boli kem logi and kem libun. Mariafe Flang, a hegelong and *kumbing* (jaw's harp) player, spoke rather dryly:

> In reality, most T'boli kem libun work harder than kem logi. When kem logi work, they spend what they earn on liquor. And when they are drunk, they forget about their families. Kem libun, on the other hand, are forced to work hard to feed their families and to send their children to school.

Milin Manguwan echoed Mariafe's views: "Kem logi earn only for themselves. Kem libun, on the other hand, must spend whatever meager income they earn, slowly, for the survival of their family."

Mina Tungay, player of s'magi, hegelong, *klintang* (small row of gongs), offered some historical context:

> When the Visayan settlers came, our kem logi learned to smoke, drink, and gamble. The irony is, it is not the Visayan kem logi who drink. They are the ones who sell the liquor! In short, my husband is a drunkard. Singlehandedly, I have worked very hard to support my children. With

a heavy heart, I was forced to sell our only carabao [farm helping bovine] in order to survive.

To Mina's words, Mariafe added: "When the Visayan lowlanders came and took our lands, our kem logi became idle except for paid labor. But each time they get paid, they buy cellphones and find teenage-girl text-mates, breaking up their own families!"

Tuning Blagay, a bead ornaments-maker, offered a slightly different view:

> I am actually thankful to the Visayans. Because of their influence, we work hard now to send our children to school. And because they sell soap, we are now also clean. They have contributed much. But their coming has also had bad effects. Thankfully, my husband is a good logi. He respects me. That is why we live peacefully even though we are poor.

To this, Lucita Sagan, a hegelong player, added: "No such thing as happiness in my life! Only I support the family!"

With a tone of resignation, Mariafe concluded:

> Since we have been forced to work so hard by doing different kinds of labor including performing music, we don't depend on our kem logi anymore. We have come to trust ourselves. Other kem libun have also gone abroad to escape [their heartaches here].

Myrna joined in the conversation:

> Many T'boli kem libun in and around Lake Sebu—even those with only elementary education—have decided to risk finding work overseas because there are very few jobs available here. They apply to become domestic helpers in Qatar, Hongkong, Riyadh, and Bahrain. The kem logi, on the other hand, have not been able to do the same because they have no skills to cook and babysit. They have no other talent besides farming. So the kem libun work overseas and send their earnings back to their kem logi, many of whom use the money on other kem libun.

Frankie Sabal, Mendung's first son, talked about what he thought was the effect of education on the T'boli:

> Education has been making us dependent on the cash economy. We now live by buying and selling just like the Visayans. Education has also been causing the rising tide of *kanya-kanya* [individualism]. There is no longer leadership, guidance, unity.

To Frankie's words, Myrna added:

> Indeed, education has not guaranteed us better lives because even if one gets a degree, there are no jobs available for the T'boli, who, as Indigenous persons, are discriminated against. But when some T'boli get educated, they also tend to become selfish, greedy, and untrustworthy.

"But education," Mariafe exclaimed, "has caused the T'boli kem libun to have more power. Now we know our 'rights.'"

Luming Tawan, hegelong player, added: "If you hit a kem libun today, you go to prison."

To this Mina added: "I live very close to the police station. If my drunkard husband beats me up, he will surely end up there."

Myrna clarified that the power of T'boli libun could not be solely attributed to modern education. Long before the T'boli had schools, there were already powerful T'boli kem libun. Diwa Ofong, also called Ye Hingol (Moving Mother, she shook when she talked), was one such libun. Each time kem libun had problems, they ran to her. She was a staunch defender of kem libun, Myrna said.

The conversation turned to the issue of *duwaya*, the practice of a logi taking on several wives: one to cook, one to work in the farm, one to entertain guests, one to play princess, and many other roles besides. Just a generation ago, Myrna said, a libun who wanted to separate from her husband approached a datu to ask for help with returning the dowries. By doing so, she ended up becoming that datu's wife and property.

Mariafe reported that the T'boli officials—most if not all of them kem logi—recently pushed for the continuation of the duwaya practice, "for as long as the kem logi can feed all of their kem libun." Mariafe exclaimed, "NO! We, kem libun protested!" "But the officials had their way," she lamented.

"Duwaya is unfair to kem libun," Frankie, Mendung's first son said. "Tradition, on the other hand, does not force people to follow. Duwaya can take place only if the first wife agrees that her husband takes on other wives. There has to be agreement."

Joining the conversation about duwaya, Mendung's second son, Manolete, said:

> Our father, Datu Sabal, was rich and generous, and was a good settler of disputes. He had many wives. Each day of the week, our father slept with one of his seven wives. It was his first wife who distributed rice to each of my father's families. Our mother, Mendung, was the seventh wife. Besides being a good singer who was invited to sing during dowry negotiations, wedding celebrations, rituals, feasts, and elections, she was a good decision maker, a highly respected one. Whenever our mother was

requested to sing, our father would say, "Go ahead, that's your work." But our mother never abandoned our father.

Frankie added:

> We salute our father. He was not jealous or resentful of our mother's success. He never said a bad word toward her. "You are our pride. Increase your pride," he said to her. [Despite this] there was a lot of trouble, a lot of jealousy [in our home]. That is why in my generation, *isa na lang* [one wife is enough].

Frankie's wife, Flor, spoke: "If Frankie practices duwaya, I will not agree with it," she said.

Joanna, Manolete's wife, added: "I, too, will not agree. But if Manolete insists on practicing duwaya, fine with me, but we will separate."

Frankie, Manolete, Flor, and Joanna—Mendung's sons and daughters-in-law—all studied in the Allah Valley Public High School. Their education may have contributed to their changing gender norms.

Myrna noted that because of the unequal T'boli gender relationships, many kem libun have opted to separate from their T'boli husbands.

> The T'boli kem libun are fed up especially when their husbands take on other wives or mistresses, or when these husbands are jealous and violent, even though they, themselves, have their own secrets. By freeing themselves of their T'boli husbands, the kem libun feel they can then focus on earning a living for their children and for themselves.

Myrna's experience of marrying a Visayan man is not an isolated case. The reason why many T'boli libun have opted to marry Visayan kem logi, she said, is because of what they have observed to be the better working relationships between many Visayan wives and husbands in the pursuit of a better life. "The Visayan kem logi don't choose what work they take," she said. "And they really work hard to earn money for their wives, especially if they have children. When I married a Visayan man, I held money for the first time. This was not the case during my first marriage. It was my husband who held the money and who decided on what we did," she added.[72]

The stories of Mendung, Myrna, and the other T'boli women and men generally support the claim of gender complementarity among the T'boli. This complementarity manifests itself in the division of roles and responsibilities—that to some extent are interchangeable—among women and men.[73] Evidence suggests, however, that this gender complementarity is undergirded by a deep inequality that may be partly attributed to the centuries-old performance of the *Tudbulul* that continues to be the strongest justification for the continued practice of duwaya (polygamy, but not polyandry); arranged marriages by fathers, uncles and brothers; unequal labor between the genders; and violence against women.

The universal women's rights as invoked by Mariafe may be problematized for its tendency to colonize local norms. On the other hand, a narrative of insoluble universal difference would be as problematic. Both universalism and relativism can be oppressive but also potentially productive for indigenous interests as some of the T'boli women have noted.

Historicizing the *Tudbulul*'s Gender Ideology

What can the *Tudbulul*'s gender ideology be attributed to? Many of the Philippine feminist scholars and activists who have asserted that gender egalitarianism existed during precolonial times date the advent of inequality to the Spanish colonial period. Myrna disagrees with this claim and argues that gender inequality, at least in the case of many T'boli, may have already been around before the arrival of the Spanish, who never directly conquered the T'boli anyway. Is there historical evidence to support Myrna's claim?

A reexamination of the Spanish colonial archives indeed reveals references to what may be considered indicators of precolonial women's high status and a relatively egalitarian gender ideology. What feminist historians have not also emphasized, however, are references to practices that signal otherwise. During the earlier part of Spanish colonization, between 1569 and 1576, specifically, Miguel López de Legazpi observed:

> Marriage among these natives is a kind of purchase or trade, which the men make; for they pay and give money in exchange for their women, according to the rank of the parties. The sum thus paid is divided among the parents and relatives of the woman. Therefore the man who has many daughters is considered rich. After marriage, whenever the husband wishes to leave his wife, or to separate from her, he can do so by paying the same sum of money that he gave for her. Likewise the woman can leave her husband, or separate from him, by returning the double of what he gave for her. The men are permitted to have two or three wives, if they have money enough to buy and support them.[74]

Legazpi's report was corroborated by the accounts of conquistador Miguel de Loarca (1582–1583) and Spanish governor Francisco de Sande (1576–1582).[75] These references to early colonial gender norms contest totalizing claims of precolonial women's high status and relative gender equality so prevalent in Philippine feminist discourse, outside of qualifications like Fe Mangahas's that precolonial gender norms "already carried the seeds of inequality."[76] Thus taking a different stance, Delia Aguilar argues, "Filipinas have always been disempowered by a patriarchal system and the myth of historical female power undermines attempts to expose and combat the roots of this oppressive social structure."[77] Myrna's claim that the gender hierarchies codified in the *Tudbulul* predated colonization may have basis after all. Entrenched in precolonial society, these hierarchies may have been reinforced, aggravated, and refined into self-conscious and endorsed hierarchies through contact with other patriarchal gender ideologies.

Impact of Muslim Neighbors

Muslim gender ideology is relevant to this discussion because of the geographic proximity of the T'boli ancestral lands and those of specific Philippine Muslim groups. A brief history of Islam's arrival in the islands and the relationship of Islamized groups with the T'boli will help contextualize gender-related discussions.

Islam was introduced to the islands during the thirteenth century. This was facilitated by the thriving Arab market that connected Central Asia, Africa, India, China, and Southeast Asia; the traffic of Sufi missionaries; and the development of Muslim communities built on intermarriages between Arab and Malaysian men and Native women.[78] Islamic schools in Sulu and Maguindanao were established during the fifteenth and sixteenth centuries for the purpose of teaching Islam and Arabic.[79] Citing Wernstedt and Spencer, Mora writes of the long historical ties between the Islamized Maguindanao peoples and highlander groups like the T'boli, the former acting as an important trading link between the highland and lowland peoples. According to this account, Maguindanao and T'boli relations were also marked by difficulty.[80] The T'boli, Blaan, and Ubu highlanders were said to have resisted the aggressive proselytizing of a succession of Muslim warrior-priests.[81] These highlanders also opposed their treatment by the Muslims as potential slaves.[82]

The Muslim traditionalist stance on gender, according to Camillia Fawzi El-Solh and Judy Mabro, is to "defend the customary social and legal inequality separating men and women by advocating particular interpretations of the Qur'an and the Hadith which assert ... women's subordinate status in Muslim society [as] 'God-willed.'"[83] In addition, traditionalists stress "'the immutable and complete difference in the nature of the sexes, which is part of God's plan for the world,' and which thus means that 'the sexes are mutually complementary.'"[84] These "perceptions of gender relations ... underlie (the) traditionalists' belief in the moral imperative of confining women's role to the domestic sphere, and of defending male prerogatives such as polygamy as ordained by God."[85]

One might ask, however, if it is not unreasonable to assume that such traditionalist Muslim gender ideology remained true to its form once transplanted in the islands. Such ideology would have inevitably undergone an indigenization that determined the local face of Islam. Carmen Abubakar wrote: "When Islam was introduced to the Philippines, it absorbed many (Indigenous) cultural elements that in time came to be recognized and accepted as Islamic."[86] What is most noteworthy for our purposes about El-Solh and Mabro's description of the Muslim traditionalists' gender ideology is its resemblance to some of the gender norms codified in the *Tudbulul*. According to Myrna, marriages between non-T'boli Muslim men and Indigenous T'boli women are "not that much different from purely T'boli marriages. In the former, the man maintains many wives, both T'boli and non-T'boli, who are not able to decide for themselves. The women also have to accept their husband's culture and convert to their husband's religion. There is no equality." While Myrna cannot generalize about Muslim and Indigenous T'boli marriages, her observations remain telling.

Impact of Christian Settlers and Missions

When the Spanish colonized the Philippines, they were unable to penetrate most interior areas, including those in Southern Mindanao.[87] This was due in part to the insulation provided by the Muslim groups that successfully repelled the Spanish colonizers and in part to the resistance staged by the Native highlanders themselves.[88] It was only a matter of time, however, before Christian influences began to seep into T'boli life. The moment Datu Piang, the Muslim leader of Maguindanao, and other Muslim datus accepted American sovereignty that led to the establishment of the Moro Province in 1903, Muslim resistance that once protected the T'boli from outside groups began to crumble.[89] G. S. Casal and D. Javier write that in 1913, 13,000 hectares of the Cotabato Valley were opened up for settlement and the first waves of Christians arrived.[90] The influx of Christian lowlanders increased further once the Philippine government—seeking to alleviate land pressures in Luzon and the Visayas and to arrest the concomitant rise of revolutionary movements—opened 50,000 hectares for homesteading in the Koronadal Valley in 1938.[91] Casal and Javier write that with the arrival of homesteaders came commercial ranching, mining, and logging interests. Armed with land grants and timber licenses, the lowlanders increasingly "encroached upon T'boli homelands and disenfranchised those who had resided on the land since time immemorial, but who, without access to instruments of ownership recognized by the Philippine government, could not obtain legal protection from the latter."[92]

The gender ideology that the Spanish Catholic colonizers brought with them to the islands, Carolyn Brewer writes, was one of "male/female dichotomy" that "spilled over into an unequal gendered power relationship between men and women, that is, men over women."[93] Feminist theologian Mary John Mananzan explains that since women were taught to see themselves as derived beings taken from the rib of man, their reason for being was mainly to serve man.[94] This meant that whereas in precolonial times women performed the roles of babaylan priestesses, during the Spanish colonial times they were demoted to helpers of priests or to spectators in cultic celebrations. Women were additionally blamed for man's sin, and made to bear man's guilt.[95] Legally, according to Dinusha Panditaratne, the Roman doctrines of *patria potestas* and *paterfamilias* prescribed woman as "subordinated to male authority within her marriage, family or clan."[96]

How did this Catholic gender ideology impact colonized lowland Filipinos who would later encroach upon T'boli areas? Cristina Blanc-Szanton writes that the lowlanders engaged in "selecting and adapting old and new cultural images and formulations, giving the images new meanings, or meshing the images in syncretic combinations."[97] She points out, for example, that if in the past parents jealously guarded their daughter's virginity because it ensured a high bride price, once they became Catholics, they continued to do the same, except that it was now to promote Christian virtue, thus demonstrating the coalescing of colonial and Indigenous gender ideologies, both of which thrived on the control of women.[98]

When the American Protestant colonizers arrived, writes Meg Wesling, they claimed to treat their women better, their gender relations alleged to be the "most progressive and best suited for maintaining a woman's "high and noble" virtue.[99] Unlike the Native (Catholic) woman whom the American schoolteacher Mary Fee saw as "not owning her own virtue, and by extension, her own body [hence] . . . can only be understood as at the mercy of the protection of the men around her," white women like Fee were said to be independent, "a class of 'civilization workers' who served as representatives of social progress and Christian salvation."[100] Such contrasts between American and Filipino women in favor of the former was used to justify American intervention, for in the Filipino women's "dependence upon American protection, paradoxically, Filipino women find their own independence."[101] Fee's project was thus to introduce Filipino women to what she saw as the superior "'modern' codes of behavior and comportment . . . that interestingly, draw on the standards of the New Woman as well as on the ideals of Victorian womanhood."[102] Here lay the relationship between feminism and colonialism, with the white colonizers claiming to "save brown women."[103] What this meant for the T'boli and other Native women was they could end their subjugation only by becoming like their Western and Philippine elite feminist sisters.

Gender concerns, however, have not been the only pressing problem for the T'boli. With the influx of lowland Christians, who have more education and hence the means to take over T'boli lands and resources, came the T'boli's need for new competencies. Since missionaries were known to provide education to Indigenous peoples, T'boli chiefs headed by Ungoy "Mafok" Kawig requested that a mission be established in T'boli lands.[104] American Passionist missionary Father George Nolan, CP—succeeded by Father Rex Mansmann, CP—and the Sisters of Saint Paul of Charters opened the Santa Cruz mission in 1960. Myrna remembers attending the mission school as a first grade pupil when girls were first admitted in 1963. She recalled that, at first, T'boli parents did not want their girls in school for fear that they would be abused by lowlanders and soldiers, resulting in lower brides' prices or no dowry at all. After a mission campaign, however, some of the parents yielded. The mission, according to Myrna, established a total of six primary schools, two high schools, and one college. It also initiated health projects, livelihood programs, and services that were denied the T'boli by the government.[105] With the mission, according to Myrna, who would serve as its librarian and researcher, "our life was good and abundant through the mission's ecofarm, handicrafts, and healthcare programs. The mission received funding from the United States, Australia, and Germany, and staff salaries alone amounted to one million pesos."[106]

Mora himself observes how the Santa Cruz mission in the 1980s was "careful to accommodate T'boli religious symbols, myths and ritual practices within its own theological vision."[107] In consultation with the T'boli leaders, Catholic liturgy and icons were fused with T'boli animism and mythology in an annual "harvest festival" in which the T'boli people enthusiastically participated, even as these celebrations reconstructed and hybridized their traditions.[108] Mora also notes how the mission's organizational and economic resources bred a dependency on the part of the T'boli who struggled to assert their place in the mission.[109] In 1991, Father Rex Mansmann was "accused of raping a thirteen-year old T'boli girl."[110] Myrna attributed the accusation to jealousy among Mansmann's fellow clergy.[111] Mansmann was tried, defrocked, but ultimately acquitted of the charges.[112]

One might say that the American-led Santa Cruz mission stood for a complex gender ideology. On the one hand, it promoted education that resulted in the empowerment of some T'boli women, like Myrna, allowing them greater leverage in dealing with T'boli men and the dominant Christian lowlanders. On the other hand, it could not shake off its patriarchal and racialized gender ideology, in which male priests and foreign-funded missions do good but are not able to dislodge deeply entrenched colonial hierarchies. Related to this Meg Wesling writes:

> To claim a privileged role of teacher [and I add, missionary] over soldier and merchant as representative Americans is to disavow the violence of the colonial project, its physical and economic devastation, and to embrace the fantasy of affection as the guiding principle of U. S.–Philippine relations.[113]

Impact of Capitalists

At around the same time that the mission was in decline, according to Myrna, the roads that led to T'boli land became paved. Electricity and telephone lines were installed. This led to a tourism boom, a real estate price hike, and an urgent necessity for the T'boli to secure titles to protect their land ownership. The T'boli leadership, according to Myrna, filed an ancestral domain claim that was approved by the government in the 1990s. Because of the government's inability to provide livelihood opportunities to the T'boli, however, many T'boli, including the all-male tribal chiefs of Lake Sebu, were forced to sell their lands or to mortgage them to lowlanders. Only a small portion of the ancestral domain now remains. Because of the influence of capitalism that introduced the notion of land as commodity to be bought and sold, the T'boli have become increasingly dispossessed. With the loss of their lands, the T'boli also lost their forest hunting grounds, their farms, their free use of the lakes, and their planting and harvest rituals. "We lost our power," Myrna lamented. All this has especially affected the kem logi, who felt more and more insecure. With the invasion of the settlers, the kem logi resorted to selling their cheap labor while developing new vices that have led to more dispossession and gender-based abuse.

Many T'boli kem libun, on the other hand, have transitioned to selling their labor and their products, whether farm produce or handicrafts.[114] Tourism in Lake Sebu and in the surrounding areas has brought employment opportunities to the T'boli kem libun and a market for their works. But middlemen are known to purchase T'boli women's works at a very low price and to sell these expensively. The International Work Group for Indigenous Affairs claimed that the settlers who have ended up owning real estate and the establishments and have been employing T'boli kem logi and kem libun as service staff have been the ones reaping the most profits from tourism.[115]

That the T'boli women have been afforded opportunities to generate income necessary to keep their families alive gives the impression of raised status for women under capitalist conditions. Many T'boli kem logi, on the other hand, have not been able to obtain such income to provide for their families because they have lost their farmlands and they have continued to liken themselves to Tudbulul for whom everything is magic. That a growing number of younger-generation kem libun have "escaped" to foreign lands to work as salaried domestic helpers in order to build concrete houses back home, send their children to school, and establish small businesses, complicates earlier claims of women becoming relegated to the household and losing control over assets with the advent of private property and capitalism. On the other hand, claims of women's empowerment under capitalist conditions become tempered when one finds out how low women's wages have been, keeping women dependent on their non-T'boli employers or on T'boli or non-Tboli husbands. There have also been reports that capitalist pressures have rendered young T'boli kem libun vulnerable to sex trafficking as ruthless modern capitalism grafts onto older forms of treating women like objects to be exchanged among men.

In the T'boli encounters with market forces, one observes a mutual reinforcement of the customary T'boli and capitalist gender ideologies. This supports assertions that unequal gender ideologies cannot be attributed to the *Tudbulul*, the Qur'an, or the Bible alone. As El Solh and Mabro note, women's status in general "cannot be isolated from other variables, such as cultural specificity, social and political structures as well as the level of economic development," not to mention women's class origin, educational background, employment status, age group, and geographical location.[116] In the case of the T'boli kem libun, the rising ethnic and class inequalities between the T'boli and lowland Christians, Muslims, and capitalists have served to consolidate their precarious status, reinforced by the continuing performance of the *Tudbulul*.

Women's Agency?

The question is, why have the T'boli kem libun like tau m'ton bu Mendung Sabal continued to sing and listen to the *Tudbulul* if this has only reinforced T'boli gender inequalities? Who is Tudbulul to them?

During the gathering by the lake, Milin sang an excerpt of a *Tudbulul* episode:

> We de Tudbulul lunay sebung, ket gono gono'n motun
> Ni libun ni enget funen, mudel sotu libun
> Ilo-en de Tudbulul, to lowom to genfun me
> Belaem kon wolu libun gonohen mung, mahil du kedeng libun
>   gonohen mung
> Mahil dur kedeng libun gonohen mung, bote de du.
>
> Tudbulul of Lunay Sebung, he comes into every house.
> Who shall own him? Every woman wants to have him.
> Women long for him.
> He has eight women with him.
> It troubles him with whom to stay for the night.

Remarking on Milin's song, Mariafe declared:

> Tudbulul is like the president of the Philippines. He takes care of everyone, especially those with problems. If he married eight to ten women,

it was because he loved them all. He began with love. He was moved by love. If he rejected some, it was only temporary. I, as listener, am moved by love to hear his stories. Women like me like him and wish him well.

Echoing Mariafe, Luming said: "Tudbulul had so many wives because he loved them all. Like him, we are all moved by love. If not for love, we can't come together."

To this, Biho added: "Tudbulul gathers us all, including you [referring to the author]."

Danilo pointed out:

> We trace our lives to Semgulang. He was the most powerful and wealthy man who did not want anyone to stand in his way. He owned Lake Sebu and people from faraway places came to see him and the T'boli tribe because of our riches as attested to by the T'boli songs and dances.

Myrna disagrees with accusations that Tudbulul is the main cause of the T'boli women's suffering. She argues that while Tudbulul, in his time, beat up his wives, his avowed intentions, as well as his wives' reception of his acts, were as expressions of love. Such reasoning, however, may no longer work today when violent actions inflicted by T'boli kem logi against T'boli kem libun has come to be generally understood by the latter not as acts of love, but as abuse. In addition, Myrna argues that while Tudbulul, during his time, did not toil to provide for his families because it was believed then that there was enough magic to go around, such view may no longer be used by contemporary T'boli kem logi as an excuse for refusing to work to provide for their families. Reliance on magic has come to be equated by contemporary T'boli kem libun with economic violence, hunger, and death. The stark differences in the intentions, contexts, and interpretations of the actions of Tudbulul and of contemporary T'boli kem logi have therefore allowed the T'boli kem libun to criticize their kem logi, while maintaining their love for their revered hero, Tudbulul.

Myrna's and the other T'boli women's exoneration of Tudbulul from contributing to their own oppression may easily be taken as evidence of "false consciousness." Saba Mahmood describes false consciousness as the internalization of patriarchal norms that contribute to reproducing ones' own domination.[117] Why, indeed, must T'boli kem libun keep on venerating a hero who has been used for centuries by generations of T'boli kem logi as a model for abusing them? Abu-Lughod cautions against quick judgments about women who, she claims, "both resist and support existing systems of power but [whose] experiences and motivations should not be misattributed to false consciousness, feminist consciousness, or feminist politics."[118] Based on these arguments, T'boli women may not be simplistically reduced to, on the one hand, victims, and on the other, resistors. Accusations of false consciousness can also easily lead elite feminists, Christians, and Muslims who claim social and/or moral ascendancy to want to save Indigenous women. Impulses to "save," Abu Lughod argues, are highly problematic and "depend on and reinforce a sense of superiority . . . a form of arrogance that deserves to be challenged."[119] Thus, Mahmood notes recent developments in feminist scholarship that tend to veer away from simplistic portrayals of non-Western women as "passive and submissive beings shackled by structures of male authority."[120] Focus has shifted instead to the "operations of human agency within structures of subordination," and to "how women resist the dominant male order by subverting the hegemonic meanings of cultural practices and redeploying them for their 'own interests and agendas.'"[121]

What follows is an inquiry into the T'boli kem libun's experiences and understandings of singing and listening to the *Tudbulul*. It asks where the T'boli kem logi's agency lies—if at all—in acts of singing and listening to a text that has been accused, time and again, of reinscribing gender inequality and T'boli kem libun's oppression.

The first thing to consider about the *Tudbulul* is that it is an epic that is orally performed. While different singers may follow the same general plot and character development, each one has a distinct way of telling the story by employing different words and tunes. Even with one singer no two *Tudbulul* renditions are exactly alike, not with the constant rephrasing of words and recasting of voices.[122] Taking the *Tudbulul* as one bounded and fixed text, therefore, will be an easy way to misunderstand it. Mendung as tau lemingon/temutul was at liberty to creatively spin every rendition of hers according to her specific audiences' constitution, the occasion at hand, and the time allotted for her performance. Mendung, according to Myrna, was particularly known for providing commentaries between the different Tudbulul episodes, commentaries that are easily missed if one examines only the "formal" song texts (if there is such a thing). By using various narrative, sonic, gestural, and affective strategies to impart Tudbulul's story, Mendung, according to Myrna, was known to sing the *Tudbulul* as a lesson to her audiences. Specifically, she sang the *Tudbulul* to urge the kem libun to stand up for themselves and the kem logi to stop oppressing women.[123] In addition, Mendung's and other singers' performances of the *Tudbulul* have provided opportunities for T'boli kem libun listeners to reflect on the *Tudbulul*'s texts against their own lived realities and to generate their own embodied, affective, and analytical responses to the singers' performances. Thus, during Biho's and Milin's performances of excerpts of the *Tudbulul*, the kem libun audiences

FIGURE 2.3. Myrna Pula and other T'boli women in Lake Sebu, South Cotabato, 2015

Photo by Grace Nono.

listened reverently but also interjected, intervened, denounced, questioned, sang back, and shrieked with laughter at what they heard (figure 2.3).

As the singer rested in between episodes, she and her listeners discussed further, each motivated with making the performance meaningful to her own life. Thus, reflecting on the *Tudbulul*'s main plot, Myrna as a listener issued her own commentary:

> There is an urgent need to put an end to duway, the practice of kem logi having many wives that results in the impossibility of peace in the family because of jealousy among the wives and children. [We must also end] violence against kem libun because women are humans who deserve as much respect as the kem logi. The prearrangement of marriages [must also stop] because they take place without the consent of the concerned parties, and because the marriages brokered through such arrangements almost always fail. [Another custom that must stop is] the demand for the giving of excessive bride prices because they burden new couples with

endless obligations, as well as bury kem libun in debt to the logi's family, making it hard for them to get out of their marriages when their husbands are abusive. This also invites early death on the part of the kem libun. [Finally, we must end] the nonacknowledgment of the rights and claims of children from second, third, fourth, and so on wives to their father's assets, because they, too, must enjoy the benefits of their ties to their fathers.[124]

The T'boli kem libun's voiced responses to the *Tudbulul* performances demonstrate how the epic's prescriptions can be contested, negotiated, reinterpreted, and subverted through creative strategies that push for more gender equality that is what the present generation of T'boli women demands. This agrees with Ellen Koskoff's view that "tensions surrounding power and control that exist between women and men can be exposed, challenged or reversed within musical performance."[125] As Mahmood, citing Butler, notes, "the reiterative structure of norms serves not only to consolidate a particular regime of discourse/power but also provides the means for its destabilization."[126] The *Tudbulul* that had been accused of being responsible for much of the T'boli women's suffering, has been—in the voices of kem libun singers like Mendung and in the ears of women listeners like Myrna—turned into a force for inciting T'boli ken libun to rise up and change their condition of subjugation.

Outside of singing, Mendung applied lessons from the *Tudbulul* to her other social functions. When she was elected a councilwoman in barangay Tubiallah, serving as libun kemukum for ten to fifteen years, she continually advised kem libun, particularly those who were oppressed by their husbands, to stand up for themselves. There was a case, according to Myrna, of a libun named Lining, who, in the 1980s, complained about her jealous husband who maltreated her. Mendung helped Lining separate without having to return the husband's dowries. By learning about the workings of the marriage law, Mendung herself ceased to be afraid of it. Having lived a difficult life under the watchful eyes of her father, uncles, and three husbands, she strove to break free from their control. She made herself aware of the arguments for not returning dowries should she and Datu Sabal separate. It was, in fact, Datu Sabal, according to Myrna, who was afraid of the prospect of Mendung fighting for her rights that could result in him losing all his properties. Mendung attributed the reversal of her fortunes to her marriage to Datu Sabal and especially to her tau munung, whose wise guidance allowed her to become financially independent so that, in the end, she supported not only herself and her children but also her husband and fellow wives' families. One must remember, however, that Mendung's story was the exception to the rule. Other T'boli women, including many women tau m'ton bu, suffer from gender-related violence until the end of their lives.

With Mendung's reputation as an empowered libun and defender of other T'boli women, she can easily be made to fit the Philippine feminists' construction of the babaylan as symbol of Philippine womanpower, except that Mendung was neither a precolonial woman nor a genericized and nationalized babaylan. Mendung's tau m'ton bu practice also did not spare her from gender-based abuse, although she did challenge her condition. Contrary to Philippine feminist claims, therefore, babaylanhood does not necessarily index a woman's high status. As Manduhai Buyanderger found out in her study of Buryat women shamans: "simply participating in the practice of shamanism does not automatically make women powerful.... It is important to look deeper into their experiences."[127] Anyway, ritual specialization does not guarantee the type of straightforward, overt flourishing of woman's power that many feminists generally envision.

The conflation of the babaylan—constructed as nationalized, precolonial women of power—with modern-day feminism, without attention to ethnic, class, and other differences, reminds one of Chandra Mohanty's critique of Western feminism's hegemonic construction of a monolithic and homogeneous category of "Woman," which results in the discursive colonization of historical Third World "women."[128] It further reminds one of Audre Lorde's critique of the assertion that "all women suffer the same oppression simply because we are women."[129] The appropriation of the precolonial babaylan identity by modern-day feminists has tended to eclipse the embodied voices of Native ritual specialists like Mendung who inhabit the turbulent and contingent present muddled by social calamities, including gender inequalities. Contrary to popular view, ritual specialists like Mendung do not lie outside history. They are not devoid of agency. They need no other contemporary women to embody them as though they are not, themselves, embodied and historical. They need no other women to idealize them as though their conditions mirror the egalitarian past untainted by historical exigencies that elite feminists imagine the precolonial times to be. They need no other women or men to save them, as though they do not have their own moral and other resources to address their needs. And yet, they also do not wish to be simply left alone. As Abu-Lughod notes, "it is too late not to interfere."[130] The lives of women and men all over have been entangled with the long histories of colonization and unequal interracial or intertribal relations.[131] Mendung herself sang, alluding to the need to be listened to, to be recognized, to be supported as a historical poor libun with abundant human and spiritual riches to offer:

> I am poor, very poor, but my song is my protection. I tell the rich people, I'm not selling my song, I'm not giving it away. All I need is recognition. The only one who allows me to see, who translates my song, is Myrna. While Myrna promotes, D'wata [Creator] looks down. I never

stop to breathe the sad harvests of the past. I have no other wealth but my song. It earns for me. It is my mother and my father too. I became famous because my song is not a game, the words are not ordinary. I'm the one who's ordinary. But never mind, my song is what people want to hear until the day I die. Generations to come will read about it. I will leave them my story. This is what I will leave on earth. Grace will promote my song. She's from Manila. I will send it to Malacañang, passing through space, on an airplane, because I dreamed it.[132]

The work of Mendung, the tau m'ton bu, to defend and empower other T'boli libun draws from deep T'boli spiritual truths perhaps older than the *Tudbulul*: the T'boli spirit pantheon that enshrines a relative egalitarianism that had not yet been realized. It draws from the reciprocal and mutually beneficial relationships between Mendung the tau m'ton bu and her tau munung, between Mendung as singer and her cousin and interpreter, Myrna.

But while gender inequality is a very real concern for many T'boli kem libun, it is neither the only one nor the one most pressing for some. The T'boli are equally if not more urgently pressed by the dispossession of their lands, identities, rituals, and traditional leadership by powerful outside forces that have been living amongst them, reminding them each day of their grave losses and uncertain future. The T'boli are heavily discriminated against by the settlers. They are not treated as equals. So while Tudbulul has his faults according to today's understanding of women's rights and gender equality, he has continued to provide the T'boli people with a sense of history, leadership, power, self-love, wealth, dignity, and hope for the future. He who walked the earth and underwent all kinds of trials. He who proved to all that "nothing is impossible if one has the will." So while T'boli kem libun detest their husbands' use of the *Tudbulul* as justification for their polygamy and abuse while having little ability to provide for their families, these men remain their brothers, sons, husbands or ex-husbands, their own. To excise them from T'boli kem libun's lives will, in the end, undermine the T'boli people's survival. This complicates individualistic notions of fulfillment, freedom, and empowerment by considering the greater needs of T'boli kem libun, not only on the grounds of gender but also class and ethnicity. It echoes African American womanist writers like Delores Williams, who have emphasized the role of the intersecting oppressions of race, gender, and class in the situations of black women. Against white feminists' focus on "patriarchy . . . as the center of gender oppression," Black Womanists have claimed that this approach has met the needs only of white women, with limited relevance for black women who have experienced domination differently.[133] Native American scholar and activist Devon Abbott Mihesuah alludes to a similar point when she writes: "Some Native women argue that, while they might be oppressed because of their gender, they are primarily disempowered because of their race, and they believe that it is more important to eradicate racist oppression than sexist oppression."[134] The T'boli libun's responses to their experiences of domination echo those of other disenfranchised and marginalized women for whom "freedom consisted in being able to reclaim lands, traditions, self-worth," because these have been deliberately denied them in the long history of colonization and domination.[135]

Shifting Gender

The shifts in the gender of Mendung's lihol in song extended to her other activities. Myrna noted that whenever Mendung sought forgiveness for her offenses, when she forgave her fellow wives and husband, when she regularly performed the *demsu* (offerings to spirits), or when she sang short songs, wove fabrics, and played the hegelong, she embodied the quality of lemnoy. But when she cleared her family's farm, cut trees, or separated married couples in favor of women, making sure no dowries were returned, Mendung embodied the quality of megel. Whenever Mendung treated cough, colds, headaches, and dysentery with herbs, or when she sang love songs, prayers, and the creation story, she performed lemnek. But when she sang the epic *Tudbulul*, chased the souls of the dying—a matter that required extra power—provided forceful critiques of T'boli men's oppression of their women, or incited the male datus to stand up for themselves against the invaders, Mendung embodied lembang. In this scheme, the problems of gender complementarity come into full view, with the mostly private qualities of forgiveness, healing, love, creation (related to reproduction), and prayers being associated with women and the mostly public qualities of physical prowess, action, major decision making, resistance to larger forces being identified with men. One must consider, however, that it is Mendung, a libun who is articulating both gendered actions, demonstrating her agency. By appropriating both genders with her voice and other actions, she as libun disrupts the gender binary's internal hierarchy, disrupting its ability to oppress. Shifting her every articulation according to each action or turn in the epic *Tudbulul*'s plot, Mendung's gendered voice demonstrated a deep relationality that reminds one of Judith Butler's notion of gender as

> a shifting and contextual phenomenon, [it] does not denote a substantive being, but a relative point of convergence among culturally and historically specific sets of relations.[136]

The one thing that distinguishes Mendung's gender relationality from Butler's is the former's acknowledgment of gendered spirit agencies as crucial to the vocation of ritual specialists, spirits that are generally dismissed or elided by colonialist scholarship.

This chapter concludes that among the Native ritual specialists' resources lie the seeds of their empowerment. This concurs with Leila Ahmed's argument about Islam that although it "instituted a hierarchical structure as the basis of relations between men and women, it also preached, in its ethical voice . . . the moral and spiritual equality of all human beings. Arguably, therefore, even as it instituted sexual hierarchy, it laid the ground, in its ethical voice, for the subversion of the hierarchy."[137]

Looking to the future, Mendung said that when the T'boli kem logi cease to oppress kem libun, and when the T'boli kem libun have learned to stand up for themselves while continuing to uphold all the good things about Tudbulul, and once the T'boli people restore their ownership of their ancestral lands, rituals, and identities, they will then realize Lemlunay, the place of justice, fairness, peace, contentment, and celebration.

> Lemlunay gono sesotu'n ne
> Lemlunay gono kemulu'n ne
> Lemlunay gono te, setambul
> Sewaten uni sembakungen
> Lemlunay gono kemulu'n
> Lemlunay ni tey lem o bung

> Lemlunay is where we go
> Lemlunay is our source
> It is where we gather to play gongs
> Gong sounds from all directions
> Lemlunay, the source
> Lemlunay, so exuberant.[138]

On Sexual Relationality

While writing this chapter about the voices of T'boli women and men, a number of gaps emerged. First, this chapter has rarely, if at all, attended to matters of sexuality. This elision may be attributed to a number of factors, including the lack of discursive tradition in Native Philippines that separates sex and gender, nature and culture, so entrenched in Western gender discourse. There is also the inherited colonial consignment of sex to the realm of taboo, if not to specialized medical-scientific discourses. A second gap has to do with the focus on the heteronormative binary of men and women and, to an extent, its relational continuum. By largely attending to this gender bifurcation, with the exception of scant references to the boyos or the T'boli feminine-masculine spirit helpers—because I, as author, have been so immersed in heteronormative sex and gender politics that imposes the horizon of possibility for what exists—this chapter has not really done much to help address the paucity of nonheteronormative voices in Native Philippine ritual specialist scholarship.

The Philippine feminists who have been writing about the babaylan have frequently asserted the predominance of women ritual specialists during the precolonial times, turning this claim into a panegyric for female power. A number of gender and sexuality studies scholars have likewise cited Spanish colonial reports about precolonial and early colonial male ritual specialists who were either temporarily effeminate or had permanently effeminate attributes.[139] Such references have been cited as evidence of precolonial transgender ritual specialization before it became desacralized or "stripped of its positive associations with religion and the sacred."[140] What have largely remained unaccounted for in literature, perhaps until now, are not only present-day Native transgender ritual specialists, but in particular, the Native female-to-male transgender Native ritual specialists. Do they exist? How do they understand the relationship between sexuality and ritual specialization? How do their understandings relate to theories that link so-called ambiguous sex with spiritual potency or those that promote "femininity as the (normative) vehicle to the spirit world" at least in the case of the male-to-female transgender ritual specialists?[141] How do their understandings relate to currently circulating sex and gender labels and frameworks?

When I brought up transgender ritual specialization with Myrna Pula, she immediately contacted Elia Cansing Capeon, a young Blaan woman chanter who we have both worked with. Elia knew someone with that experience. Elia introduced us to a present-day Blaan female-to-male transgender *nungaru* (someone who knows, spirited person) who introduced us to another. What follows are my initial findings based on encounters spanning three years.

I call on my meetings with these two female-to-male transgender nungaru to raise a number of issues. First, just because they and others like them have not been reported until now does not necessarily mean they are an ontological anomaly but that they represent a clue to a Philippine tradition that may have been overlooked, at least in babaylan literature. Second, the seemingly astonishing happenings that these persons report—representing a whole other level of preternatural occurrences—heighten issues of interpretation that are always situated and determined by the interpreter's social location, in addition to what may be conscious or unconscious assumptions of superiority. Readers, for instance, who are convinced of the existence of spirits and their effects on the physical world must face challenges that include idealization, or the kind of demonization perpetrated by many missionaries when confronted with Native ritual ways. On the other hand, those who are committed to a materialist ontology might dismiss indecipherable claims of reality, though they might still renounce judgment and salvage respect for matters that they know are beyond their knowledge and experience.

The Blaan

The two Native female-to-male transgender nungaru I write about are of Blaan ancestry. Living in areas contiguous to the T'boli, the Blaan peoples have inhabited the hills, mountains, and valleys of the provinces of Sarangani, South Cotabato, Davao del Sur, and Davao del Norte in the southwestern portion of Mindanao.[142] Catherine Gueguen writes of the coming of Christianity to the area as concomitant with the 1905 establishment of the archipelago's southern administrative boundary. During the American occupation (1898–1946), missionaries traveled to these areas, followed by active proselytizing during the 1970s. These Christianization campaigns were accompanied by massive inflows of Christianized lowlander populations from Luzon and the Visayas. The onslaught of Christian settlers armed with land titles took place alongside the granting of tribal territories as concessions for logging, mining, and stockbreeding activities.[143] Transnational pineapple and banana plantation companies like Dole began to occupy the best farming areas.[144] The significant decrease in the Blaan's land area including those of sacred sites had pushed many Blaan further into the mountains.[145] To cope with the problems of logging, mining, militarization, and tribal disunity, some Blaan communities have reportedly upheld their customary laws.[146] Others have maintained syncretic religious activities that attest to the "durability" of Blaan practices "linked to the idea of sacredness."[147] Many Blaan are also said to now maintain "double residences," one in the lowlands where they may be employed and another in the highlands, "where a kind of 'traditional space' could be re-instated."[148]

Bie and Gunintang: Two Nungaru–Ambaling Lagi

In June 2018, Myrna, Elia, and Bie Gulae visited my home in Bunawan, Agusan del Sur, in time for a thanksgiving ceremony officiated by several Agusan-Manobo baylan for the successful year of transmitting Indigenous knowledge from elders to the youth in our community-based school. Responding to the warm welcome that he received from the locals, Bie offered a *malem* (song) in his low-pitched and husky *talo* (voice in Blaan) in the Blaan language that Elia and Myrna retold in Visayan and English for the benefit of others.

> Even if we don't know each other, even if we have not met each other before, because of the spirits' desire, all of us are gathered here. I will try my best to welcome you back. In my whole life, I never dreamed that I would meet Grace and all of our Native friends here. My wish is that all Natives and all people on earth will have unity so that the spirits will also have unity among them as they provide guidance to us. I am grateful for your hospitality here in Agusan, even if there are only three of us who arrived from the boundary of South Cotabato, Davao del Sur, and Sarangani.

When Bie, Myrna, Elia, and I finally sit down to talk, Bie introduces himself as a nungaru or someone who knows, a person with knowledge, *garu* means "knowledge." What this means is he has a *magin* (tutelary spirit helper in Blaan) whom he describes through a malem as a male "child who holds the world, his mother from the lagoon, the hill of Ta Fanday." Bie uses his knowledge to cure simple ailments and to mediate tribal cases. He however distinguishes a nungaru from an *almoos* (full-fledged ritual specialist) whose vocation, he says, entails so much more than what a nungaru does. He also explains that a "real" almoos usually does not admit to being one [the vocation is not something to brag about]. Nor will an almoos volunteer his or her services to anyone. Both the almoos and the nungaru may offer assistance only when specifically requested.

Bie further introduces himself as an *ambaling lagi*, the B'laan designation for a female-to-male transgender person. To demonstrate what he means by ambaling lagi, on noticing Lucy, who is our school's lesbian Manobo tribal leader, Bie exclaims, using one of his few Tagalog words, "Pareho!," meaning "The same!" Of his activities as an ambaling lagi, Bie says that they have included hunting, clearing forests for swidden farming, plowing fields, and planting corn. He claims that he once built thirty-eight houses with massive posts with the help of only his magin, who supplied him with the extra strength. Of his relationships with women—a discussion that I observe incites much giggling among Bie, Elia, and Myrna—Bie says that the presence of his magin has sometimes resulted in his gaining a younger and handsomer appearance that has attracted many women. At one point, he recalls, a married woman pursued him relentlessly, resulting in this woman's husband shooting at Bie, thankfully missing. Also related to his magin, Bie claims to have once owned many properties that he gave away as dowries and bride prices for the hands of several women. At one point, he says, he had a total of eight wives who all slept with him—four on each side—but with whom he did not have *sdeme* (sex), copulation being prohibited by his magin and by the *uldin* (sacred law), along with stealing, cursing, and selfish acts. Perhaps frustrated with Bie, his wives began to fight with each other, leading Bie to send them all home.

None of this, however, was how Bie's life began. According to him, he was born and raised a girl named Jolita, with a *kie* (vagina). Jolita was often beaten up by his father for not doing "girls' chores," like cooking. Protesting at one point, she refused to eat. On the fourth day of her fast, her head hurt exceedingly. At that point, a magin who was a man-child without genitals appeared and stayed until Jolita felt better. This commenced Jolita's relationship with the magin. When Jolita turned eight years old, she suddenly grew a *bato* (penis) with flesh coming from the placenta of the man-child magin. Bie concealed this bodily transformation from his parents who according to tradition arranged for Bie to marry a man. Not only was this marriage against Bie's wishes, it was against those of the magin that had prohibited him from engaging in romantic and sexual relationships. So Bie was married off by his parents, causing him symptoms of insanity. He refused to have sexual relations with his husband, not only because of the absence of attraction on his part, but out of fear that his bato would be found out. The couple separated after one year and five months, at which point Bie's parents arranged for him to marry another man. This second marriage turned out to be another unconsummated union, also lasting a year and five months. When Bie was arranged to marry a third time, the magin gave him a letter in the form of a leaf with drawings of two valleys and a mountain, signifying that Bie would give birth to two girls and one boy. Bie had sdeme with his third husband. His bato according to him would disappear and be replaced by her kie on such rare occasions as full and new moons, the only times when Bie felt aroused, a feeling that would last only for an hour. As indicated by the magin, Bie gave birth to two girls and a boy. So as not to be in demand for more sex, Bie found his husband a second wife and even provided for the dowry and the bride price. As time passed, this third husband became entangled with horse and carabao thieves and was shot dead. For the fourth time, it was arranged that Bie should marry. This would become another sexless union that also ended after one year and five months. Explaining to his fourth husband why he had no desire for him, Bie showed his bato. This fourth husband cried, Bie recalled. They separated on good terms.

In 2002, a woman who Bie referred to as his best friend—perhaps someone he was intimate with—died. This caused Bie so much grief that he ran amok and shot someone who had nothing to do with his friend's death. The barrel of the gun didn't fire, though, because, according to Bie, his magin would not let it. The magin reprimanded Bie for his actions and ordered him to go home and to do only what was good, like helping people; in other words, reminding Bie of the nungaru's mandate. Bie fought with his magin and, according to him, he almost died at that point. As a result of Bie's transgressions against his magin and the uldin by spending too much time and money on women and perhaps by engaging in intimate relations, Bie was punished. He lost his wealth and with it his bato. Bie claims that his male genitalia have not returned to this day. Whenever he sees beautiful girls, he feels desire for them but he cannot do anything about it. He definitely feels no desire for men. If his bato returns, he says, he will accept it wholeheartedly. He may even marry a woman then, but only if his magin allows him to. He does recall his magin telling him to watch out for the future, for someone meant for him may come into his life.

In a situation of loss and privation—masked only by Bie's playful manner—is how Myrna, Elia, and I find him in July 2019 when we visit Barangay Blaan, Malungon, Sarangani. Bie shares a tiny split-bamboo hut with his granddaughter. His mother whom he cared for had just died. Deeply ashamed of his current state, Bie tells us that his magin had actually visited him recently. He cannot, however, tell people about it for fear that they might flock to his house and he will have to send them all away because his current dwelling is too small to accommodate anyone. Bie's goal is to build a bigger structure where he can treat minor ailments. His magin further instructed Bie to gather eight bottles, perhaps because it plans to give him medicines to administer to those who seek his help.

In Barangay Blaan, Myrna, Elia, and I also have a chance to meet Gunintang Freay, whom Bie had talked about during our first encounter in Agusan. Like Bie, Gunintang is a Blaan nungaru and an ambaling lagi. He lives in Barangay Kimlawis, Kiblawan, Davao del Sur, a portion of which had been written about as the Blaans' last retreat after they have been driven deeper into the mountains by mining-related violence.[149] Gunintang is much older than Bie, his face kind and handsome, his voice soft and serious. Slung below his waist is a *fais* (long dagger) with a shiny corrugated silver blade and a wooden scabbard decorated with red cloth, brass rings, and horsehair. I ask Gunintang if he might be willing to share his story with us for a possible book publication and he says that even with his fellow Blaan he does not share his story if he senses that they will not believe him. But if the person who asks believes or will not use his story for ill, "why will I not tell the truth?" he says. Gunintang discusses sex and gender issues in a conversational manner, with Elia retelling Gunintang's Blaan in Visayan. When it comes to deeply sacred matters, however, Gunintang's mode of communication shifts from speech to malem, which I suspect is when his talo heightens in its relationality. In his soft and delicate talo, Gunintang shares a malem to introduce to us his primary magin, whom he addresses as *tua lagi* (old man):

> Atngan ksitu mi tua lagi asnitongan ago gi dalan
> Ye man ando:
> Ge i tnanda go amda di munan na fandronggo
> Dugu ifagotgo fais
> Du ye fais go silanggoble ku ta mdarong i bong kasfati dibong banul
> Du ye i fagot gu i klung am du bla yo idad tase to nanon fat to inubum

> The first time old man and I met on the road
> He told me:
> You are the one I decreed long ago who I would approach.
> You are the one I have allowed to hold my long dagger
> A long dagger that I will not give you unless the wars of the world are forthcoming.
> It is what you will use to fight [the forces of oppression]
> along with four people you will lead.[150]

Gunintang says that he is often in the mountains where it is peaceful. There, he calls on tua lagi through his malem to continue to learn from him and to carry out instructions like cultivating a swidden rice farm with very specific measurements. Gunintang tells Elia, Myrna, and me what he claims many almoos believe these days, that we are now just a few steps away from a big war or from natural calamities. Gunintang also predicts the sudden appearance of a powerful almoos who is a woman. Once he and Bie find this "true" almoos, he says, they are to join her. What the different almoos should do these days, he says, is perform rituals and pray. Similarly, what good people or the believers should do is help others. Gunintang adds that there will come a time when he will call the almoos from the different tribes to the sacred house in the mountain to perform a thanksgiving blessing there.

Of Gunintang's sexual history and relationships, it is his wife, Mining Capeon, Elia's husband's cousin, who talks to us. Gunintang, according to Mining, was born a girl. Her early contact with spirit, however, made it clear that she was not to marry or bear children. Not knowing about this dictate, Gunintang's parents arranged for her to marry a man. Gunintang dutifully followed, moving to her husband's place where she gave birth to a baby girl. Being in violation of the spirit's wishes, however, this marriage would not last. At some point, Gunintang's husband was shot dead. This signaled Gunintang's return to Barangay Kimlawis where young girl Mining, who had not had her first menstruation, was also arranged to marry a man. Gunintang came to live in the house of Mining's family. When it came time for her to be asked to leave, she refused, saying that even if the man betrothed to Mining killed her, she would not depart. Mining's marriage did not proceed. Meanwhile, Gunintang's genitals changed suddenly. When Mining and Gunintang lay down together, Mining was surprised to find out that Gunintang had grown a bato. Gunintang asked Mining to hold it, which she did, proving to herself that indeed, Gunintang had turned male. Mining then had a dream in which she was told she would not marry except the person who was truly meant for her. She would also not give birth to a child. After that dream, Mining told her parents that Gunintang had turned male and the two of them would like to marry. Mining's parents disapproved but Mining told her father that he might as well ask Gunintang for a dowry. Gunintang was asked to provide a total of nineteen items—twelve to replace what the man betrothed to Mining had given, plus seven of his own. Gunintang was able to provide everything, leading Mining to suspect that perhaps Gunintang had *garu* (knowledge). In fact, Gunintang's dowry was a violation of the uldin because someone with knowledge is exempt from giving such dowries. When Gunintang married Mining, Gunintang's magin told him, "treat your wife well because she is your partner for life, your pillar." Although Gunintang is not required to be celibate, he is prohibited by his magin from having relationships with other women. Mining, on the other hand, dreamed that the time will come when Gunintang will no longer be able to singlehandedly carry out the spirit's wishes, at which point she will assist him.

I ask Gunintang and Bie how many sex designations there are among the Blaan. Bie says there are two sexes: libun (female) and *lagi* (male), with two additional genders: *ambaling libun* (male who becomes female), and ambaling lagi (female who becomes male). I also ask if they have heard of any other nungaru–ambaling lagi in the past or in the present and they say that they have no knowledge of any past nungaru–ambaling lagi. There are numerous present-day ambaling lagi, they say, but these have no garu. Elia remarks that she has a nungaru uncle who is an ambaling libun, but this one, she says, married a libun. Gunintang feels that there may no longer be any more ambaling lagi like himself and Bie, specifically those who undergo sex change through spirit intervention. He does not state his basis for saying so. Asked what the relationship is between their sexual orientation and their ritual specialist practice, Bie responds that his nungaru vocation is the reason why he is an ambaling lagi. The growth of his bato and its disappearances and reappearances have been the direct consequence of his relationship with his magin. I ask the two if their sexual orientation may have given them an advantage over other nungaru who are strictly libun or lagi, alluding to theories that link so-called ambiguous sex with spiritual potency. Bie's response is that, on the contrary, a nungaru–ambaling lagi like himself has a much harder time and is at a greater disadvantage because of the controls and strictures to which he is subjected. He asserts, however, that being an ambaling lagi is no less appropriate a sex orientation for a nungaru compared to his libun and lagi counterparts. This is because the ambaling lagi and the ambaling libun both originate from Creator

D'wata (figure 2.4). Their mandate is to do what is good, to help those in need, to stand for peace.

While at Barangay Blaan, Bie, Gunintang, Elia, Myrna, their families, and friends decide to hold a *demsu fankiton*, a water ritual at the Mailog River. On foot we trek through a bulldozed highway and pass by large trucks and quarrying equipment. We turn into a narrow dirt path and hop on stones over mud. We then climb a steep ravine with only small roots to hold on to before descending into a thin, shallow stream canopied by little trees and carpeted by roots, pebbles, and crystal-clear water. After moments of silence while clearing some weeds, Bie offers his malem: "You who watch over the waters, don't be surprised at us for our goal is good. Inspire someone to grant the desires of the nungaru and the almoos so that we can help those who believe." Gunintang also offers a malem: "I ask permission from the guardian of the headwaters. We are here. Don't be surprised at us for our aim is good. If you have signs, send the good ones, like good weather." Walking back, Gunintang, who was sluggish on our way to the river, energetically leads the pack.

During our final evening, I have a difficulty falling asleep. At around three in the morning, not long after I doze off, I am abruptly awakened by a rather loud but beautiful malem. I recognize the talo as Gunintang's because I heard him sing just a few hours before and because the talo is coming from the direction where I know he is sleeping. Even without Elia's translation I understand some of the malem's words, like *tabangi* ("help" in Visayan), so I suspect that the song has the same intent as Gunintang's malem hours before, when he asked for assistance to attend the full moon ritual at Bulul Lumut. After an hour or more of trying to recover my sleep while listening to the song, I doze off again, waking up at past seven to the beautiful sounds of the *faglong* (Blaan two-string lute), singing, cooking, bathing, and storytelling that have graced Myrna's, Elia's, and my mornings since we arrived at Barangay Blaan. As soon as I arise, I look for Gunintang to compliment him on his singing at three o'clock that morning. This, he vigorously denies having done. I ask Myrna, Elia, and Bie, who were sleeping close to me if they heard the same malem that I did, and they too say no. I tell them that the singer used some Visayan terms and this Gunintang claims to never do because he sings only in Blaan. After further questioning, Elia concludes that I may have heard the talo of Gunintang's magin, which she wishes she could have heard so that she could interpret the spirit's messages to me. I say that the message seemed similar to that of Gunintang's song the night before, thanks to the spirit's use of words I was familiar with. Reflecting further on the matter, I think to myself that if indeed the talo I heard came from Gunintang's magin, this may be another case of relational voice that emerged from the negotiation of Gunintang's and his magin's gendered voices. Unlike Mendung, who sang lucidly while mimicking her

FIGURE 2.4. Bie Gulae and Gunintang Freay Samlang, Malungon, Sarangani, 2019

Photo by Grace Nono.

spirit helper's voice, Gunintang was in deep sleep when his material voice was borrowed by his magin in order for it to be heard, recognized, and understood by its intended listener. Mimesis, therefore, can take on a bilateral or multilateral valence, a mutuality of causes and effects, between spirit and human. And like other forms of mimesis, this one is not synonymous with faithful imitation. By mimicking Gunintang's talo, the magin imposed a sonic layer that thickened its befriended's voice, making it louder and more forceful, yet still recognizable as one that belongs to Gunintang.

Further Insights on the Nungaru–Ambaling Lagi

The embodied voices of nungaru–ambaling lagi Bie Gulae and Gunintang Freay in acts of singing, speaking, ritualizing, prophesying, and healing rectifies the historical impossibility of Native female-to-male transgender ritual specialists suggested by the silence on such subjects in five centuries of babaylan discourses. These voices further contest narrativizations of a precolonial golden age of gender pluralism followed by a colonial and neocolonial age of heteronormativity, when transgender ritual specialists are supposed to not exist or when transgender subjects are stripped of associations with the sacred. On the other hand, Bie's and Gunintang's historical reality may not be considered an indication that the nungaru–ambaling lagi are thriving. Their gender identity continues to be elided in the bifurcated sex and gender framework of the educational system, government institutions, and most religious organizations. Their spiritual experiences are considered inadmissible by materialist sex and gender discourses. As Native subjects Bie and Gunintang have been challenged by Indigenous patriarchy that arranged their young selves' marriages to men in ways that they could not resist. Their communities have themselves been faced with land pressures, militarization, and privation.[151] Bie too has not been able to live up to the uldin and to his magin's wishes resulting in the loss of his wealth and preferred sex identity. All these should temper tendencies to idealize Bie and Gunintang as symbols of power and antiheteronormative resistance. And yet neither are Bie and Gunintang victims who might become elite feminist and transgender politics' targets for salvation. Although undergoing a low point in his life, Bie remains playfully hopeful. Gunintang, on the other hand, despite historical traumas that the Blaan people have undergone, is dignity personified, his faithfulness and commitment to uphold his nungaru mandate, unyielding. Both Bie and Gunintang appear to be also open to forging mutually beneficial relationships with other groups committed to ritual, service, and peace.

Of theories that link so-called ambiguous sex with spiritual potency, Bie's and Gunintang's oral discourses based on their experiences show no signs of acquiescing. These two nungaru are no more powerful than their male and female counterparts and are, in fact, more hard-pressed, according to Bie. Do their experiences in any way demonstrate womanhood as the normative vehicle to the spirit world? Not with their disinheriting their own femaleness, a move that did not inhibit them from becoming nungaru. Might one say then that the two took on maleness because their primary magin were masculine? Their stories appear to suggest so. That said, if a nungaru's magin is feminine, the nungaru or almoos may also take on a more feminine character, not because femininity is the normative vehicle to the spirit world but because a nungaru-ambaling lagi's sex is a relationship, a living negotiation between the sex a nungaru is born with and the gender of the magin that the nungaru becomes closely associated with.

How does the nungaru–ambaling lagi relate to current gender and sexuality scholarship? The following section tries to determine the appropriateness of applying Western sexual orientation or desire and gender identity frameworks to Bie's and Gunintang's experiences. In 2003, David Valentine cited anthropologists who "pointed out that Western sexual identities and identity labels cannot make sense of—and indeed, are complicated by—non-Western sexual practices and desires."[152] The critique of these anthropologists was directed at other scholars who used Western sexual identity labels as a "means of organizing and interpreting cross-cultural variations in embodied personhood according to Eurocentric ontological categories and modernization narratives."[153] The critique equally addressed scholars and activists who imagined later labels and categories to be more progressive, supplanting "outmoded 'traditional' understandings of sex, sexuality, embodiment, gender and identity," which, accordingly, "hark back to an earlier (and implicitly, outmoded and false) model of homosexuality which conflated sexuality and gender."[154] Both practices of imposing Western frameworks and labels and of deeming earlier language as false and inferior, have constituted a "theoretical imperialism" that "masked and marginalized a more heterogeneous and uneven class of phenomena in different social contexts that Western and/or more privileged conceptual frameworks could not encompass but that they render unintelligible."[155] Valentine reminds his readers that Western sex and gender categories, especially those undergirded by the separation of gender and sexuality, are themselves local, recent, "specific understanding[s] of sex, gender, and identity," with race, class, and linguistic biases.[156] Though these categories have been "theoretically productive tool[s]," they have, "ironically produced a system whereby those who are already disenfranchised—through poverty and racism—cannot be fully accounted for in contemporary theorizations about gender and sexuality."[157] Critiques like Valentine's and those of anthropologists he cites have led to the general tendency to "follow the basic anthropological tenet of using one's informants' categories to describe them."[158]

In full agreement with Valentine's recommendations, this study has made use of the Native Blaan titles of ambaling lagi and ambaling libun and the T'boli designation of boyos. At the same time, it does not assume indissoluble difference between Native Philippine and Western labels. Totalizing difference, like totalizing sameness, assumed, for example, in certain constructions of "Women" and "babaylan," has tended to reinstate the privilege of colonizers and national elites as "universal self-determining subjects."[159] As Andrea Smith notes, citing Hiram Perez: "Queer theory, when it privileges difference over sameness absolutely, colludes with institutionalized racism in vanishing, hence retrenching, white privilege."[160] In addition to employing Native labels, this study has also made strategic use of the English term "transgender" to refer to people whose gender identities do not match their biology or the sex they were assigned at birth.[161] This usage that is, itself, contested in the Philippines, does not aim to impose a Western category on non-Western experience, but to mark a site of negotiation between Western and non-Western frameworks and labels.[162] Let us take up the hegemonic understanding of sex and gender as individual traits. Beatriz Preciado writes: "gender-producing subjects understand themselves as delimited spaces and as private property, with a gender identity and a fixed sexuality. The programming of a dominant gender starts from the following premise: an Individual = a body = a sex = a gender = a sexuality."[163] While this formulation is not totally irrelevant to Philippine experience, the spirited bodies of Native nungaru–ambaling lagi Bie and Gunintang strongly suggest sex and gender as relational, corporate, intersubjective. Bie and Gunintang are ambaling lagi not by their own individual biologies and historical agencies alone but by their magins' interventions on their bodies. This relational understanding of sex may loosely be associated with Judith Butler's notion of gender as "'a relation,' a set of relations, and not an individual attribute."[164] However, much of Western and elite nationalist sex and gender discourse is incapable of imagining a larger social that includes nonhuman agents that interact with humans in the construction of sex and gender. This sanctioned blindness to the ontological reality and agency of nonhumans has been also directed to so-called nature, treated in some feminist discourses as prediscursive and as presocial. Bie's and Gunintang's sex changes, achieved—according to their own accounts—neither through hormonal therapies nor surgical procedures but through spirit intervention, point to "nature" as a conglomeration of transformative agencies, one that demands an expanded understanding of transgenderism to account for Indigenous experiences. Judith Butler does argue that "the very concept of nature needs to be rethought, for the concept of nature has a history, and the figuring of nature as the blank and lifeless page, as that which is, as it were, always already dead, is decidedly modern, linked perhaps to the emergence of technological means of domination."[165] So-called nature, to many Indigenous communities around the world, is not only agentive in the abstract sense but outright political, its constitutive elements actively negotiating, contesting, and transforming the social fabric.

To say that Bie's and Gunintang's experiences of sex and life in general is relational is also to say that these are not theirs alone to be concerned about. At the heart of the nungaru, and many Native ritual specialist vocations, is the loss of individual identity and freedom so highly prized by the Western Enlightenment. To be a Native ritual specialist is not only to become subject to numerous taboos and rules of conduct, it is to accept the lifelong mandate to serve both humans and spirits, the violation of which could result in disciplinary measures, including death. Sex is not a matter of rights or liberation but service through one's vocation. Bie is required to be celibate, other than for the purpose of procreation. Gunintang is allowed sexual intercourse but only in the context of monogamous marriage; his wife, Mining, is tasked with helping him fulfil his responsibilities. The nungaru's home life itself is relational in the sense that Bie wants to build a bigger house that can accommodate an extended family that includes nonblood relations. The nungaru's house serves not as a private abode for nuclear family members but a community ritual space and a sort of hospital. Here is homelife not geared toward reproducing free and autonomous subjects profitable for the capitalist state, but members upholding tribal communitarianism and mutual service. I would argue that this in itself constitutes a kind of freedom, one based on a larger understanding of the self. This manner of life, however, has become severely challenged by neoliberal individualism and the patriarchal and heteronormative nuclear family setup. Younger-generation ritual specialists now increasingly juggle community service with individual careers and nuclear-style families.

While this study acknowledges the changing sex, gender, and family norms that Native ritual specialists increasingly contend with, it is uncomfortable with portraying Indigenous experiences as always "evolving" and "refigurable" according to Western modernist conceptions of history and progress. To portray Indigenous realities as not also resistant to external influences and pressures that have attempted, time and again, to destroy Indigenous communities, governance, values, and resources betrays the centuries-old Indigenous struggles to keep ancestral ways alive in the face of continuing domination.

Bie's and Gunintang's voices, therefore, point to a disconnect between nungaru (and other Native ritual specialist) experiences and many feminist assumptions based on understandings of sex and gender as matters of individual rights, freedom, and power, promoted through top-down feminist politics inaugurated by the histories of colonization. I have already pointed out babaylan feminism's archaicizing, idealizing, and flattening of a living, complex, and heterogeneous institution of Native ritual specialization. I will push my commentary further by stating that the kind of agency with which many feminists have constituted the precolonial babaylan, based on hegemonic notions of freedom, may not exactly be the same agency that Native ritual specialists like Bie and Gunintang possess. Saba Mahmood's illustration of the learner submitting to a "painful disciplinary regime, as well as to the hierarchical structures of apprenticeship, in order to acquire the ability—the requisite agency—to [perform one's role] with mastery" is closer, in my estimation, to the experiences of the nungaru and other Native ritual specialists who have gained their identities, first and foremost, by becoming subject to "specific relations of subordination" in exchange for the wellbeing of their communities.[166] The Native ritual specialists' submission to spirit can easily be interpreted as the absence of agency that has distinguished uncivilized heathens from civilized and modern subjects. Numerous campaigns—both military and religious—have been waged to transform and/or eliminate such ways of being. On a related note, Native ritual specialists have been the stuff of romanticized portrayals as figures of resistance of the anticolonial, antimodern, antipatriarchal, and antiheteronormative sort. This study concurs with Mahmood's problematizing of "reading agency primarily in terms of resistance."[167]

3

SONG TRAVELS

Mumbaki Mobility and the Relationality of Place

It is the end of the 2015–2016 winter in Wallingford, Connecticut. Most of the snow has thawed and green leaves have begun to sprout on the treetops. This morning, family, friends, and colleagues of the recently departed American anthropologist Harold Conklin (1968–2012) are gathering to celebrate the passing of the "giant man," who, through decades of anthropological research, helped "put Ifugao (a province in the Cordillera Administrative Region in Northern Luzon) on top of the Philippine map."[1] A semitraditional version of the *baki* (Ifugao ritual) Lawet is being readied by Mamerto "Lagitan" Tindongan, a middle-aged, male, transnational *mumbaki* (Ifugao ritual specialist), whose practice in places outside the Philippines complicates the discursive confinement of Native ritual specialists in ancestral lands. Lagitan has lived in Ohio and other parts of the United States for over twenty years. He was, however, initiated into the baki priesthood in Ifugao by his father, mumbaki Bruno "Buwaya" Tindongan, who was Conklin's Ifugao language instructor and informant.

On the wooden floor panels, Lagitan sets up an altar with an assortment of objects: striped bright red Ifugao woven fabrics arranged crosswise, a carved Ifugao wooden bowl and a coconut shell cup used during the baki, octahedron-shaped wood blocks, a votive candle, precious stones, a Pakistani drum, a Tibetan singing bowl, three of Conklin's books, and a bottle of Japanese sake (rice wine). Lagitan accompanies his motions with the *choyat* (chant during the altar preparation) while fifteen to twenty ritual attendees—Ifugao and Ifugao descendants, other Filipinos and Americans—circle around him.

Agamid/Tobotbar
Choyaton chaan gamongngato,
Bayahato, ya pamahanato
Mabaybayah an bayah
Ya mapampahan an pamahan
Ta pun-alichawhan chaa tun naat-atben
Matungulan hi Kabunian, wad Chalom,
Napungut ad Lagud, ikiyyangan,
Ya bibiyo tun ad Wallingford
Ot Hiya[2]

Charge/Petition
I set you up relics,
rice wine and wooden bowl.
Be tasty, wine.
Be a container, wooden bowl
so that all the deities will come through you,
deities in Kabunian, from Chalom,
from Lagud, from Kiyyangan,
and spirit beings in Wallingford.
So be it.

Lagitan then invokes the *Liblibayan* group of deities that oversee the wine and the water to make sure that none of those who partake of the sake will suffer from stomach aches.[3]

Agamid/Tobotbar
Baiyon cha'yun Liblibayan
Hu'yapan yuy palihi'
Ta achiyu tagachon chi awa' chi nabukan,
Ya balu'wachang
An manginum hi bayah ti naiho

Charge/Petition
I petition you, Liblibayan.
Drink the wine
so that you do not hurt the abdomen of women
and men
who drink this wine because it is untoward.

The next group of deities that Lagitan invokes are the *linnawa* (ancestral spirits) especially his Ifugao ancestors, who are Conklin's adopted lineage. He also asks the ritual hosts, Bruce, Conklin's son, and Allen and Aleta Cayong-Abayao, the house's owners, to audibly call on the spirits of their direct ancestors.

Agamid/Tobotbar
Baiyon cha'yun linnawa
Chommachommangon chayu
Waey naalliwan, nalemtaan
Ya cha'yu won nun-aayyagan ayu
Ta umali ayu ta uminum ayu bayah
Mun-awer ayu gamong ya tayabban
Ta achi ayu mangiluya inagaga'iho
Hey iluyayu ya hey mitaguwan mi
Ya mitaguwan chi pi'mogmog ya pi'liya' mi
Tuntunon yuy Bagor yuh Kabunian
Ta iyalupe chay bayah ya tayabban
Hitun naat-atben matungulan
Hi Kabunian, wad Chalom,
Napungut ad Lagud, ikkiyyangan
Ya bibiyo tun ad Wallingford
Lawet chi abaiyan yun linnawa
Ot Hiya

Charge/Petition
I call upon you ancestral spirits
from both sides of the family lineages.
If anyone is missed, forgotten,
then you call one another
to come and drink rice wine.
Take our offerings of relics and chickens
so you will not cause any harm.
Give us long life
and plenty of animals and rice harvests.
Locate your Bagor in Kabunian
so they will take the rice wine and chickens
to the different deities
in Kabunian, from Chalom,
Napungut from Lagud, from Kiyyangan
and the spirit beings from Wallingford.
It is for Lawet that you are called, ancestral spirits.
So be it.

Lagitan then invokes three groups of spirits. The first comprises the spirits of the mountains, rivers, and highways of Wallingford, Connecticut, where the ritual is taking place. The second are composed of what Lagitan calls the ascended masters close to him: Guanyin, Shiva, Jesus, Mary, Sanat Kumara, and his Native American spirit helpers. In the third group are the major Ifugao deities from the spirit realms of Kabunian, Lagud, Chalom, and Kiyyangan, like Lidchum and Bugan. Also part of this third group is Lagitan's Ifugao mumbaki lineage. Lagitan then summons Hinogwakan—head of the malawetan group of *maknongan* (Ifugao deities) that reside in Lagud, the cosmic downstream where the dead go—to Wallingford, so that the deity can fetch Conklin's soul to take it to Lagud.[4]

Lagitan tells me later that whenever the Lawet is performed in Ifugao, the mumbaki's long *buad* (chant) would not only summon Hinogwakan, it would guide the deity, step by step, from Lagud to the site of ritual. Once it arrives, the mumbaki would lend it his voice to while in a state of mediumistic trance. In Lagitan's Lawet version in Wallingford, however, only an abbreviated buad is performed to summon Hinogwakan, in part because Lagitan is not well versed in the directions from Lagud to Wallingford, Connecticut—a noncustomary maknongan route—and in part because he feels summoning the maknongan is enough for it to come. A few minutes into the chant, Lagitan claims that Hinogwakan has arrived. He, however, refuses to let the maknongan enter him, barring it from chanting through his voice. "I do not want anything to mess with my [individual] body," he says.

Allen the house owner and Lagitan slaughter two chickens while the latter recites the *pun-ngorpan* (invocation during the animal slaughtering) for the sake of the sacrificial animals and for the intercession of the ancestral spirits. There is supposedly one other set of invocations before this one but Lagitan does away with it for brevity.

Agamid/Tobotbar
Ngorpon chaan oloh mun manu-atu
Manekon at manekachar ah
Umub-ubbuwan ah
Achi-a mi'yapa, achi-a mun-uchuwong
Pohchom punchilihom chi chalam
Ta pun-atbayan chaa tun naat-atben matungulan
Hi Kabunian, wad Chalom, Napungut ad Lagud,
ikkiyyangan, ya bibiyo tun ad Wallingford
Unnot hey itaguwan min hina'ama
Mi'taguy imogmoganmi
Ya pi'liya' mi

Ta umanamut amih halaungan mi
Ya ma'id ah ar-ali, ma'id chi mahapehapet
Lawet chi punngorpan chaan manuato
Ot Hiya

Charge/Petition
I slaughter you chicken.
Grow and be strong.
Be a hen.
Do not be pitiful, do not be sad.
Make your blood free of iniquity
so all the deities will communicate through you
in Kabunian, from Chalom, from Lagud
from Kiyyangan, the spirit beings in Wallingford.
May our family live long.
May we have plenty of animals
and rice harvests
so we will all go home
without harm, and without curse.
It is for Lawet that I slaughter you, chicken.
So be it.

While the cooking of the sacrificial chickens is underway, Lagitan speaks in conversational English to thank Allen and his wife Aleta for hosting the ritual. He also offers words of comfort to Bruce, Conklin's son, a physician and geneticist, for his great loss. He explains that what he is doing is a semitraditional baki, in consideration of its location in the United States. He then shares his memories of Conklin.

"I was very angry with him when I was growing up," Lagitan blurts out emphatically, his voice, ringing loudly across the house. We, the ritual participants are stunned. "Conklin always took my father Buwaya away from me! I thought my father was the most powerful man in the village, but here was Conklin who ordered him night and day! I asked my father why he always had to serve Conklin. His reply was 'so we can earn some money.' My parents had seven children and worked very hard to send all of us to school. Years later, when I attended college in Manila, I learned about labor rights. And when I attended graduate school in the United States, I learned about colonization. My anger burned for the 'big man.' To make matters worse, Conklin, who was given an Ifugao name during his adoption, came and went as he pleased. But none of us could come to America where he lived!" Lagitan here alludes to the unequal power relations on which colonial and neocolonial anthropology was and to an extent continues to be premised.

A heavy silence falls on the room. You can hear a pin drop. I glance at Bruce and at Patricia Afable, an Igorot anthropologist connected with the Smithsonian Institution. What could they be feeling at this moment with Lagitan's brash disclosure? Are they not offended at this younger mumbaki's harsh words that seem to undermine Conklin's memory?

Lagitan goes on to speak about his anger spilling over to me during the early phases of my dissertation research. "We fought," he says. "She may be Filipino from Mindanao, conducting ethnography with more parity, for ends like decolonization that may be different from those of her predecessors, but this was still research! I was still being observed and represented!" I hold my breath. I cannot believe what is happening. He continues: "Perhaps to clarify her intensions, Grace did something that usually does not happen. She took me to her dissertation defense in New York." In that dissertation defense, Lagitan interpreted his own experience as a transnational mumbaki in the United States, in response to the widely criticized practice of outsider "experts" speaking on behalf of Native voices that become muted through the use of foreign languages, categories, and theories that do not necessarily reflect Native experience. Related to this is the practice of according expertise to the scholar alone and not acknowledging the deep collaboration with Indigenous research partners that goes into every ethnographic study.

Turning his attention back to the celebration of Conklin's life and death, Lagitan requests me to offer a chant to help honor the dead and console the living. This I do, as a student of oral chant taught to me by elders in my home province of Agusan and in other parts of Mindanao and the Philippines. I, after all, am not just a researcher and scholar. Like Lagitan, I also carry knowledge that my mentors authorized me to practice.

When it is Bruce's turn to speak, he refers to Lagitan, who had the gall to sing back to his father, as his "brother," after Conklin's adoption by the Ifugao people. He thanks the Ifugao people, especially Buwaya and his family, for assisting his father in almost half a century of anthropological work. This is reciprocated by Lagitan with words of gratitude for Conklin who helped him fully reconnect with his father's baki through the anthropologist's writings.

Once the chickens are cooked, Lagitan performs the *gonob* (food invocation) to signal that the animal offerings are ready to be eaten. He, Bruce, Allen, and Aleta then call on their direct ancestors.

Agamid/Tobotbar
Gombon chaan longahon chi manu-atu, ya hinamalatu
Linnawan chi aamod ya aapu nachommodmang
(Lagitan, Bruce, Allen, Aleta called in their direct ancestors at this point)

Tuntunon yuy Bagor yu
Ta ilongaho chay hinamar ya tayabban
Hitun naat-atben matungulan
Hi Kabunian, wad Chalom, napungut ad Lagud,
Ya bibiyo tun ad Wallingford
Lawet chi agnoban yun Linnawa nachommachommang
Bu-ad chi aammod
Bu-ad aman hi Bu'way, oletaon hi Otteng, Oletaon hi Bandaw, ya hi
   apun hi Himmayud
Ibu-ad uy bu-ad yu
Ta chutuon Hinogwakan ad Lagud
Chi cholan chi nabanagan hitun ad Wallingford
Ta iyenay luphu' chi manu' ad Lagud
Ta mataguwan min hina'ama,
Mataguy imogmogan ya miliya'
Ti nabu-ad chi Bu-ad yun aamod
Ot Hiya

Charge/Petition
I call upon the steam of the rice and the chicken.
Spirits of ancestors from both family lineages,
locate your Bagor
so they will share the steam of the rice and the chicken
to the different deities
in Kabunian, Chalom, and Lagud
and the spirit beings in Wallingford.
It is for Lawet that you are called, ancestral spirits.
Bu-ad of my lineage,
bu-ad of my father Bu'way, uncle Otteng, uncle Bandaw, and
   grandfather Himmayud
let me use your bu-ad
so Hinogwakan from Lagud will be guided
to the house of the bereaved in Wallingford
so he will take the burnt skin of chicken to Lagud
so we will live long
with plenty of animals and rice harvests
because I called your bu-ad, my elders.
So be it.

To close the ritual, Lagitan chants the *palayah* (chant to close the altar).

Agamid/Tobotbar
Palayahon chaan gamongngatu ya pamahanatu
Achi man mapalayah chi mimogmogan ya miliya'
Hey mapalayah ya pachug, lobo', ya beter ad Lagud
Ti ten palayahon chaan gamongngatu ya pamahanatu
Ot Hiya

Charge/Petition
I fold you up, relics and wooden bowl.
May our animals and harvests remain aplenty.
May curse, sickness, and famine stop in Lagud
because I am folding you up relics and wooden bowls.
So be it.

In the communal meal that follows, the serving table overflows with *pinikpikan* (ritual chicken dish flavored with coagulated chicken blood, burned feathers and skin, and smoked, cured, aged meat). There is also a slow-cooked pork dish, blood stew, tropical vegetables with fermented fish, and dishes with Chinese and Western influences. Lagitan tells me that this spread departs from that of the traditional Ifugao Lawet where nothing is served except meat. While the guests enjoy the food, children play ball and sample Lagitan's *atlatl* (spear thrower). Bruce, Allen, Aleta, and the other guests remark at how the semitraditional baki satisfactorily performed the function required for the occasion, giving everyone a sense of Ifugao in the United States (figure 3.1). Conklin would not have had it any other way, they say.

Sometime after the event, I am told that immediately after the semitraditional ritual, many of the participants got sick in the stomach. Lagitan was hit the worst. Did he not, however, invoke the Liblibayan group of deities that oversee the wine and water to make sure that none of those who partake of the sake would suffer from stomach aches? When I talked to Lagitan, he suspected that it might have been the departures in the food preparations that caused the unfortunate incident.

Mumbaki and Place

This chapter inquires into the voices and experiences of two generations of Ifugao mumbaki in Ifugao, Philippines, and in Ohio and other parts of the United States, places that have been actively constructed by local and global power relations and by conditions of colonization, migration, and ongoing Indigenous struggles to assert ownership of ancestral lands, identities, and lifeways. It demonstrates

FIGURE 3.1. Lagitan during the semitraditional ritual for Harold Conklin, Wallingford, Connecticut, 2016

Photo by Grace Nono.

that places are built on translocal connections that move along multilateral lines rather than in unidirectional or linear fashion, or from imagined colonial centers to passive peripheries, and conversely, from imagined traditional homelands to modern diasporas.[5] The power relations that constitute such places may be found at play in Native encounters with religion, anthropology, education, market economics, science, tourism, migration, and marriage. All of these have exposed the mumbaki to various forms of prejudice, impressing on them a sense of racial, civilizational, gender, and religious inferiority, as well as material inadequacy, which coalesce with Native forms of class hierarchy. In response, the mumbaki presented here have negotiated their compromised positions in creative ways, including the assertion of physical mobility with the aid of portable songs and recitations that allow rituals to be performed outside of Ifugao and across national boundaries. This goes against the "assumed isomorphism of space, place and culture," and constructions of Native ritual specialists as confined to ancestral homelands where they are believed to lead uncolonized and nonmodern lives.[6] Besides physical mobility, these ritual specialists have responded to their difficult circumstances by raising their cross-cultural competencies, a kind of mobility as well as strategy for continuity, revitalization, and resistance to the reduction of traditions to singularities and Indigenous Peoples to homogeneities.[7] There is also relational mobility, the forging of relations with unlikely quarters aiming toward strategic alliances that offset oppressive logics. Thus, within translocal structures of domination, the Ifugao mumbaki presented here have not been passive victims but subjects of their own histories, negotiating, accommodating, resisting, and creating new conditions of power and possibility.[8]

While this chapter argues for Indigenous mobilities—physical, ideological, and relational—it draws a distinction between dilettantism, that is, the dabbling in "babaylan" practices often driven by class, ethnic, and racial privilege, and the careful and committed cultivation of reciprocal, back-and-forth relations between lands and peoples.[9] In the case of mumbaki Lagitan, the importance of Ifugao as the primary site of his elders and ancestors is retained, while at the same time expanded to include new homes in other places. This concurs with assertions that places in the modern world have not lost their significance as sites of rootedness, even as they are increasingly the locations of exile, displacement, and diasporas.[10] The mumbaki's chant, often portrayed as an element of a relatively unchanging Indigenous ritual tradition, is central to this study that presents it both as descriptive and prescriptive of transformations within the baki tradition, a dynamic participant in larger cultural developments.

The Translocal Production of Ifugao

Lagitan's experience of mobility did not commence with his immigration to Ohio. Ifugao itself made available for him cultural, linguistic, and ideological forms of mobility during his early years there. Centuries of transnational flows, connections, and networks with their attendant hierarchies helped shape and shift local cultural practices and identities.[11]

The province of Ifugao, claimed by the Ifugao people as their ancestral domain since time immemorial, is a landlocked mountainous area that is between 1,000 and 1,500 meters above sea level (figure 3.2). It is bounded on the east by Isabela, on the west by Benguet and a part of Mountain Province, on the north by another part of Mountain Province, and on the south by Nueva Vizcaya. Surrounding it are major land and water forms that have contributed to Ifugao's relative inaccessibility. On the eastern side between Ifugao and Isabela is the Magat River; on the western side between Ifugao and Benguet is Mount Pulag; on the northern part between Ifugao and Mountain Province are Mount Amuyao and Mount Polis; and on the southern side between Ifugao and Nueva Vizcaya is the Lamut River.[12] None of these natural barriers, however, have exempted the Ifugao people from longstanding relationships with other tribes. It is said that long before colonization, highland peoples like the Ifugao traded highland gold and forest

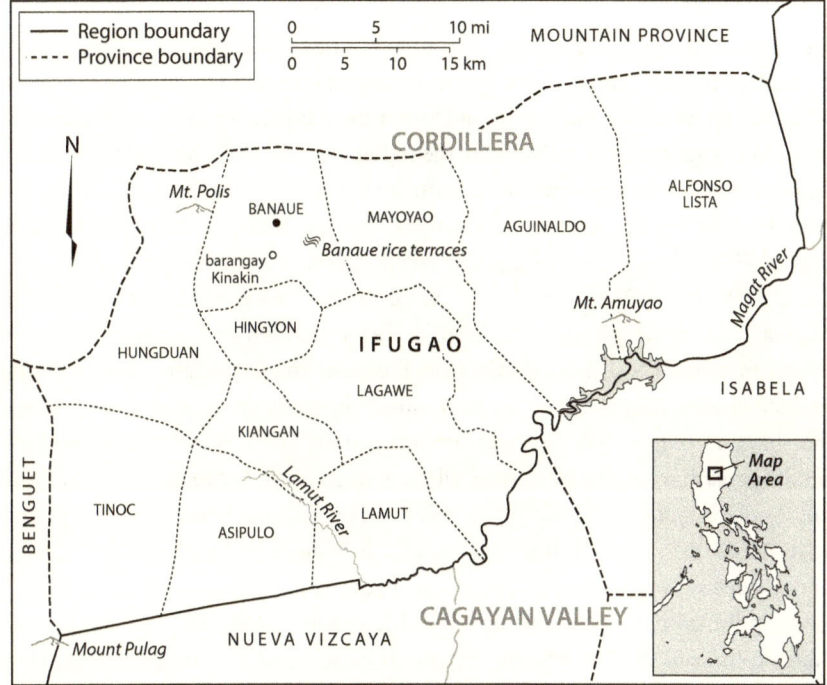

FIGURE 3.2. Map of Ifugao, showing Banaue

Map by Bill Nelson.

products with lowland staples and livestock.[13] This mutually beneficial relationship that engendered cultural similarities is said to have been destroyed by the divide-and-conquer strategies of colonization.[14]

Colonization and Missionization

The first written reference to the Ifugao people dates back to 1752, two centuries after the Spanish colonizers first set foot on the Philippine islands. The delayed attempts to infiltrate these highlanders had been attributed to both the inaccessibility of their territory and to the fierce resistances of Ifugao warriors.[15] The long drawn-out conflict between the Igorrotes (the Spanish name for savage mountain tribes, after i-golot, archaic Tagalog for mountain dwellers) and the Spanish was attributed by William Henry Scott to the latters' desire for the Igorrotes' gold, religious conversion, and regulation of trade between the Igorrotes and the already colonized lowland populations.[16] Spanish military offensives were launched from colonized lowland areas like Cagayan Valley and Nueva Vizcaya, resulting in the 1889 establishment of Ifugao as a separate politico-military unit. These military campaigns were accompanied by missionaries, leading to the establishment of the Dominican Catholic Mission in Lagawe, first in 1852, and again in 1894 with the arrival of a second group of Dominicans. Education was emphasized by the colonial government to facilitate the reducción policy.[17] The continued resistance of Ifugao warriors, however, eventually weakened the Spanish military presence, leading to the eventual withdrawal of the colonial forces during the early part of 1898.[18] When the Philippine Revolution erupted on different islands between 1896 and 1898, all Spanish nationals in Ifugao were ordered to leave for Manila.[19] The triumph of the Philippine Revolution led to the collapse of over three centuries of Spanish colonial rule. Freedom and sovereignty, however, remained elusive. Treachery by the new imperial power, the United States, caused the Filipinos another half a century of occupation. The United States framed its act of aggression as benevolent assimilation based on the propaganda that Filipinos needed America to civilize them because they were not ready to govern themselves. William Howard Taft wrote: "'Our little brown brothers' would need 'fifty or one hundred years' of close supervision 'to develop anything resembling Anglo-Saxon political principles and skills.'"[20] Many knew, however, that the United States colonized the Philippines because of its strategic location with regard to Japan, China and India, and because of its rich natural resources.[21] The Filipinos rose to arms yet again against the new colonizer, igniting the Philippine-American War that according to independent Philippine sources claimed 1.4 million lives from "1899 to 1905 . . . [exclusive of] the thousands of Moros killed in the first two decades of U.S. colonial domination."[22] This bloody history is mostly downplayed by American official reports.

If the Ifugao people were generally successful at defending their land, people, and traditions against the Spanish colonizers, the Americans and their lowland Filipino wards had more success at infiltrating Ifugao ranks through the "softer" colonial strategies of education, missionization, and market economics. No matter how "soft" this mode of domination was, however, it was no less vicious, serving as the "essential matrix of racialization" that Sylvester Johnson wrote, is "what makes empire socially real and efficacious."[23]

When the Americans assumed their rule over Ifugao from lowland Bayombong, Nueva Vizcaya, a civil government was established with headquarters in Banaue.[24] New batches of missionaries arrived, particularly the Anglicans, who deliberately chose to be assigned in mountain regions to convert the non-Christian tribes there.[25] In 1907 and 1910, Belgian missionaries from the Congregation of the Immaculate Heart of Mary (CICM) also arrived in Ifugao, reestablishing the Lagawe mission in Burnay in 1927. In 1946, Belgian missionaries resumed their evangelization work in postwar Lagawe.[26] It was only in 1990—almost half a century after the 1946 Philippine independence—when the foreign missionaries finally passed on their functions to the local clergy.[27]

The long history of Christianization of the Ifugao people may be said to have affected the baki in two general ways. The first led to the framing of baki as sin, to be fully excised from the lives of the Ifugao people. Herman Dinumla, descendant of great mumbakis Bahug and Anggodon, and now a lay pastor in the Banaue Evangelical Church as well as a Bible translator for the Summer Institute of Linguistics, explained this position. His church promotes Ifugao identity and traditions in the form of dances and songs made to carry Christian themes but is clear about doing away with the baki because the baki, according to him, relates with multiple maknongan, contrary to the Christian message of invoking only one God made known through Jesus Christ. Dinumla's church has thus sought to eliminate the baki through the combined approaches of pastoral work, Bible translation from English to Ifugao, Bible college education, radio broadcasting, and medical work through a missionary-founded hospital.[28] Pastor Dinumla's views are shared by pastor of the Christ is the Answer Church, Evangeline Ballangi, who makes clear that her church acknowledges only one good spirit, that is, the Christian Holy Spirit. She says that everything else—even the good spirits that the mumbaki calls on—is considered by her church as evil.[29] Pastor Evangeline herself is descended from a mumbaki grandfather named Pugong and is the sister of the recently departed mumbaki Huwan Candelario.

A second general impact of Christianization on the baki is the framing of its adherents as dialogue partners of the Roman Catholic Church. This development may be related to the papal apologies to Indigenous Peoples for the church's "role in the brutalities of colonization," and for its "contempt for (Indigenous) cultures and religious traditions" resulting in grave threats to their culture and identity.[30] Also related to this is the Catholic Church's tradition of inculturation—the church-sanctioned encounter between the Gospel and the peoples' cultural traditions—that some Ifugao Catholics cite as having helped them reconcile Ifugao spirituality with the Christian faith.[31]

World Heritage Recognition, Tourism, and Changing Land Use

Besides colonization and missionization, the translocal production of Ifugao may also be gleaned from the world heritage recognition of some of its sites, contributing to the global tourism boom and the changing manner of land use. For centuries, the Ifugao economy was primarily agricultural. The management of fields, terraces, private forests, and swidden farms comprised the main economic activity in Ifugao's steep and sloping landscape.[32] These gave birth to magnificent landmarks like the Ifugao rice terraces that date back to the eighteenth century, according to Spanish records, and to as early as the tenth and sixteenth centuries, based on genealogical mapping and other oral sources.[33] Several baki were developed by the Ifugao people to immortalize their rice terracing traditions.[34] These are the *hongan di page*, or calendric agricultural rites linked to rice production and consumption, and the *hongan di tagu*, or rituals for humans associated with health, property, and changes in family and individual status, including death.[35] In 1973, the Banaue rice terraces were declared a National Cultural Treasure, and in 1995, the rice terraces of Nagacadan, Hungduan, central Mayoyao, Bangaan, and Batad were declared a UNESCO World Heritage Site. In 2001, the Ifugao chant *Hudhud*, traditionally performed during rice field weeding, harvesting, funeral wakes, and bone-washing rituals, was also declared a Masterpiece of the Oral and Intangible Heritage of Humanity.[36]

The national and international recognition of the Ifugao rice terraces and the *Hudhud* has led to global tourism becoming Ifugao's primary industry. This development has bequeathed to Ifugao numerous business and development opportunities. It has also exposed it to threats of commercialization.[37] Related to this, Maria Stanyukovich contends that the declaration of the *Hudhud* as a Masterpiece of the Oral and Intangible Heritage of Humanity has contributed to the muting of some of the epic's sacred versions in favor of a genre exclusively aimed at entertainment.[38] She further argues that by reframing the *Hudhud di Qani* (Hudhud for harvest) as a nonritual performance stripped of its associations with Indigenous religious traditions, and by "censoring the shamanistic versions of the *Hudhud* like the *Hudhud di Nate* ('funeral song/song of the dead')," the "time-honored intertwining of the priestly and oralist functions in Ifugao society" has become increasingly eradicated.[39]

During the second half of the twentieth century, observers bean to notice the depletion of the terraces' water sources, imperiling rice production, leading to the decline of harvests.[40] The government responded to the latter by importing cheap, commercial rice from other parts of Southeast Asia. Some quarters contended, however, that this resulted in the decreased demand for mountain rice. Neither has the introduction of commercial fertilizers, pesticides, and high-yielding lowland rice varieties that are capitalist commodities with "no ritual value" address the problem, only lessening the incentives for terraced agricultural production that constitute majority of the baki's contexts.[41] Finally, the increased abandonment of the farming vocation by the younger generations in favor of professional work in urban areas posed yet another threat to terrace farming and its attending rituals.[42]

Anthropologists

In addition to missionaries and tourists, anthropologists have represented another significant translocal presence in Ifugao, resulting in the Ifugao people becoming one of the most studied in Southeast Asia.[43] Like the early missionaries, the early anthropologists in Ifugao came from imperial centers, carrying with them their white privilege that facilitated the collection of information in ways that aided the colonial project. Many anthropologists, however, set themselves apart from missionaries, priding themselves in being scientists. Anthropology's rational and secular approach to the baki has resulted in baki being framed not as a sin to be extirpated but as a cultural practice to be documented and analyzed for posterity before it dies out with the onset of modernity. The following section discusses how a number of anthropologists have depicted the baki in their writings.

In 1946, Roy Barton wrote about the Ifugao cosmology, the pantheon of maknongan, and the baki as "religion." This religion, according to him, was one of the "most extensive and pervasive . . . that had been reported outside of India, at least in ethnographic literature."[44] Barton was particularly struck by what he saw as the "god-creation [that] has proceeded on an almost unlimited scale," with probably over 1,500 gods as of 1946. This development he attributed to the "amalgamation of streams of immigrants or from intermarriage between neighboring peoples and . . . borrowing such as results from contact or commercial intercourse and exchange."[45] Barton further took note of the discrepant teachings among the various priests and the different practices even by the same priests at different times, noting how this was not surprising, considering the oral nature of Ifugao religion and its centuries of accretions due to the absence of one sacred book to refer to.[46]

Revealing a deep condescension, Barton wrote of this Ifugao religion as "a distorted reflection of the Ifugao himself. . . . It reflects his ignorance and not his knowledge, his slothfulness and not his industry, his wishful thinking and not his resourcefulness, his credulity and not his inventiveness, his helplessness and not his strength. Out of his weaknesses the Ifugao has created fantastic conceptions of refuge from a harsh reality and has made them his gods."[47]

The problem with the term "religion," however, is it is often an inaccurate translation of Indigenous experiences.[48] The matter is summed up by Tisa Wenger, who writes that the view of religion as a "separate sphere of life that is largely disconnected from community or land," or as a "matter of individual conscience," or as a "commodity that can easily be chosen and changed," is "in many ways a product of American cultural history," hence, not universal.[49]

Of the mumbaki, the American anthropologist Harold Conklin described these as "a few men in each community [who] acquire sufficient knowledge and repute to serve as almost full-time ritualists or 'priests.'"⁵⁰ Ifugao author Lourdes Dulawan stresses the *kadangyan* (wealthy) origin of the mumbaki, a class status derived from inheriting rice fields, heirlooms, animals, household implements, and cash. If one is not a kadangyan, that is, if one is *nawotwot* (poor: someone who does not own land, or who was captured by enemy groups, or who earns his or her keep by serving the rich), one must first acquire wealth and distinction before becoming a mumbaki.⁵¹ Lagitan's recollection of how his father, Bruno "Buwaya" Mainah Tindongan, became a mumbaki is intertwined with Buwaya's engagements with Conklin.

Estimated to have been born on October 5, 1925, Buwaya was from the hamlet of Bayninan, Banaue, Ifugao. Born a nawotwot because he inherited only a few rice fields from his mother, Adchunglay, who herself inherited little as Mainah's daughter from his second wife, Buwaya was not expected to become a mumbaki. Notwithstanding his low social position that barred him from receiving baki instruction, he liked to practice the chants on his own. His kadangyan uncle Paiyaya and his cousin Ottengan took notice of this and offered to initiate Buwaya later in his life. Ottengan taught Buwaya the performance of many baki, but withheld the *ohag*—the specific chant performed to summon the maknongan to the place of ritual—because this was reserved for the kadangyan priests.⁵² Buwaya felt belittled by his cousin. The strain in their relationship worsened when Conklin, who began to conduct research in Ifugao, decided to hire Buwaya as his research assistant because Buwaya was assertive and knowledgeable in English and Tagalog, languages that he picked up while working outside of Ifugao. The boost in Buwaya's status infuriated Ottengan, causing him to bully Buwaya further. It so happened that between 1972 and 1973, Conklin celebrated for himself the *Chinupchup*, the highest form of hongan ti tagu. This rite features the ohag and is performed only for the kadangyan. Five pigs were sacrificed and all the mumbaki in Bayninan were invited to participate. As Conklin's research assistant, Buwaya was tasked with audio recording, then transcribing, the ohag. This allowed Buwaya to learn the ohag that was denied him by his cousin.

When the children of Buwaya—Lagitan included—excelled in school and in their professions, raising their family's social status, Ottengan's brother Bandaw offered to complete Buwaya's baki education. Bandaw felt that since Buwaya could soon become kadangyan, he must be taught the rest of the baki. Bandaw was the first person to hire Buwaya to perform the ohag.

When Conklin asked Buwaya to record the ohag, it had the unintended outcome of disturbing Native class hierarchies that were the customary contexts of the baki. It also introduced a new approach to learning the baki. In addition to the customary process of learning the baki through years of listening, imitating, memorizing, helping in rituals, being initiated, performing alongside senior practitioners, then applying one's knowledge on one's own family members before others, Buwaya, as a result of his work with Conklin, came to learn the baki with the aid of recording technology.

Formal Education, Market Economics, and Immigration

Lagitan was registered in the Ifugao spirit world even when he was inside his mother Indudun's womb. This was achieved through a rite that his father Buwaya performed.[53] Born a nawotwot like his father, he was not expected to become a mumbaki. When Lagitan turned nine, he enrolled in the Kinakin Elementary School. Previously known only by his Ifugao name Lagitan or Lagget, he was given the hispanized name Mamerto. Renaming had been a common colonial strategy that disturbed Native identities and inscribed the Natives' subordinate status in the colonial or neocolonial order where they could not properly name themselves. When Lagitan turned thirteen, he was baptized in Banaue's Roman Catholic church. At sixteen, he began to attend the Banaue High School, a Catholic institution. Recalling his early experiences in school and in church, he said, "Our priests and teachers taught us that the baki was both unscientific and demonic. This effectively made me lose my interest in rituals." Lagitan further recalled how he and several other Ifugao children were sexually molested by their parish priest and by an elementary school teacher.

Growing up in Banaue, Ifugao, famous for its woodworking tradition, Lagitan learned how to carve at the tender age of eight. Under the tutelage of older Ifugao master carvers, he observed how his mentors maintained deep connections with the forests and with Ifugao ancestral spirits. When the global tourism industry boomed, the capitalist middlemen encouraged Ifugao carvers to mass-produce their works to meet the demands of the market. Due to the rising tourist consumption and to economic necessity, Ifugao woodcarvers like Lagitan deforested their own lands.

After graduating from high school, Lagitan moved to Manila to study aeronautical engineering. As a highlander in the big city, he experienced ethnic discrimination from lowland Filipinos who saw him as inferior. It may be noted that the word "Filipino," after King Philip of Spain, was first used to refer to the Spanish inhabitants of the islands before it was applied to Indios or the Natives who were colonized and Christianized. During the late nineteenth century, the *ilustrado* or the educated and "enlightened" Filipinos rallied for the Philippines to become assimilated by Spain, and for Filipinos to be recognized as equal to other Catholics and Hispanics within the larger Spanish Empire.[54] Promoting themselves as the local authorities and mediators "between the islands' peoples (including the non-Christian tribes) and colonizer Spain, these ilustrados, Paul Alexander Kramer contended, "both undermined and confirmed Spanish colonial hierarchies."[55] Seeking recognition as "overseas Spaniards" by demonstrating their "civilization" through their "education, artistic achievements, eloquence in Spanish, and loyalty to Spain," they "delimited the boundaries of who would ultimately be recognized as 'Filipino.'"[56] The Igorots would be some of the most affected by the ilustrado invention of the "Filipino." A respected diplomat once wrote about non-Christian highlanders like the Ifugao: "The fact remains that the Igorot is not Filipino and we are not related, and it hurts our feelings to see him pictured in American newspapers under such captions as 'Typical Filipino Tribesman.'"[57]

Discouraged by his encounters with lowland Christian Filipinos, Lagitan returned to Banaue to establish a butterfly collecting and export business that would help forest dwellers earn money without cutting trees. His efforts prospered. At the peak of his business in 1985, he had, according to him, about three hundred employees in the provinces of Ifugao, Mountain Province, Quirino, Zambales, and Nueva Vizcaya. It was at that point when he met Cynthia White, an American Peace Corps volunteer from Delaware who was stationed in Ifugao.[58] Lagitan and Cynthia wed and had their first child, Joannah. At the encouragement of Lagitan's American brother-in-law who was then taking a graduate course at Ohio University, Lagitan applied to the same institution's International Affairs (Development Studies) master's program and was admitted. In 1991, Lagitan immigrated to the United States, hopeful about his prospects in the Land of the Free.[59]

The centuries of colonization, missionarization, anthropological documentation, global and national heritage recognition, and formal schooling of the Ifugao have demonstrated colonial and neocolonial efforts to render what was seen as an uncivilized and heathen people intelligible to the empire and to the modern nation in ways that reinforced white and elite lowlander supremacy. In the process, Native traditions like the baki have become associated with sin, degeneracy, irrationality, and primitivism. Native functionaries like mumbaki Buwaya have been demonized for carrying forth ancestral traditions viewed as antithetical to colonial Christianity and modernity. To save an Ifugao youth like Lagitan from becoming like his parents, but also to keep him in subordinate status, he was baptized, renamed, schooled, sexually molested, and trained in the United States for imperial citizenship. As the Ifugao people struggled to maintain their ways while redefining their identities in the face of imperial and elite nationalist norms and pressures, some of them have made good use of their compromised positions to learn new competencies. In Buwaya's case, he became a salaried Ifugao language teacher and informant to a white anthropologist, a move that helped him and his wife send their children to school. He also learned to use modern technologies that he was able to deploy for his own purposes, that is, to learn chants that summoned the maknongan, catapulting himself to full mumbaki status. With this newfound social power bolstered by his new knowledge and foreign connections, Buwaya became an accomplished seventh-generation mumbaki, as well as a *mun-uyad* (bonesetter), farmer, miner, woodcutter, hunter, Ifugao language teacher and informant to Conklin for forty-four years. As for Lagitan, his formal education in the Philippines helped raise his parents' social status, contributing to Buwaya's acceptance as a full-fledged kadangyan mumbaki. Lagitan's exposure to business and development discourses also ushered him to the next stages of his life as a citizen of the United States, where he would later practice the baki. In all these, one witnesses operations of agency when Natives redeploy, even in circumscribed ways, empire's technologies for their own ends.[60]

The Translocal Production of Ohio

Filipino immigration to the Americas predated the founding of the United States and the American colonization of the Philippines. During the height of the Spanish Empire, Spanish trading ships called Manila Galleons plied the Pacific Ocean for 250 years (1565 to 1815), linking Manila and Acapulco.[61] It was during this long stretch when shipbuilders, seafarers, and slaves called Manilamen, deserting the galleons, were reportedly seen in California and Louisiana where they established bachelor communities.[62] At the close of the Philippine-American War in 1903, when freedom fighters continued to resist the new colonial regime in the countrysides, several Filipino families availed themselves of the Pensionado Act that allowed them to send their children to the United States as scholars of the US government.[63] One of the United States' declared goals on its "purchase" of the Philippines from Spain was to train a group of highly educated civil servants who would promote American ideals across the empire. In 1904, a delegation of 1,100 Christianized lowlanders and "non-Christian tribes" were shipped to the United States to represent the Philippine islands during the St. Louis World's Fair that commemorated the 100th anniversary of the "purchase" of Louisiana by the United States from France. Housed in a reservation, the Christian and non-Christian Filipinos were exhibited alongside relief maps, forestry and mining exhibits, and reproductions of Manila's cathedrals and the walled city.[64] The greatest attraction among them was the tribal village where tattooed and G-string-donning Igorots from the Cordillera highlands were presented to the world's public like zoo animals and circus freaks. These were made to perform tribal dances and to eat dogs to showcase their uncivilized state that justified the forced American annexation of the Philippine islands.[65] Between 1906 and 1934, Filipino men called Sakadas who represented cheap labor were shipped to Hawaii's sugar plantations, California's farms, and Alaska's canneries.[66] At the onset of the Second World War, US military recruitment to the Merchant Marine and to the United States Navy increased dramatically, with Filipino immigrants becoming qualified for US naturalization.[67] The Great Depression in the United States led to the US Congress passing the 1934 Tydings-McDuffie Act. This granted the Philippines independence, which took effect on July 4, 1946, following a ten-year transitional period of commonwealth government. With the passing of the 1965 Immigration Act, Filipino nurses and other professionals traveled to the United States, where many of them were given permanent resident status.[68] In 2018, over four million Filipinos were reported to reside in the United States, constituting the third-largest Asian American subgroup after the Chinese and the Indian Americans.[69] Most of these Filipinos reside in California, Hawaii, Illinois, Washington, New Jersey, New York, Nevada, Florida, and Virginia.[70] Ohio—a midwestern state bordered by Indiana, Kentucky, Michigan, Pennsylvania, and West Virginia, a place known in Native American lore as "where people brought their dead for their souls to rest in a good way"—had not been favored by most Filipinos.[71] It was in Ohio, however, that Lagitan and his family came to settle in the early 1990s.

Colonization and Missionization

When Lagitan moved to Ohio, he did not expect to come face to face with the forces of domination all over again. Soon after he arrived, he came to know about Ifugao's and Ohio's shared histories of colonization. Ohio had been the home of the Shawnee, Miami, and Delaware peoples who, in the 1500s and 1600s, fought the encroaching Spanish, French, and English. The colonists brought with them venereal disease, measles, mumps, and smallpox, which ravaged the Indian populations.[72] During the War of Independence (1775–1783), the Ohio Indians supported the English military against the American frontiersmen. When the latter won and Ohio "was to be American henceforth," the new government declared that the "Indians had forfeited their right to land and could continue to remain in Ohio only in whatever terms the American government chose to grant."[73] Further attacks on the Natives forced them to retreat from southern and southwest Ohio.[74] When the New England veterans of the American Revolution were allowed to "redeem the land warrants given them in partial payment for their military service in the Ohio country," they directly challenged the Ohio Indians.[75] The Shawnee and the Miami struck back, leading to a cessation of migration to Ohio Country during the 1780s. The Indian coalition, however, was defeated in 1794 and white settlement resumed in the eastern and southern parts of the state.[76]

Formal Education, Employment, Health, and Family

During his first years in Ohio, Lagitan experienced intense isolation. He knew of some Filipino students at Ohio University, but, according to him, they were mostly from well-off families in lowland Philippines with nothing much in common with a nawotwot highlander like him. In one of his classes that he remembers clearly, the American professor presented a documentary film about the Banaue rice terraces that demonstrated Indigenous life as more sustainable and, in some cases, more advanced than modern Western ways. This intrigued Lagitan, who began to suspect he may have traveled across the world to better appreciate Ifugao ways. The film's message also clashed with his reasons for enrolling at Ohio University's International Affairs program, which was so that he could find employment in an international development agency to help "develop" backward Ifugao. He wondered, however, why despite the positive talk about the Banaue rice terraces and Indigenous life, this professor never asked him to speak about his experiences. He was just a little brown boy who must learn quietly from a superior white man, his potential to contribute to the production of knowledge rendered nil.

Lagitan's feelings of alienation intensified when after finishing two master's degrees, in International Affairs and in Geography, he applied for jobs at the World Wildlife Fund and at Conservation International, but was not even granted interviews. "The WWF claimed to promote indigenous knowledge but had no interest in hearing what an indigenous person like myself had to say, or in honoring work experience that I obtained outside of the U.S.A.," he protested. Lagitan became further disillusioned with the idea of working for big development organizations when he found out that they depended on money from rich countries that attached commercial and political strings to aid. Unable to land a job despite his educational attainments, Lagitan ended up doing low-wage contract work like carpentry, plumbing, and woodworking. For fourteen years he worked as an assistant to a famous white American wood and bronze sculptor, working on pieces from start to finish, even signing the sculptor's name. Seeing the pittance that he as nameless immigrant apprentice received from the huge amounts that his works fetched, Lagitan resigned. He embarked on his own woodcarving career and received good reviews for his works. Without marketing support, however, his income further dwindled. To make matters worse, soon after his arrival in the United States, he was struck with Ménière's disease, a malady of the inner ear with symptoms that include severe headaches, exhaustion, energy depletion, vertigo, loss of hearing, tinnitus (ringing in the ear), loss of balance, and vomiting whenever his pupils moved. Consulting two American specialists, these told him that

Ménière's has no known cure. Even if he underwent surgery, there was a 40 percent chance that the procedure would fail.

As though his problems were not enough, Lagitan's marriage to white American woman Cynthia became more and more difficult. Cynthia felt that she was doing all the work and was not getting enough support from her partner. In a conversation with her, she noted the dramatic change in Lagitan from a successful butterfly businessman in Ifugao to having two master's degrees from Ohio University, to becoming a woodcarver who could not earn enough money to support his growing family. Later, when Lagitan would become involved with neo-shamanism, according to Cynthia, things got even worse, because Lagitan would refuse to accept payment for the healing that he did. Cynthia reported, "My job has always been to support the family. I've been the general manager, making sure everyone [all four children] were where they're supposed to be. Occasionally Lagitan supports from income derived from renovations and contractor jobs, but these have been intermittent. You never know when it's coming. Meanwhile, I had to get student loans to pay for my doctoral studies, the mortgage, the bills, the children's school supplies."[77] Burdened with so many responsibilities, Cynthia gave up supporting Lagitan's art, which put a major strain on their relationship. Alongside many other problems, this eventually led to their divorce.

According to Lagitan, his Ménière's disease, the stresses of graduate school and family life, his meager income, and his experience of isolation and severe homesickness made his first decade in the United States a "living hell." After fleeing the Philippines to escape a life of subordination to missionaries, anthropologists, schoolteachers, Filipino lowlanders, and the Ifugao kadangyan, Lagitan had hoped that his immigration to America, Land of the Free, where justice and equality were rumored to reign, would give him voice and reprieve. He was mostly wrong. Except for the four beautiful children that he and Cynthia raised, the beautiful wooden house that he built with his own hands, and his critical (but not commercial) success as a sculptor, Lagitan has been hounded by the third-class status assigned to him as a racially marked immigrant, who, despite his educational qualifications, could obtain only temporary, low-paying, assistant-level jobs. In a racially rigged order, little brown man Lagitan was feminized and placed very low on the social ladder. To make things worse, his Ménière's could not be helped by the purported superior Western scientific medicine.

In an effort to overcome his debilitating illness, isolation, and material deficiencies, Lagitan turned to groups that could offer him acceptance, belonging, solace, and support. He forged connections with some Native American artists, and turned to white and mestizo American neo-shamanism that he claims eventually led him back to Ifugao where he would reclaim his baki inheritance and take it with him to the United States.

Native Alliances

The reverence for the land and the shared histories of colonial invasions, demonization of Native traditions, assimilation, and resistances were among the things that drew together Ohio-based Ifugao woodcarver and mumbaki Lagitan, Ohio-based Cherokee warrior and artist Don Cox, and Shawnee poet, filmmaker, and artist Tom Coy, the three of them, the "erstwhile people without history."[78] In ways comparable to the Ifugao warriors' fierce resistance against the Spanish invaders, Coy's ancestor, Shawnee warrior chief Tecumseh (1768–1813), gathered the Indians to fight against the white colonists responsible for the Native American genocide, dying bravely in an encounter in Ontario. Coy says of his experience growing up: "It wasn't popular to be Native American. We were discriminated or hanged and killed. The Christians thought that to be Native American was to be a witch. If you practiced your traditions that was centered on Earth Mother, they put you in jail. You couldn't be an Indian. [So] many of us gave up on our ways and became Christians. Most of us now have become integrated into the white race. Most no longer practice Native ways or are clueless about them. There are Sunday School Indians who may get together on weekends, like a club, but there's no place where you can go to be with just Indians. There are also government Indians who own casinos but these are all about the money." Don Cox observes that the Indian nations are now "trying to get their children to speak their languages again, to practice and pass on the knowledge of weaving, pottery, dance, and rituals. Because of this, they are getting stronger. We [the Native American nations], used to fight each other but this only allowed the white man to wipe us out." Coy adds, "to say that there are no more Indians is a white man's story. Indianness is in our hearts. They can't kill us. They can't wipe us out."[79] Today, Cox asserts, "if you have a drop of Cherokee in you, you fight for it, you give back of yourself to the Nation."

Neo-Shamanism

While trying to find a cure for his Ménière's disease, Lagitan had a chance encounter with Ramona Compton, a half-white, half-Lakota licensed psychotherapist who, he claims, gave up her professional practice once she realized that shamanic healing—associated by some with neo-shamanism, a "conglomerate of different cultural forms of shamanism" adapted to Western society—was a more effective way to address her clients' needs.[80] Seeing Ramona's soul retrieval services advertisement during a 2005 health EXPO reminded Lagitan of the *Ayag* (baki to retrieve lost souls) that he witnessed in Ifugao while he was growing up. For the first time in his life, he said, he considered learning his father's baki. But because he had no means to go home to Ifugao yet, he decided to first undergo Ramona's soul retrieval process. Of the ceremony, he recalled Ramona connecting with the Ifugao maknongan who guided her to the place where she claimed part of Lagitan's soul was left behind. To cut a long story short, this soul retrieval ceremony did not cure Lagitan of his Ménière's disease. What it did, however, was lead him to rediscover his father's baki. That same year, Lagitan met Susan Sheppard, a Native Lenapee spirit medium who channeled a message from an Ifugao prince-looking spirit named Gety, who said that he needed Lagitan to finish a mission that he had not fulfilled because of his untimely death. Gety would become one of Lagitan's spirit helpers. In 2007, Lagitan underwent nine Munay Ki initiation rites under Ramona Compton, who conferred on him the title of *laika* (earth keeper, shaman, medicine person) in the Westernized Andean tradition. During Lagitan's Munay Ki initiation, Ramona connected not only with the Andean spirits, but also with Lagitan's Ifugao ancestors and deities, in effect, commencing Lagitan's reconnection with the maknongan years before he would become initiated in the baki. Lagitan recalls that during his Munay Ki initiation, Ramona also saw three Native North American spirits that came to witness the event, spirits that would become part of Lagitan's transnational group of helpers.[81] In late 2005 and early 2006, Lagitan began to work with white American neo-shamanic healers and teachers Crow Swimsaway, a cultural anthropologist, and Bekki Shining Bearheart. Crow and Bekki were the first people to introduce Lagitan to neo-shamanic journeying. During a visit to Crow's and Bekki's Ohio home, they explained that they began their neo-shamanic work by becoming involved with European reconstructionists of pre-Christian spiritualities.[82] These reconstructionists were people drawn to tribal, earth-centered ways and connections with individual ancestries, and who asserted the shamanic roots of all people, which did not mean, Crow clarified, that everyone was a shaman. Shamanic journeying, according to Crow and Bekki, is about connecting directly with spirits, rendering the practice of long apprenticeship with living shamans unnecessary. They had thus been drawing on several traditions picked up during brief encounters with living traditional shamans and revivalists. One thing they have not done though is work with Ohio Natives because they claim that many of the local old ways had been lost. In 2007, Lagitan learned *kolaimni* from medicine woman Mechi Garza, who was of Cherokee, Choktaw, and Irish descent. Garza described kolaimni as "connecting with light," based on the understanding of the body as surrounded by an electromagnetic sheath.[83] Of the different healing methods that Lagitan had come to learn, kolaimni, he said, had become his primary healing modality. In 2008, Lagitan also studied with Patricia Minor, a white Irish American woman who identifies herself as Catholic as well as a *paqo* (fourth-level priest) in the Westernized Q'ero tradition. Patricia is also a core shaman trained by Michael Harner, an interfaith minister, and a certified practitioner and teacher of the reiki energy healing modality introduced to the United States by a Japanese woman. When I met Patricia who, like Lagitan, has not been to Peru nor met any Q'ero, she said: "What we practice today is what Don Benito [Corihuaman] formulated for the Western world. One implication of this is that one person, not a whole village, can initiate a person into paqo-hood." When I asked Patricia which spirits were closest to her though, she replied, "Jesus and Mary." She had in fact attuned Lagitan to what she called the Inner Sanctum that she claimed was directly taught by Jesus.[84] The Inner Sanctum, according to Lagitan, has helped him heal the wounds inflicted by Catholicism, particularly the demonization of the baki, and the sexual molestation of Ifugao children like him by their Banaue parish priest. One of the things that Lagitan appreciates about his forays into neo-shamanism is how this has led him back to Ifugao rituals. At the same time, he had very real issues with the baki. He consulted Patricia, who proposed that he communicate directly with his Ifugao ancestors. Lagitan recounted a 2011 séance in which he asked questions to his Ifugao ancestors who answered back through medium Patricia:

> First, Patricia saw my prince-looking Ifugao spirit helper who identified himself as Gety, my namesake (Lagitan, Lagget). Then she saw my ancestors, with my paternal side showing up first. These were powerful mumbaki, she sensed. Through Patricia, I asked my paternal ancestors several questions, first, about animal sacrifices. The reason I asked this was because I knew that the expense incurred in sacrificing animals is one of the main deterrents to the continued practice of the baki in Ifugao. I also asked this because in America, many people, including my youngest daughter, are averse to killing animals, hence, my inability to make much sacrifices. In response to my question, my ancestors spoke through Patricia that animal sacrifice is, in fact, not necessary. Animals, according to them, were first offered without being butchered. Over time, people started butchering their live offerings and this became the tradition to this day. I was satisfied with their answer. In fact, I had, proven to myself and to my father that I could call and ask help from the maknongan without having to sacrifice animals.
>
> My second question had to do with cursing in the baki that I do not agree with. In response, I was told that cursing was definitely not part of baki's original purpose, which is love. Again, this answer resonated with me, having fought many battles in my life and having witnessed Ifugao kill each other especially during tribal infighting, using different means, including the baki. There have been mumbaki who charge money to perform curses. Fortunately, my father was not one of them. In my view, the baki's power had weakened because of this corruption. What

is important now, in my opinion, is to get the power of the baki back by reclaiming its original purpose. The kind of baki that I would like to pass on to my children and to whoever is interested is one that is based on love and peace.

Finally, I asked why I came to the United States if my role was to serve my fellow Ifugao. I was told that I have other roles to play in my lifetime, but these were not elaborated on. When I finished conversing with my ancestors using my Ifugao language, it was awesome for me to watch Patricia come out of her trance instantaneously.

Working further with Patricia, Lagitan came to know the other roles that he would play in his life. This included, according to him, bridging different cultures and healing the earth. In 2011 and 2012 Lagitan underwent the Hatun Karpay initiation that conferred on him the title of paqo or fourth-level priest in the Westernized Q'ero tradition. All these experiences have helped Lagitan recover much of his self-esteem and voice. Recounting his journey from Ifugao to Ohio and how this impacted his embodied voice, he said:

> Growing up as a poor boy in the hamlet of Bayninan, Kinakin, Banaue, my *hapet* [voice] was maayun, reflecting my *munpalukipid* [meek] status. When I entered school, first in Kinakin, then in Banaue where I garnered academic honors and leadership roles, I became *munpahiya* [fearless, arrogant, politician-like], my hapet becoming more *magangoh* [loud and authoritative].[85] This change became more pronounced when my butterfly collecting and exporting business got big. Looking back, from being a nawotwot boy in the hamlet of Bayninan who moved to barangay Kinakin, then to the municipality of Banaue, then to the big city of Manila, I was always faced with the threat of being bullied, so I fought my way through, strategically deploying my voice to gain respect and recognition. When I moved to the U.S., my character and hapet changed again during my marriage to an assertive white woman, during my unequal relationship with a white American artist, with my failure to get a stable job despite my academic qualifications, and with my debilitating illness and loneliness. From my hard-earned power in Ifugao, I turned sheepish again, sinking back to my maayun voice and munpalukipid self.

The changes in Lagitan's hapet further indicated shifts in his gender identity. Whereas during the height of his butterfly business in Ifugao he was looked up to as a leader in the male circles of businessmen, woodcarvers, and mumbaki (as Buwaya's son)—circles where men prided themselves with being the heads and providers of their families, and where comparison, competition, and rivalry in the acquisition of material wealth and social status were encouraged—all this drastically changed when he came to the United States. From his experience of what may be considered normative masculinity in both the Philippine and North American contexts, Lagitan's diminished ability to sell his labor in the United States and to perform the role of financial provider for his wife and children significantly subdued his masculinity, impacting his gender identity, marriage, and family life.[86]

It was his encounters with neo-shamanism, according to Lagitan, which helped him regain his life purpose. His laika and paqo initiations gave him a new sense of belonging. "I felt accepted," he said, recalling the neo-shamanic circles that he participated in. One can only guess that part of the reason why Lagitan was readily accepted by some of the white American neo-shamanic circles he was a part of was because he gave life to so many romantic imaginings about the "shaman," or what Alcida Ramos refers to as the "hyperreal Indian" image of an exotic man, mysterious, soft-spoken, nonmaterialistic, a "victim of the system, innocent of bourgeois evils, honorable in his actions and intentions," while, at the same time, assimilable, thanks to the domestication processes provided by American university education, marriage, and citizenship.[87] Lagitan himself may even be credited with playing up the "shaman" stereotype that has given him a sense of power.[88] For all its positive effects, neo-shamanism has been criticized on several grounds, including its perpetuation of romantic and nostalgic images of the shaman as otherworldly and not also immersed in more "mundane" issues like class and race. It has been critiqued for its tendency to extract practices from Indigenous Peoples with whom neo-shamans may not have mutual and reciprocal relationships. Still another critique of neo-shamanism has to do with its reduction of Indigenous practices to core (psychological) elements like altered states of consciousness, stripped of sociohistorical and politico-cultural contexts, flattening racial, gender, and class differences.[89] Furthermore, associating modern, neo-shamanism with white shamanism implies a nonwhite version that is "old," premodern, and backward. This old-new distinction exposes the racialized hierarchy that states the "West creates history," the "East preserves history," and a "tertiary group of minor 'religions'"—like Native ritual traditions—is "lacking in history."[90] Finally, the practice of connecting directly with spirits rather than with emplaced human communities who work with such spirits but who may be of a different color, language, culture, and class, exposes white America's tendency to produce "exclusive forms of (white or whitened) community."[91]

In 2011, Lagitan decided to go home to Ifugao after voluntarily requesting his father, Buwaya, to give him a *liyah* (initiation) in the baki priesthood. This, for Buwaya, was a much-awaited event. He had been looking for someone to pass his baki to. Lagitan recalled of his liyah:

I came home in May, a month not known for initiations because these usually happen in July, toward the end of the harvest season. My father, Buwaya, said it was alright to hold it then because I was only coming home for a short while. The liyah took place in the afternoon in our Ifugao house in Kinakin. Only my father, my older brother, Pedro, and I, were present besides the baar or the non-mumbaki ritual helpers charged with killing and preparing the animal offering and serving the food. My father connected me to our ancestors, and through them, to the bagor or maknongan. We sacrificed one chicken, and upon checking the bile, my father said that my initiation was auspicious. I was accepted as a mumbaki. During this liyah, I felt the presence of spirits, but unlike my Munay Ki initiation, this was not a major spiritual experience for me, perhaps because I was already connected to my Ifugao lineage through the Munay Ki. My father, on the other hand, had an intense experience. Despite the pleasantly cool weather, he sweated heavily while invoking the deities to descend. After about four to six hours, we finished, as day turned into night.

Lagitan, the eighth-generation mumbaki, traces his lineage through Buwaya's mother Adchunglay's side, to the following ancestors *chin-nadne-nadne* (a long, long time ago): Bumanghat of Bayninan, who initiated his son Pachinngon of Bayninan, who initiated his son Paiyaya of Bayninan. Since Paiyaya of Bayninan had no son, he initiated his son-in-law Mainah of Bayninan. Both Paiyaya and Mainah initiated Mainah's son Bistol (brother of Buwaya's mother) of Bayninan, who initiated his son Ottengan of Bayninan. Ottengan and another Paiyyaya of Bayninan initiated Ottengan's first cousin Buwaya of Bayninan, who initiated his son Lagitan. Everyone in this mumbaki lineage was born kadangyan except Buwaya and Lagitan, who were not expected to become mumbaki because of their nawotwot origins. By acquiring wealth and distinction, these two rose in status. In the same year as his initiation, Lagitan purchased rice fields, big jars, gongs, and expensive bead heirloom jewelry that are the customary markers of the kadangyan rank. Having no interest in these, however, he gifted them all to Buwaya, who continued to be reminded by some of the hereditary kadangyan of his nawotwot origins, a matter that Lagitan attributes to jealousy.

Buwaya was already ailing in his heart, liver, and lungs when Lagitan came home to Ifugao to be initiated. He was unable to walk, his feet swollen. But he regained energy after realizing that his baki would live on through his son (figure 3.3). He felt encouraged to continue his practice after many years of stopping because his youngest daughters, who believed the baki was antithetical to Christianity, urged

FIGURE 3.3. Ifugao Mumbaki Bruno "Buwaya" Tindongan in Banaue, Ifugao, 2007
Photo by Gaston Damag.

him. Lagitan offered Buwaya healing using methods he had learned from his neo-shaman teachers in North America. Lagitan also gave Buwaya five out of the nine Munay Ki initiation rites that he had received. Buwaya and Lagitan did a ritual together to strengthen Buwaya's connection to the Ifugao ancestors and deities. Buwaya recovered following the exchange of healing and religious/medical knowledge between him and his son.

Crossing Borders: The Baki in Multiple Locations

Following his Ifugao initiation, Lagitan's next task was to memorize the baki of the Ifugao priesthood. The baki, he explained:

> are the oral means through which the Ifugao priests summon their spirits. The maknongan know the baki's sound. When they hear it, they know that they are being called, so they come immediately. The baki were taught to the Ifugao by the maknongan like Lidchum, the head of Kabunian (Skyworld).[92]

Knowing that he did not have Buwaya's "photographic memory" that allowed the old man to effortlessly recite the names of deceased ancestors and their descendants up to eight generations Lagitan resorted to recording his father's baki with his iPhone for subsequent memorization. Like Buwaya during his time, audio recording has been a crucial pedagogical tool for Lagitan because of its ability to capture not only the baki's words but especially its sounds, which are what provoke the spirits to listen and come to the site of ritual. In addition to audio recordings, Lagitan planned to acquire copies of Conklin's researches that were informed by his father Buwaya. He knew, however, that neither audio recordings nor text transcriptions can replace learning in context, that is, sitting with, listening to, and participating in rituals performed by the elderly mumbaki.

When Lagitan traveled back to Ohio after his Ifugao initiation, he carried in his bodily and digital memory his father's baki. Because baki is invisible, it did not require a special visa to cross borders. Because it is weightless, it did not encumber its carrier's luggage. As a "portable practice," baki travels well, traversing geographical and cultural boundaries with ease.[93] A very important aspect of the baki that Lagitan transported to Ohio was the maknongan's names that he was to memorize so that he could call on them whenever he or others were in need. The maknongan are no strangers to travel, a kind of discarnate analogue of Lagitan's terrestrial mobility. They go where an initiated mumbaki summons them through voiced invocations and offerings. Such translocality also means that, despite the baki's geographical circulation, the importance of Ifugao as the baki's customary site of performance is not in any way diminished; Ifugao, where Lagitan's ancestors lived and died, and where they continue to serve as the living Ifugaos' intercessors to the maknongan they are aligned with. In addition to the maknongan's names, Lagitan transported to Ohio his knowledge of making *bayah* (rice wine) and of building Ifugao houses. Since there is no terrace rice farming in Ohio, Lagitan has not spent much time learning the hongan di page or the calendric agricultural rites linked to rice production and consumption. What he has focused on instead are the hongan di tagu, or rituals for humans, particularly those for healing, protection, and negotiation. As of 2013, Lagitan had committed to memory three or four of Buwaya's twelve hongan di tagu. As of 2019, Lagitan felt comfortable performing eight hongan di tagu plus two rice-related rituals. Baki mastery takes time. In Lagitan's case, this has been partly due to his lack of practice because of the limited number of Ifugao in the United States who request him for rituals that are the opportunities for baki mastery. Another reason has been his ability to already pray and heal using modalities other than the baki—kolaimni, reiki, neo-shamanic journeying, tai chi, qigong—modalities into which he has been incorporating baki elements. From one vantage point, Lagitan has not yet attained full baki mastery. From another, he has transformed his connection to the mumbaki lineage so that it can speak to a broader and more diverse community.

Death of a Mumbaki

On January 23, 2013, a month after Lagitan was introduced to me by Hospicio Dulnuan—an Ifugao based in New York who used to be Lagitan's performing arts teacher—I receive a Facebook message from Lagitan in Ohio. In the message he tells me that he is about to board a plane to the Philippines because his father Buwaya had just died. He invites me to join him in Ifugao. I decide to travel to the northern mountains to catch the final days of Buwaya's wake and to meet Lagitan for the first time.[94]

It is slightly drizzling when the bus pulls up at the Banaue terminal, where Lagitan awaits my arrival. I glance from my window and see a svelte brown man with hair as black and long as mine. That must be him, I think to myself and I am right. After our introductions, Lagitan ushers me to a tricycle that takes us to his younger sister Estela's house a few hundred meters away. We eat a light breakfast then head over to Lagitan's family home in barangay Kinakin, where the second and final part of the vigil for Buwaya is taking place. From the asphalt road, we descend on foot and on slippery stone steps, down to about a hundred meters below, into a sound world of human mourning, the slaughter of sacrificial animals, endless cooking, serving, and convivial chatter in Ifugao, Ilocano, and English. We join the throng of between fifty and several hundred attenders of the vigil, comprising elders, middle-aged community members, and children. The center of all the activity is the wooden Ifugao house on stilts with galvanized iron roofing, under which lies Buwaya's body, dressed in Barong Tagalog, inside a beautiful wooden coffin adorned with Ifugao woven fabrics.[95] "We made a compromise here," Lagitan tells me upon our arrival. He means that some of the manner in which the vigil is conducted subscribes to the preferences of his Christianized and Westernized family members, while others are more in accordance with those like him who are just as Westernized and Christianized but who equally uphold Buwaya's baki. This compromise also means that at the place of vigil, one hears gong beaters taking turns at playing and dancing to simulate eagles that once inhabited Banaue, but also phonograph music that plays American country western Christian hits like "Standing on the Promise of God" and "How Great Thou Art." In one of the evening vigils, Lagitan organizes a liwliwa chanting session so that the elders can sing and listen about Buwaya's life and deeds.[96] While this transpires, however, the singers' voices are drowned out by a Mel Gibson movie and by evangelist fire and brimstone speeches by "Christ is the Answer" members who have the benefit of a loudspeaker. "The liwliwa," these evangelized Ifugao, claim, "are nonsense. They have no Biblical basis and constitute the devil's work."[97] Thus, Ambrosio, Lagitan's brother-in-law, mutters: "The family and community are divided. Some are against the baki, while others are for it. We are told that there would have been more vigil attenders had the family not invited mumbakis to perform rituals." To this, Lagitan says, "The Ifugao are just as disenfranchised as the Native Americans. Many are confused, having been told by the colonizers that their ancestors are demons."[98] Lagitan, however, believes that the Ifugao continue to have strong connections with their ancestors.

Of the vigil of eight nights and days—three hosted in Lagitan's younger sister Estela's house, where Buwaya died, and five in their home in Kinakin, where Buwaya lived—I am told that two baki were performed: Pamotbotan on the first day, when Buwaya's body was brought out of the house for public viewing; and Changlis or Bu-ar on the sixth day, to call the ancestors to take the animal offerings and the intentions of the attenders of the vigil to the maknongan. On the day following Buwaya's burial, Lawet is also performed. The rest of the vigil is devoted to Christian services and Bible sharing. Lagitan tells me that during one of the baki ceremonies before I arrived, Buwaya's soul was asked for the spiritual reason of his death (outside of the medical findings). This responded through a medium-mourner that "It was the Pahang deity that took me because I never performed the Pahang ritual. Even when I was sick, the Pahang was not celebrated. I could have lived longer had the Pahang been performed." Buwaya's two youngest daughters, whose religious beliefs led them to ban their father's baki, making sure, out of good intentions, that Buwaya only saw a medical doctor and not a mumbaki when he got sick, wept hard upon hearing this. It turns out from the traditional Ifugao perspective that Buwaya's illness was not something that could have been cured by a doctor because it was the ritual-seeking ancestors who caused it and who could have cured it. On the day of Buwaya's burial, a mourner becomes possessed by Buwaya's soul again. Through this medium, Buwaya chants his gratitude to all the mourners, saying that he is satisfied with how the wake is being conducted (figure 3.4).

Fetching the Soul of the Departed

The flurry of sounds subside once the attenders of the vigil leave for their homes within and outside Ifugao following Buwaya's eight-day wake and burial. Before the sun is up the following morning, Estela, Lagitan's younger sister, knocks on my door to see if I would like to record the baki that is about to commence. I hurry to the Ifugao semitraditional house, laptop in hand, passing by children playing and adults sweeping the yard with palm brooms that make scratching

FIGURE 3.4. Lagitan with Huwan Candelario after Buwaya's wake and funeral, Kinakin, Banaue, Ifugao, 2013

Photo by Grace Nono.

sounds. I climb the narrow bamboo ladder into the dark, cramp, and smoke-filled interior where the mumbaki, together with Lagitan's oldest brother, Pedro, have already gathered. I set up my laptop while Lagitan readies his iPhone recorder to document the proceedings. The baki that is about to take place is the Lawet, similar to the semitraditional ritual that Lagitan would perform in Wallingford for Harold Conklin two years later. The Lawet is performed to summon Hinogwakan, the maknongan responsible for ushering the soul of the departed to Lagud—the Cosmic Downstream where the dead go—as well as to cleanse the surviving kin of impurities. I am told that this baki has to take place very early in the morning while the stream is still clear, and while the water trails are not yet muddied by the farmers. This way, Hinogwakan would not have a difficult time finding his way. The Lawet is officiated by Huwan Candelario (pastor Evangeline's brother), an elderly mumbaki who served as Buwaya's mentor in the past. Huwan is assisted by Jose "Nabbud" Pagaddut, Buwaya's nephew, a younger mumbaki from Talop, Kinakin, and by Lagitan. It is important to have several mumbakis in attendance, I am told, so that if the one who does the calling becomes possessed by the maknongan, the other mumbaki would be able to converse with the deity and do its bidding.

The wood crackles as the fire burns at the hearth, casting a soft glow on Huwan's blanket-draped silhouette. This elderly mumbaki faces the *punamhan* or wooden box where the maknongan's power is believed to be stored. The punamhan contains betel nut, leaves, ashes, and the blood of sacrificial chickens. Also sprawled on the wooden floor is a *chuyu* or pamahan, a wooden container for the bayah, coconut shell cups called *ongot*, and Huwan's sugarcane shoot. Squatting on a low wooden bench, Huwan lets his left elbow rest on his left knee. His left palm supports the left side of his head, while his right hand holds a cup, supposedly of rice wine. Lagitan tells me that if the deity invoked by Huwan enters him, his left elbow will slip off his knee. Then the other mumbaki would know that whatever words are heard from Huwan's voice would no longer be his, but the deity's. In a slightly rhythmic vocal drone that does not depart much from his speaking tone, Huwan begins to chant Lawet's lengthy invocations and petitions that would last four hours, with rests in between. Nabbud joins him in an equally monotone rhythmic iteration of what seems to be an endless narration of deities' names. Huwan and Nabbud repeat the invocations three times: first, at the ritual's onset; second, when the sacrificial animal is being slaughtered; and third, before the ritual food is partaken. This means pausing twice along the way, giving the ritualists and participants time to wash their throats with what would have been bayah, but because Lagitan's family was not able to ferment mountain rice for the occasion, they are substituting bayah with the imperial beverage of Coca-Cola.[99] The pauses between the prayers also give the mumbaki a chance to tell stories while the cooking of the animal offering is in progress. Toward the end of the baki, during the part called gonob, Huwan performs the buad or chant with a slight melody.

Huwan begins by paying respects to his mumbaki lineage and by narrating how an ancestor in Lagud made rice wine. He then chants how the maknongan discuss among themselves who should travel to Kinakin to fetch Buwaya's soul. In this deliberation, Hinogwakan agrees to be the one to go, claiming, "I am sturdy in taking back rice souls." Hinogwakan examines the river tributaries to determine which path to follow. Guided by Huwan's chant throughout his journey, the deity passes through Ifugao's old settlements, Baliwon, Moma, Ha-pid, Ca-ba, Nunkitumman, Lagawi, Kiyyangan, Mun-gayang, Bayyukan, Ampa-chang, Bunne, Atuggu, Numpolyah, Ar-aligangnga, Og-wag, Luyaan, Mabu-lud, Chugong, Nattiw, Tabla, Inhalanay, Bay-yaw, Bukkon, Gi-lut, Bangaan, Bungubungna, Bayninan, Puitan, Numpi-ot. He asks the inhabitants of each village he passes where Buwaya's bereaved family is calling him from. Eventually, he arrives in Punlutaan (the sitio of Kinakin) where the Ifugao house stands, and where Huwan, Nabbud, Lagitan and his oldest brother Pedro await his coming. The moment Hinogwakan arrives, he asks: "Chanay bayah yu?" (Where is your rice wine?) There is no rice wine, of course. There is only Coca-Cola. Still, Huwan offers the customary response: "Nehnay bayah an nunchachaan moya untuuwot mangininum" (We have rice wine ready, so let us drink). A few moments later, Huwan's buad states that Hinogwakan is getting intoxicated. At this point, Huwan, Nabbud, Pedro, and Lagitan present the deity with the sacrificial animal, a duck. Hinogwakan, as voiced by Huwan, cleanses and blesses all of Buwaya's descendants, giving them assurances that he will take good care of Buwaya's soul. The deity journeys back to Lagud following the river, Buwaya's soul with him, no longer needing Huwan's chant to guide him on his way.

If one compares Huwan's 2013 Lawet for Buwaya with Lagitan's 2016 Lawet for Conklin, one of the biggest differences is the length of time spent on each ritual. Huwan's version took between four and five hours, while Lagitan's took a fraction of that time. Huwan's baki had also fewer nontraditional elements compared to Lagitan's semitraditional version. Before returning to the United States, Lagitan and I discuss the possibility of my visiting him in Ohio to experience his use of the baki there.

A New Home for the Baki

I spend almost all of my August 2013 visit to Ohio accompanying Lagitan in what seems to be endless driving across vast plains, cornfields, wooded hills, rivers, and lakes between his family home, his barn in another county, festivals where his wood sculptures are exhibited, the farmers' market where we purchase supplies, his spiritual teachers' houses that we visit, tai chi classes that he teaches, and the Unitarian Universalist Church that he and his children occasionally attend. I see that Lagitan has grown comfortable in his adoptive land and is well loved by his children, neighbors, and friends. The following sections describe Lagitan's actual application of aspects of the baki in Ohio, with notes on how these depart from Buwaya's and Huwan's versions in Ifugao. Also included are notes about a distance healing session that Lagitan offered for someone in California, a blessing that he conducted in Pennsylvania, and an oral performance that he delivered in New York, all of them featuring aspects of the baki.

Property Protection in Athens

It is market day in Athens, Ohio.[100] Many locals congregate and chatter around stalls that sell organic greens, local meat, seafood, and freshly baked bread. As

Lagitan and I walk around, people greet him warmheartedly. Some have read about his sculptures in the local papers. A husband and wife had their porch built by him. There is a former Peace Corps volunteer who had been to the Philippines and who speaks Tagalog. We also meet a fellow healer of his, and an epileptic who he treats right there and then. Lagitan seems well liked by most of these white Americans and their children.

Before shopping, I ask Lagitan if it is safe for me to leave my laptop inside his pick-up truck. He responds positively because all he has to do, he says, is invoke the Puchung to protect the vehicle and the belongings inside it. The Puchung, he explains, is a group of Ifugao guardian deities whose names are recited by the mumbaki in every ritual in order to gain their general protection. Outside of ritual, the Puchung may also be invoked without offerings by a mumbaki or by a non-mumbaki who is a Puchung holder or is aligned with a Puchung lineage. As guardians, the Puchung, according to Lagitan, are customarily commanded to inflict pain on transgressors' bodies. For example, if someone steals an object after the Puchung have been commanded to attack, the thief's hands or eyes or other body parts may swell or suffer from pain for as long as the stolen object is not returned. The person who commanded the Puchung is the only one who can perform the *ihapud* or healing for whomever the Puchung has afflicted. Ihapud proceeds with the Puchung holder chewing *moma* (betel quids) until they become red then spitting them on the affected body part.

Because of Lagitan's desire to eradicate cursing from the baki—cursing that he believes has weakened the baki's power, not to mention that it does not solve any problem—Lagitan now commands the Puchung only to cause transgressors' hearts to be "touched." In this way, he says, they will change their minds about committing wrongdoing, or if they have already done so, they will correct themselves voluntarily. Lagitan tells me that when he lost his digital recorder during Buwaya's wake in Ifugao and had a strong sense of who had stolen it, he invoked his father's Puchung lineage. "I asked the Puchung to touch the person's heart and to make him return the recorder, deviating from the traditional prayer that commands the Puchung to harm the culprit. And it worked!!! The man returned the recorder to my sister Estela."

After extolling the Puchung's guarding powers to me, Lagitan goes ahead and silently invokes his Puchung lineage that Buwaya attuned him to—Puchung Chumor, Puchung Chorhangon, Puchung Inlaoh, and Puchung Ammoket—commanding them to protect his truck and its contents while we shop. In addition to omitting the "curse" part, Lagitan's Puchung departs from Buwaya's and Huwan's versions by being performed silently in his mind. This Lagitan does so as not to attract undue attention from Americans unfamiliar with the practice.

Police Negotiation in Logan

It is 9 p.m. and I accompany Lagitan in fetching his daughter Amihan from the Rootwire Music and Arts Festival in Logan.[101] While driving home, we notice the police stopping cars. We are told that they are looking for drugs or drunken drivers or perhaps, without admitting it, racial Others to profile. Lagitan is stopped by a white American policeman, allegedly because his truck's headlights are broken. I sit on the front seat nervous at how this long-haired, little brown man would handle the situation. Lagitan is ushered outside his vehicle and asked for his driver's license. After a brief exchange, he returns and is told to drive carefully. Once we are back on the road I ask him what just happened, and he says, "As soon as I saw the police car tailing behind us, I called the Puchung. I felt, however, that this was not going to work, or that they were not the right deities to call, or that they were not going to protect us, so I called the friendly Halupe [negotiators] instead. What happened was I befriended the cop, and no ticket was issued." In other words, feeling that a particular group of spirits did not have the leverage to achieve the result he needed, Lagitan adjusted and called on another group with the more pertinent specialty of negotiation.

The Halupe, Lagitan tells me, is a group of Ifugao deities that are invoked to deliver offerings to the maknongan or *bagor* (Ifugao deities). They are the deities' errand boys and girls who belong to two groups. The first, the Maule, are the gentle and kind ones, the peacemakers who are summoned to help resolve conflicts. The second are the Mabungot, the fierce and cruel warriors, who are called to counter, for instance, an enemy's curse. Just like the Puchung, the Halupe's names are traditionally recited by the mumbaki at every baki, in the full hearing of the ritual participants, amidst animal and other offerings.[102]

Lagitan's invocation of the Halupe during the incident with the Logan police took place outside of ritual. Without the customary offerings of rice wine, chicken, or pig, Lagitan said that all he did was feel gratitude in his heart. In place of the lengthy recitations that could freak out the authorities, Lagitan just performed an abbreviated and silent version in his mind.

The next evening, Lagitan and I are on the road again. For the second time around, we are stopped by traffic police. After an exchange of words, the officer issues a ticket. Once back on the road, I ask Lagitan what just happened. "I didn't call any maknongan," he said.

Mural Blessing in Philadelphia

On May 4, 2013, I receive an email from US-based muralist Eliseo Art Silva who invites me to deliver a babalylan blessing during the unveiling of his new mural,

Alab Ng Puso: 100 Years of Filipinos, in Philadelphia. Eliseo explains that this is the first memorial to honor the more than one million martyrs of the Philippine-American War.[103] He tells me that June 15 is the target date, to commemorate the end of the battle of Bud Bagsak and the Philippine-American War. Perhaps because I had been writing books about ritual specialists and performing songs taught by some of them, Eliseo may have thought that it was appropriate for him to ask me to perform the babaylan's role. I clarify that I am not a babaylan, only someone who had been taught one little aspect of some ritual specialists' vast knowledge. I also tell him that there may be someone in the United States more suited for the role he has in mind. I email Lagitan to ask if he might be interested in this invitation, and he says yes. That Eliseo's earlier mural in Filipinotown, Los Angeles, California, was blessed by Lagitan's Ifugao performing arts mentor, Hospicio Dulnuan, who had introduced Lagitan to me, encourages Lagitan to respond affirmatively to the invitation. Eliseo and Lagitan discuss the logistics of Lagitan's participation via email, agreeing that Eliseo and the Philadelphia Art Council would provide Lagitan with airfares, food, and accommodations, as well as a fee for his time and effort.

A few weeks later, Lagitan tells me about his plan to invoke the Ifugao war deities during the mural unveiling. "Why them?" I ask. He thinks that the Mabungot are appropriate because the mural memorializes the more than one million deaths during the Philippine-American war. "The Mabungot and Halupe," he says, "are invoked not only to resolve conflicts but also to help the souls of those who have died in wars or accidents who may still be confused, not knowing that their bodies had expired. Lingering on earth, these souls can interact with the living and cause them illness." Since calling the maknongan requires a mumbaki to present offerings or he can be in "shit trouble," Lagitan plans to request the Philadelphia organizers for a live chicken. He also expects to perform a baki with rice wine offering once he is back in Ohio.

As the event gets closer, Lagitan emails me that Eliseo and the Philadelphia Art Council could no longer pay him anything for his time and effort, not even cover his gas, accommodations, and other needs. But they would still like him to come. Despite my admonitions, Lagitan feels that he should still go. When a tai chi student of his, Kimberly Boyer, offers to drive him to and from Philadelphia, he takes this as a sign that he is making the right decision.

When I visit Ohio two months after the Philadelphia mural unveiling, I have a chance to talk to Kimberly, who tells me that the mural blessing deeply upset Lagitan, and not only because of the long drive and the uncertainty of the accommodation and reception at their destination. Kimberly recalls the details of the mural unveiling that she understood was organized "to bring awareness of history and to honor and unite the Filipino-American community."[104] She recalls:

Before Lagitan came onstage, a Catholic priest gave a blessing, and all were reverently silent. The moment Lagitan appeared, I felt a nervous energy and people seemed to panic. Barely thirty seconds after he started talking, people came up to me, asking me to stop him. "There's no time for him," they said. Looking at them, they seemed to be more of the conservative types who shuffled in their seats, unreceptive, seemingly ready to be offended. I felt a kind of fundamentalist fear of the esoteric.[105]

I ask Lagitan for his recollection of the Philadelphia event. Among the things he tells me is that the event organizers provided him with a mannequin chicken rather than the live bird that he had requested. "How can I practice all kinds of baki in this continent if all that people can offer are artificial animals?" he asks incredulously. He also tells me that before he delivered the Ifugao blessing, which was what everyone expected of him, he was first smudged by Kimberly with Wyoming sage. Then he opened the four directions, after which he launched into a talk before an audience composed of VIP guests and other prominent members of the Filipino-American community. His talk, he admits, was unplanned. This was provoked by an incident that happened outside the bathroom after he changed into his Ifugao G-string. Many eyes became focused on him, he said, and people started to have their photos taken with him. His impromptu talk, therefore, was meant to dispel associations of Natives with inferiority. It was to tackle, head on, the othering that highland Igorots, like himself, had received from lowland Filipinos who were the mural unveiling's main audiences and organizers. Such othering was immortalized by statements like that of Philippine diplomat Carlos P. Romulo: "The fact remains that the Igorot is not Filipino and we are not related, and it hurts our feelings to see him pictured in American newspapers under such captions as, 'Typical Filipino Tribesman.'"[106] Statements like these have provoked outrage among the highlanders. When he delivered his talk to the audience, he said, people's eyes started rolling. When he said that he was an eighth-generation mumbaki as well as an initiated earth-keeper and fourth-level priest in the Andean tradition, "more eyes rolled until these eyes were no longer looking at me," he said.

I contact Eliseo to get his perspective on the matter and to ask why Lagitan was neither compensated for his efforts nor reimbursed for his expenses. Eliseo explains to me in an email that he tried his best to get Lagitan compensated for his services, "but our funds were not enough . . . Lagitan, [however,] volunteered to come without compensation, and a good friend of his covered his trip," Eliseo reports. Eliseo adds that "Only a very limited number of people did not appreciate Lagitan's participation in the [mural] dedication . . . the types who have internalized oppression [colonial mentality]."[107] Eliseo shares with me the contact information of two groups of people who attended the event, those who he thought appreciated Lagitan's participation and those who did not. Out of ten people I contact for their opinions, only one responds. On July 29, Aida Navidad Rivera, president of the Philippine Folk Arts Society, and state chair for the Pennsylvania National Federation of Filipino American Associations, wrote about Lagitan: "His presence at the dedication of the mural added to the authenticity of the occasion. He was invited by Eliseo to perform an ethnic ritual. However, the solemnity of his ritual was diminished if not lost because of the following reasons: 1) he delivered a speech before his ritual; 2) the ritual was too long and he tried to translate in between acts—he was there for a blessing not [to] conduct a class; there were VIP speakers and other numbers in the program waiting; 3) he finished by promoting his book and his upcoming event; this is absolutely out of place."[108]

Had the blessing taken place in Ifugao, the mumbaki invited would have been free to say whatever it was that he wanted said during the occasion. In Philadelphia, however, mumbaki Lagitan was asked to perform the role of an actor within a circumscribed script that he did not write, with props assigned to him, like the artificial chicken. His presence was seen to lend "realness" and "authenticity" to the event, but the moment he delivered real commentary, he was shunned. Lagitan sang back to the populations that have derided and discriminated against his people for centuries and paid the price for deviating from the script.

Lagitan's blessing in Philadelphia was an abbreviated version of its Ifugao counterpart. It was also performed outside of ritual and uttered without offerings. In addition, it was fused with other elements such as smudging and opening of the four directions, elements that he derived from other spiritual traditions.

Healing at the Athens Unitarian Universalist Church

Lagitan jumps on his truck to catch the Athens Unitarian Universalist Sunday morning service. His daughter Amihan and I tag along.[109] As soon as we arrive, I behold the beautiful rough-hewn brick UU church that glistens under the morning sun after an evening of rain. A woman minister leads the multicultural and intergenerational fellowship that has made Lagitan and his children feel welcomed and accepted. After the service, Lagitan introduces me to Andree Cavender, a white American woman UU member. Andree tells me that in early 2012 she was diagnosed with uterine cancer. She had surgery but was told afterwards that some of the cancer remained. Andree had a healing session with Lagitan after which she underwent further tests that showed her to be cancer-free. While Andree is realistic that she could not prove it was Lagitan who helped rid her of her cancer, neither can she prove that it was not. All she knows, she says, is that Lagitan is a good man with good children.

Immediately after the service, Lagitan is requested for healing by another UU member, Jen Bowman. Jen tells Lagitan that nine years ago, while she was pregnant, she fell and has since suffered from extremely painful mobile ribs. I join Jen and Lagitan climb up the stairs to the church's mezzanine. Lagitan tells Jen to sit comfortably on a chair, then raising his palms, he silently invokes his spirit helpers. First, he calls on the spirits of the four directions that he first came across in the Q'ero teachings.[110] Then he calls on his three Native North American spirit guides, as well as his Japanese-looking martial artist guide, and his Ifugao prince-looking spirit helper named Gety. He also calls a lynx and a fish. The next group of spirits that he calls are his ancestors, particularly his mumbaki lineage from Buwaya's mother Adchunglay's side.[111] He then invokes what he refers to as the Ascended Masters that include the Ifugao deities Lidchum and Bugan (heads of Kabunian or Skyworld), Yomogyog and Bugan (heads of Chalom or Underworld), and Tadona and Inuke (who live in Kiyyangan and are always invoked by the mumbaki). Finally, he calls on the local Ohio spirits that are called *Pinacheng* in Ifugao. He tells me later that whereas in Kinakin and Bayninan in Ifugao, he would call the different Pinacheng that inhabit each mountain, river, or tree, in Ohio the practice is to just call the name of each mountain, river, or road where the spirits dwell. After mentally invoking the spirit helpers then asking them to use him as their instrument or channel, his palms begin to pulsate. He proceeds with his primary healing method, kolaimni by scanning Jen's energy centers with the palms of his hands. He searches for dark areas that to him signify heaviness, disturbance, or illness, and scrapes them off with his hands. He then blows light on the different energy centers, a practice that he says he learned from the Q'ero teachings.

What I find interesting in all this is to witness, at first hand, how people in Lagitan's adoptive land approach him for help with their health issues and how Lagitan, in response, claims to tap into Ifugao, Q'ero, Native North American, white American, Judeo-Christian, Indian, Japanese, Chinese, and Atlantean sources of healing. Some people may no longer consider this practice baki, but Ifugao elements are certainly woven into it.

Distance Soul Retrieval for a California Resident

Lagitan helps me launch my second book, *Song of the Babaylan*, at the Los Angeles Public Library in Southern California. During the program he speaks about his experiences as a mumbaki in the United States.[112] When we open the floor for audience participation, a woman friend of his, Janet, originally from Tukukan,

Bontoc, Mountain Province (adjacent to Ifugao), steps to the front to share her story. Janet has lived in the United States since the late 1980s. Like Lagitan, she was married to an American Peace Corps volunteer. To the audience of mostly Filipino Americans, Janet talks about her painful divorce and the helpful advice she received from Lagitan. She then recounts that sometime in 2012, the belly of her daughter, Cuyappi, began to swell. Alarmed, Janet took Cuyyapi to the Mount Sinai Hospital in Los Angeles to find out what the problem was. Much to Janet's distress, Cuyappi was diagnosed with stage four ovarian cancer. Cuyappi, however, did not seem to believe the doctor's diagnosis. What she did instead was seek help from Lagitan. Since Lagitan was in Ohio, and Cuyappi and Janet in California, Lagitan suggested that they do distance healing. They all set a date, and the moment for the scheduled healing arrived. As soon as the session was over, Janet realized that she had slept through the whole process. Then her phone rang with Lagitan at the other end, telling her, "Your daughter's soul was left alone in the Tukukan River, but I was able to bring it back." At that point, Janet remembered that while she was sleeping, she dreamed that she was taking care of a child who fell into a deep well. She called on others to help save the child but no one came to the rescue. She dove into the water, herself, and pulled out the child who she thought had died, but in the end, lived. She realized that the child was her own daughter, Cuyappi. Reflecting back on her dream, Janet concluded that "Both Lagitan and I saved my daughter."[113] Lagitan, himself, offers his own recollection of that session:

> First, I set up an altar with water and salt on it. I lighted sage and a candle to represent the four cardinal directions and the four elements of life: water, earth, air, and fire. I intuitively included other objects: healing stones, statues, Ifugao traditional clothing, in the altar. Then I opened the seven directions: south, west, north, east, below, middle, and above. Beating a drum in a slow rhythmic drone to help me focus, I silently called on my spirit helpers and teachers, particularly, my Ifugao spirit helper, Gety, as well as the Ifugao ancestors and deities, past healers, ascended masters, star beings, whoever came to mind. After the sacred space was created, I followed the kolaimni healing sequence by first scanning Cuyyapi's energetic centers to check if there was any major blockage. Because Cuyappi's diagnosis was severe, I focused on the problem with my mind. While doing the energy balancing and while working on her heart center, the image of a child appeared. She was playing by the river. I called her and convinced her to go home because her mother was waiting for her. I also asked the spirit of that river to release her. In Ifu-

gao tradition, what I did was Ayag or soul retrieval ritual. I had participated in several Ayag while I was growing up. Although I did not follow the traditional Ayag process, I believe that I was guided by my Ifugao spirit helper and ancestors in that particular healing.

Ayag, says Lagitan, is an Ifugao baki performed to retrieve a soul that may have lost its way or that may have been trapped in a specific Pinacheng's dwelling. It does not need animal sacrifices but requires *gangha* (gongs), *tor-ge* (women's loin cloth), *wonoh* (men's loin cloth), *uloh* (blanket), *boong* (beads), *hinamar* (cooked rice), and *iklug* (eggs that have been boiled). In Ifugao, once the cause of the illness is determined by a *munhapud* (diagnostician) as soul loss, a mumbaki is then called. This mumbaki, together with members of the sick person's family goes to a place of high elevation, one that overlooks the specific Pinacheng's abode suspected of holding the lost soul. Offerings of shelled and sliced eggs are laid over cooked rice. A temporary clothesline is set up to hang the traditional clothing and bead ornaments on. The gongs are struck two or three times. Then the mumbaki shouts toward the Pinacheng's dwelling to ask if the lost soul is there, and if it is, for the Pinacheng to send it to the ritual participants so that they can all go home together, leaving their offerings behind. The mumbaki and his entourage then eat, beat the gongs again, and repeat the shouted appeal one more time before heading home.

Months after the healing session with Cuyappi, Lagitan scanned the young woman's energy centers long-distance and saw that she was cleared. He told her, however, that what they did was not a substitute for medical attention. Cuyyapi's father, who was a senior manager at a pharmaceutical company, could not agree more. He had Cuyyapi undergo surgery, but the doctors found no cancer.

Exhibition and Book Blessing in New York

Lagitan and I are having a back-to-back event at Topaz Arts in Queens, New York.[114] He is unveiling his wood sculpture exhibition entitled *Unearthing the Magic* and I am doing another launch of my second book. Lagitan performs oral chants from Ifugao, Northern Philippines, while I sing those from Agusan and other parts of Mindanao, Southern Philippines, where I come from. Lagitan chooses to chant *gopah* and *baltung* for the occasion. The gopah, he says, are oral chants performed to deliver blessings. They are rendered by a *mungopah* (gopah chanter) who does not have to be a mumbaki but who often chants with a mumbaki present, the one who calls on the maknongan. There are two kinds of gopah that convey blessings. The first has fixed words and takes place during the Challong and Ohag (types of baki). The second is more improvised and is performed during a *gotad* (feast), where it is made funny to incite laughter among the audiences. The baltung, on the other hand, is a chanted call and response traditionally performed during the Ulpi, or baki after the rice planting. Lagitan likens the writing of my book and the sculpting of his wood to rice planting. They are just the beginnings of the process, he says. The ideas and feelings contained in our works have to be cultivated in the bodies, hearts, and minds of our readers and spectators until they bear fruit. For the event, Lagitan performs the gopah and baltung without offerings. He also shortens the chants. And because there are no other Ifugao present besides him, no one is able to respond to his calls.

I am surprised to hear Lagitan's hapet thunder, shaking the audiences with its power. This is a far cry from his earlier attempts to chant in his shy, meek, and uncertain voice. It's as though he is helping his voice emerge and connect with the seen and unseen presences, offering blessings to all those who have gathered.

I ask Lagitan afterward how he feels about public performances like this one. He says, "I was unsure at first. I didn't think this was the real purpose of my initiation. I used to consider performances like these as unrelated to spirituality. But after I heard people's reactions, I began to change my mind. I now see oral performance as part of why I was initiated. Sharing knowledge through them is just another form of service. So I will perform the baki, gopah, and baltung whenever I'm invited for the purpose of healing, educating, peacemaking, even entertainment in the case of gopah and baltung. Performing the chants and recitations publicly does not diminish their sacredness and efficacy." Lagitan's insight complicates claims that entertainment cannot also be sacred, or that the time-honored intertwining of the priestly and oralist functions in Ifugao society has been eradicated.

Song Travels
The Baki, Recontextualized

As an initiated Ifugao mumbaki in the United States, Lagitan has had to fashion a baki according to what is available to him in his immediate surroundings. In place of the Ifugao sacred mountains and water holes, and the spirits that dwell in them, he has had America's land and water forms and the local spirits that he invokes during his ceremonies (alongside Ifugao and other deities). In place of the elderly mumbaki who train novices like him, he has had his iPhone and text transcriptions to aid his baki memorization work, complemented by his occasional homecomings to Ifugao where he continues to train with the older mumbaki. In place of his fellow Ifugao in Banaue who request rituals from a mumbaki, he has his white American, Native American, and Filipino American friends who seek him out for healing, blessings, spiritual advice, or joint ceremonies. In place of pigs, he has his egg-laying hens in his backyard that he sacrifices whenever there is a need to. I have witnessed Lagitan butcher chicken for dinner while instructing his children Torin and Amihan how to decipher the bile for spirits' messages (figure 3.5).

In place of the Ifugao moma, Lagitan orders betel nuts, leaves, and lime from an Indian store in California. For his rice wine needs, he ferments his own rice. In the summer of 2013, Lagitan also began to build an Ifugao house, a process that was shot on film and covered on Facebook with at least a thousand followers. In 2019 this Ifugao house was transferred to Santa Fe, New Mexico, where Lagitan has performed ceremonies to help heal historical traumas and to mend hurts inflicted on the earth by humans. All this confirms baki as a ritual that can take place translocally, not only in Ifugao but anywhere else in the world where an ordained mumbaki invokes and petitions ancestors and deities to the place of ritual.[115]

FIGURE 3.5. Lagitan reading chicken bile with his daughter Amihan, Albany, Ohio, 2013

Photo by Virgil Apostol.

The Baki, Technologized

Lagitan's immigration from Ifugao to Ohio that is twenty to thirty travel hours away, requiring several thousand dollars in roundtrip fare, has severely limited his face-to-face apprenticeship with his mumbaki mentors. When Lagitan was initiated into the baki in 2011, he spent a total of one month in Ifugao. When he came back home in 2012 after being told that his father was dying, he stayed for another month. When his father Buwaya and eldest brother Pedro died months apart in 2013, Lagitan stayed a total of two months. Such discontinuous presence in Ifugao and sporadic baki training have been largely compensated by Lagitan's review of his iPhone recordings and text transcriptions that he has been able to take with him to the United States. Audio recordings have been crucial to Lagitan because of their ability to capture the baki's sonic nuances that are what the maknongan recognize and respond to. They have additionally afforded Lagitan memories of his father and feelings that accompanied rituals in Ifugao.[116] Finally, these recordings and their text transcriptions have allowed Lagitan to share the baki in more sustained ways with his children in a place where few Ifugao rituals take place.

Video calling has been another means for Ifugao people in the United States to access the baki back home. Lagitan's performing arts mentor, Hospicio Dulnuan, has been calling on mumbaki friends in Ifugao to perform rituals for him, long-distance. When I visited Hospicio in his Long Island home in 2011, he recalled how he requested Kindipan and another mumbaki in Ifugao to conduct the Pahang ritual for his continued healing, following his groin surgery due to clogged veins that caused him extreme difficulty in walking. Recalling the baki that he sponsored and attended on Skype, Hospicio said:

> My nephew, Jun, here in Ronkonkoma, set up Skype on his large TV screen. He then connected with my family in Ifugao who were directly overseeing the ritual proceedings. Skype allowed mumbaki Kindipan to ask me questions and to give me instructions in real time, while the baki was going on. Kindipan sacrificed seven native hens and showed me the chicken biles—their sizes, positions, and colors—all of which indicated an auspicious outcome.[117]

Hospicio's and Lagitan's experiences support claims that technology is a crucial way for Indigenous traditions to remain relevant in the modern world, allowing influences to travel not only in one direction—that is, from colonial centers to the colonies—but equally in reverse, "from the margins to the metropole."[118] The impetus for baki's survival also does not only move outward, that is, from Ifugao to the United States, but inward as well, through the efforts of U.S.-based mumbaki like Lagitan and baki adherents like Hospicio to keep the ritual alive both in the United States and in the Philippines.[119]

Lagitan's experience further indicates that while the technologization of the baki facilitates mumbaki pedagogy and continuing practice, it does not replace contextual learning with elderly mumbaki in Ifugao. Notes and recordings are helpful but can only partially capture the baki that is first and foremost about the embodied and intimate relations between lands, humans, and spirits.

Baki's Pedagogy, Individualized

Due to the vast distances that separate Lagitan from other Ifugao in the United States, much of this mumbaki's practice has been for "personal growth." "Even if I'm not doing baki for other people," Lagitan says, "I'm advancing in my spiritual development by continually communicating with the maknongan. I memorize their names and call on them for my personal needs."

Lagitan's approach to learning and mastering the baki in the United States finds parallels with the neo-shamanic approach.[120] Marete Jakobsen observes neo-shamans to be "not part of a close community of expectant people waiting for their skills to develop. It is a highly individualized process" wherein the "individual assesses his/her own development."[121] Being an initiated mumbaki, however, Lagitan's process in the US is complemented by continuing instruction by elderly mumbaki whenever he is Ifugao where his knowledge finds ready application among his relations.

The Baki, Hybridized

Of his baki initiation, Lagitan says: "It has given me a sense of inner peace and fulfillment to know that my Native tradition is alive in me. This is especially so because not a lot of educated Ifugao retain their respect for the baki. Having internalized colonial domination, they see the baki as demonic, barbaric, and primitive. [But] there is also truth in the baki. And it is important to know one's identity, my Ifugao identity that I took for granted while I was back home, but that intensified when I came to the United States where one experiences one's difference more acutely."

Faced, however, with situations outside the purview of Buwaya's and Huwan's baki, like cancer, while getting exposed to neo-shamanism's proclivity for mixing transcultural elements, Lagitan says: "I do not stick to my Ifugao tradition alone. I do not want to restrict my spiritual growth. I blend Ifugao Indigenous knowledge with those of others." Thus, Lagitan invokes not only the Ifugao deities but also the spirits of the four cardinal directions, Guanyin, Mary, Jesus, Saint Francis of Assisi, Shiva, Gandhi, Sanat Kumara, and many others. His ritual, at least for most of his clients in the United States, has also tended to consist more of scanning and clearing of energy centers and blowing of light, matters drawn more from kolaimni than from the baki. "I could not apply Buwaya's and Huwan's versions because my clients in the United States do not necessarily relate with the baki," he says. He further declares: "A healer makes no cultural distinctions. Whatever works for a person in need must be done, whether the healer sticks to his or her own tradition or combines that tradition with those of others. I started to drop the cultural barriers. I like to be inclusive. In fact, it was my other initiations that helped me understand my father's baki better."

Such assertions by Lagitan can be framed in support of Indigenous cross-cultural competency, continuity, sovereignty, and revitalization, as well as of resistance to the reduction of Indigenous traditions to singularities and Indigenous Peoples to homogeneous groups.[122] Indeed, Lagitan's hybridization of the baki can contribute to baki's continuity, particularly in noncustomary contexts. On the other hand, one can argue that hybridization—when not carefully undertaken—can further contribute to baki's marginalization when the Ifugao language, texts, sounds, processes, and relationships become subsumed by more dominant ways. One can further argue that Lagitan's hybridity, with its assumed cosmopolitanism, complexity, modernity, toleration, and queerness, can become the new norm against which the baki in Ifugao—assumed to be more traditional, rigid, simple, absolutist, and heterosexual—becomes measured. This is problematic and reinstates the relegation of Native identity "to a primitive past, a premodern precursor to the more modern, sophisticated mestizo identity."[123] Andrea Smith, citing other scholars, writes:

> [Gopinath's work] troubles the normative notion of the home as a place "to be escaped in order to emerge into another more liberatory space," in favor of "remaking the space of home within." Echoing Silva's and Puar's analysis, she reads a variety of texts to argue that the narrative of leaving home to attain personal liberation again rests on the logic of the self-determining universal subject transcending particularity. "The equation of liberation with leaving and oppressing with 'staying put' cannot be upheld. In rejecting this progress narrative of freedom through exile and the renunciation of home, these texts instead enable a queer reworking of the very space of home itself." Thus, if home can be remade, perhaps we could go farther than Gopinath and argue that the home is always already being remade: this remaking is not necessarily dependent on the diasporic subject.[124]

From the beginning of this chapter, the translocal production of Ifugao has been emphasized. The Ifugao baki itself has undergone changes due to its encounters with colonization, missionization, anthropologization, tourism, and other transnational processes. To frame Lagitan's cosmopolitan baki in the United States as superior to its Ifugao counterparts is to reinstate colonial and neocolonial privilege.

Baki Relations, Expanded

While the baki certainly remains a marginal presence in the United States, there has been a growing awareness about it in some quarters, thanks to Lagitan, Hospicio, and other Ifugao who continue to uphold it. Some Filipino Americans and Filipino Canadians, who trace themselves to lowland ancestors associated with greater colonization and privilege but who have become interested in decolonization and indigenization, have attended Ifugao rituals in Ifugao and/or in North America, becoming some of baki's new allies. In November 2013, Lagitan received a request from Shawnee artist and once Turtle Clan chief Tom Coy to lead an earth healing prayer. In August 2016, Lagitan was also honored with an invitation to lead the closing prayer during a Lakota Sioux meeting to protest the Dakota Access Pipeline.

Besides propelling the baki to a wider public, Lagitan's baki has expanded its spirit relations, a matter that may not be totally novel if one considers Roy Barton's claim, half a century ago, of the expansiveness of the Ifugao pantheon and god-creation attributed to the "amalgamation of streams of immigrants or from intermarriage between neighboring peoples . . . borrowing such as results from contact or commercial intercourse and exchange."[125] Perhaps what sets Lagitan's experiences apart from those of earlier mumbaki is the extent to which he is carrying out the task of expanding his spirit relations in light of his mission to help bridge the baki with other traditions.

The Mumbaki, Regendered

Feminizing the subjugated is a known technology of empire. Anne MaClintock writes that "imperialism cannot be understood without a theory of gender power . . . gender dynamics were, from the outset, fundamental to the securing and maintenance of the imperial enterprise."[126] Men have been reported to experience feminization under colonial regimes.

During his early years in Ifugao, Lagitan witnessed his tribal traditions demonized and derided. He also saw his father belittled by the local kadangyan and ordered around by an American employer. Lagitan's Native name was further changed, and his young body molested by a Catholic priest and a schoolteacher. Later in the big city he was bullied by lowland Filipinos who saw themselves as superior to highlanders like him. All these experiences formed part of Lagitan's encounters with feminization. On the other hand, each time he excelled in school or in business, he gained the normative masculinity and machismo that he shared with many other Ifugao males—the mumbaki included—who competed against each other for social prestige and spiritual power. The moment he came to the heart of empire and was married to an assertive white woman and became an assistant to a famous white sculptor, Lagitan felt feminized again. It was only during his forays into neo-shamanism, not to mention his initiation into the *pa'o* or Ifugao female priesthood twice in his life that he experienced yet another shift in his gender identity. With the encouragement of his predominantly women American neo-shamanic mentors, Lagitan claims to have foregone his aspiration for normative masculinity in favor of a balance between his masculine and feminine aspects, a form of gender relationality.[127] Indeed, Lagitan's generally *maayun, maule, ma'ma'uya* (kind, gentle, friendly) voice, svelte appearance, long hair, and soft manner inspired by Guanyin and Mary may remind some of the *bayog, bayoguin, bayoc,* and *asog* or the effeminate male ritual specialists reported by the Spanish chroniclers during the period of conquest.[128] This is only part of the story, however. Lagitan is equally a male mumbaki who invokes Genghis Khan and Shiva. He is an atlatl champion, a hunter, woodcarver, handyman, father, and guru-like figure increasingly surrounded by women students and admirers who serve and lavish him with their attention, which he enjoys, eliciting anger among those who claim he had hurt them.

The Baki, Muted

In contrast to the robustly voiced Ifugao baki performances by priests who simultaneously and repeatedly invoke and petition hundreds of deities and ancestors, chanting and reciting in different vocal registers and timbres, many of the rituals that Lagitan has come to lead in the United States have been relatively muted events, constituted more by mental communication with spirits and the inner intentions and visualization of ritual participants.

Silence is known to be deployed for different purposes. The relative muting of Lagitan's baki in the United States may be seen, in part, as an index of his marginal status as an immigrant of color in largely racist white America. It can also be considered a strategy for relating to his transnational clientele, many of whom neither understand the Ifugao language nor share the Ifugao cosmology.[129] As Jakobsen notes of neo-shamanic circles where people typically come from disparate linguistic, cultural, and religious backgrounds, silence—as opposed to "sounded interpretations that tend to restrict cosmology [and] could create havoc"—allows for multiple ritual interpretations to thrive. On the other hand, what may be referred to as "silent baki" is silent only to those who do not hear it, which is most people. For there are mumbaki like Buwaya, Lagitan claims, who, because of their Puchung's intervention, have heightened sensory perceptions so that they can hear beyond the "normal" limits of human audition. The maknongan themselves respond to calls, even when they are made in silence. The proof of this lies in the effects of Lagitan's silent use of aspects of the baki in the United States—the efficacious healing, the protection, and mediation—comparable to the effects of the sounded baki in Ifugao. None of this, however, diminishes the importance of sound in ritual. "Sound is powerful," Lagitan affirms.

The Baki, Abbreviated

As a modern Native subject, Lagitan as mumbaki is no stranger to the drive to be efficient, to "cut through to the chase," to strip what is deemed as unnecessary.[130] Thus unlike the baki in Ifugao that could very well last the whole evening, Lagitan claims to have devised a way to perform his rituals in ten minutes and with the same results. "Tradition is not wrong but is impractical these days," he says. His main strategy for abbreviating the baki has been to bypass the "spirit intermediaries"—mostly the ancestors and the spirits of the land—in order to go straight to the maknongan, the "highest gods." "I want to put aside the 'canes' and to connect directly with the highest deity of my choice," he says. Perhaps unknowingly, Lagitan is invoking a parallel argument used by monotheistic religions that consider only God as worthy of mention and devotion.[131]

Lagitan's abbreviation of his ritual is another characteristic of neo-shamans, Jakobsen notes. These are "modern people [who] cannot invest all the time that the (Eskimo) apprentice *angakkuq* had to spend. There has to be a short-cut. The secret teachings of the traditional shaman are presented in a weekend course."[132] But because Lagitan is not just a neo-shaman but also an inheritor of the Ifugao baki, he is equally committed to learning his father's and Huwan's lengthy baki. "I would still like to learn them," he says. "I believe that reciting over and over something that generations of mumbaki have recited in the past is one way to connect with one's ancestors," he adds.

Animal Sacrifice Made Optional

Lagitan's treatment of animal sacrifice as optional has been prompted by the high cost of pigs, chickens, and the like, contributing to the waning of ritual performances in Ifugao. It is equally provoked by the rising popularity of vegetarianism in the United States. Lagitan's youngest child, Malaya, for example, has objected to the slaughtering of her pet chickens. Thus, instead of offering butchered animals during rituals, Lagitan has resorted to offering three boiled eggs. His resolve to do away with the requirement of animal sacrifice is bolstered by his newfound ability to directly communicate with the maknongan and to know whether or not they have accepted his offerings, even without the benefit of reading the bile of dead chickens.

Trance Possession Refused

Of his early days in Ifugao, Lagitan recalls: "I remember my grandfather's mumbaki brother invoking the spirit of the fire then leaping on embers without getting scorched. I further witnessed other mumbaki getting possessed by the maknongan while chanting the baki, then answering the questions of the ritual participants." Today, trance possession remains commonplace in Ifugao, as observed during Buwaya's wake. Lagitan, however, has decided to do away with this feature of the baki in his own practice, citing as his main reasons the fear of losing control and the physical discomfort when one is entered into and departed from. Lagitan further reasoned: "I have my own body and do not want it to be occupied by another. It is enough that I receive the message." Lagitan's argument reveals a conception of the body as an "object in a coherent and fixed field" traceable to seventeenth- and eighteenth-century developments in Western modernity, in contrast to the older but also current conception of the body as porous.[133] Lagitan's resolve to do away with trance possession may have been influenced by his American neo-shaman mentors, all of whom directly communicate with spirits without being entered by them. Unlike traditional shamans, many of whom get possessed by spirits, Jakobsen writes that neo-shamans are more about mastery over spirits or *possessing* of spirits.[134] A Protestant-inflected secular modernity can be gleaned here, with the gods replaced by humans at the center of action.[135]

Notwithstanding Lagitan's insistence on keeping his body free from external interventions—if that were at all possible—the relationality of his hapet as it carries traces of other voices is more apparent. Lagitan, therefore, attributes the maayun quality of his hapet to his mother, Indudun, and her side of the family. This he contrasts with Buwaya's hapet, which is more magangoh, as Buwaya's mother Adchunglay's voice was. The magangoh voice, Lagitan says, is appropriate for the *hapo* (baki invocations) and the buad, gopah, *alim* (baki chants) that require power in the prolongation of the breath and the slowing down of notes, referred to as *mun-ur-ur-ule*. The maayun voice, on the other hand, he says, is well suited for the baki recitation of ancestors' names that require *magala* (fast) delivery. Both sounds are carried by Lagitan's embodied hapet at different moments during and outside the baki. That Lagitan's voice contains those of his significant others reminds one of Martin Daughtry's assertion that voice is "not the essence of a unitary self, but an instrument—(constructed in part through our mimetic, dialectic, dialogic, and polyphonic relationships with the voices . . . that surround us from birth)—through which our different personalities, our many overlapping 'selves,' are projected out into the world."[136]

The Baki Purified and Universalized

Lagitan's baki practice advances what he calls the Law of One that he first picked up from the Q'ero tradition, and that he claims is shared by many ascended masters, including Ifugao ones. He notes that while it is important to know one's cultural traditions and identity, it is also important to know that we are "one" with everyone. Related to this "oneness" is Lagitan's commitment to rid the baki of destructive practices. He claims that the baki has been corrupted by mercenary practitioners' calling on the power of the baki to kill and harm others for profit. This, he believes, has weakened the baki's power. His project to purify the baki from curses and to encourage customarily destructive deities to take on more benevolent roles constitutes for him the reclamation of baki's power.[137] Baki's original purpose of love and peace not only agrees with some of the values of neo-shamanism, it is aligned with some of the core messages of so-called world religions.[138] This contributes to baki's greater acceptability and transposability across geographical and cultural settings.[139]

Lagitan's interventions on the baki have been bold and have not come without a price. He feels that his continued Ménière's attacks may be caused in part by the maknongan's resistance to some of his innovations. He remains steadfast in his resolve to align the baki with love and peace. "This is the baki that I would like to pass on to my children and to whoever else is interested," he reiterates. Lagitan's commitment to the baki, coupled with his willingness to challenge spirits who direct power harmfully, invites a renegotiation of power relations and with it a remaking of history.

The Relationality of Place

For the mumbaki to summon through voice performances deities from regions of the Indigenous cosmos to different sites of ritual, and for these deities to be known to come and intervene in human affairs, suggest place as a vibrant point of intersection, an inherently layered and multiple space. That forces of domination have invaded and settled on Native lands, provoking variegated responses from Native Peoples, further configure place as internally heterogeneous and people as plurally emplaced. The assumed isomorphism of place, people, and culture, and the discursive incarceration of Native ritual specialists in Indigenous lands believed to be uncolonized and premodern, are being vigorously challenged by the relational, ideological, and physical mobilities of Indigenous Peoples. None of this, however, implies that specific places have lost their relevance, places like Ifugao where empire and elite nationalism are alive and well, contested at each turn by Indigenous agencies that uphold lands, lives, and ways.

It is the first quarter of 2021. Much of the world is devastated by the COVID-19 pandemic. The escalating death toll is compounded by the violence of authoritarian and racist regimes against peoples of color and the poor. Lagitan was already in Ifugao when the health crisis erupted. He has since been requested to offer distance healing to folks who have been afflicted by the virus in the U.S., France, and the Philippines. He applies energy healing to some of them, calling on sacred symbols and other procedures from his eclectic repertoire. In addition to his healing activities he has been invited to mediate in local land disputes. He has accepted, calling on the appropriate maknongan to "touch" peoples' hearts. But Lagitan is heartbroken because of the recent passing of his mother Indudun, his mentor Huwan, and his peer, Nabbud. He regrets having only recorded eleven of Huwan's buad due to procrastination and because of his worsening hearing problem related to his Ménière's disease. His family's house is being renovated and his land cleared for the building of huts that will become part of an Ifugao Center for Living Culture that he and his immediate kin are establishing for a translocal clientele. Lagiyan dwells in the Ifugao mountains that spoke to his ancestors, whose legacy he honors and carries in many different directions.

AFTERWORD

The decolonization of social relations is a call that has arose at different junctures of this book. It is the process of undoing the social hierarchies that have defined the interactions among the agents colonization and empire; the national and local elites, including the forces of resistance among them who have nonetheless preserved colonial power structures; and subjects like the Native ritual specialists whose embodied voices have been largely written out of public discourses.

Over the last five centuries, Native ritual specialists in the Philippines have been constructed as babaylan and relegated either to the silent pasts or the silent margins. Persecuted as agents of evil and superstition or valorized as symbols of woman power, gender pluralism, and land-based anticolonial resistance, these Native ritual specialists and their oral discourses have not had many opportunities to publicly contest hegemonic constructions about them. In the foregoing pages, a handful of baylan, tau m'ton bu, nungaru, and mumbaki have deployed their embodied voices to sing back to dominant discourses about the babaylan, voice, sex and gender, and place, asserting their oral epistemology, historical agency, and authority.

How might one respond to these acts of singing back?

One can listen, with full acknowledgment that listening is not a passive and value-free process but an act in direct correspondence with the auditor's social location. When one listens without such awareness, an auditor can leave a site of encounter with his/her foreclosed ideas intact, if not bolstered. The listening that this book proposes emerges out of sustained dialogue. It embraces self-critique and rectifies deep-seated prejudice.

What else might one do?

One can learn to sing along with these voices that are irreducible to musical tropes, and participate in their power. The promise of singing together is immense. It includes the healing of social relations, and the building of a differentiated yet coordinated chorus of voices that sing back to larger forces of domination.

Notes

INTRODUCTION

1. Mario Alvaro Limos, "The Fall of the Babaylan: How One of the Most Powerful Class of Filipinos Came to an End," *Esquire*, March 18, 2019, https://www.esquiremag.ph/long-reads/features/the-fall-of-the-babaylan-a2017-20190318.

2. This description is based on Robilyn's personal report and on a copy of the video documentation supplied by Department of Foreign Affairs officer Tes Marfil.

3. Carolyn Brewer, *Shamanism, Catholicism and Gender Relations in Colonial Philippines, 1521–1685* (Aldershot, UK: Ashgate, 2004), 40.

4. Christi-Ann Castro, "Colonized by Rote: Music Education in the First Two Decades of the U.S. Colonial Rule in the Philippines," in *Philippine Modernities: Music, Performing Arts, and Language, 1880–1941*, ed. José S. Buenconsejo (Quezon City: University of the Philippines Press, 2017), 124.

5. Castro, "Colonized by Rote," 18; Diana Taylor, "Acts of Transfer," in *The Archive and the Repertoire: Performing Cultural Memory in the Americas* (Durham, NC: Duke University Press, 2003), 17, 18.

6. Leslie C. Dunn and Nancy A. Jones, introduction to *Embodied Voices: Representing Female Vocality in Western Culture*, ed. Leslie C. Dunn and Nancy A. Jones (Cambridge: Cambridge University Press, 1994), 1.

7. Dunn and Jones, introduction, 1.

8. bell hooks, "Talking Back," in *Talking Back: Thinking Feminist, Thinking Black* (Boston, MA: South End, 1989), 5.

9. Zeus Salazar, "The Babaylan in Philippine History," in *Women's Role in Philippine History: Selected Essays*, 2nd ed., trans. Proserpina Domingo-Tapales (Quezon City: University of the Philippines University Center for Women's Studies, 2001), 214–15; Antonio Hila, *Musika: An Essay on Philippine Music* (Manila: Cultural Center of the Philippines, 1989), 11.

10. Francisco R. Demetrio, "Philippine Shamanism and Southeast Asian Parallels," *Asian Studies* 11, no. 2 (1973): 131, 151; Fay-Cooper Cole, *The Wild Tribes of Davao District, Mindanao* (Chicago: Field Museum of Natural History, 1913), 62, 133, 153, 160, 174; Fay-Cooper Cole, *The Tinggian Social and Religious and Economic Life of a Philippine Tribe* (Chicago: Field Museum of Natural History, 1922), 300; Nicanor Tiongson, ed., *Philippine Encyclopedia of Philippine Art*, vol. 1, *Peoples of the Philippines, A–J* (Manila: Cultural Center of the Philippines, 1994), 100, 192–205, 206–233, 239, 251, 265, 360, 381, 405; Nicanor Tiongson, ed., *Philippine Encyclopedia of Philippine Art*, vol. 2, *Peoples of the Philippines, K–Z* (Manila: Cultural Center of the Philippines, 1994), 45, 72, 151, 167, 186, 231, 272, 287, 379, 431, 447; William Henry Scott, *Barangay: Sixteenth-Century Philippine Culture and Society* (Manila: Ateneo de Manila University Press, 1994), 84–5; Ben J. Wallace, *Shifting Cultivation and Plow Agriculture in Two Pagan Gaddang Settlements* (Manila: National Institute of Science and Technology, 1970); Marino Gatan, *Ibanag Indigenous Religious Beliefs: A Study in Culture and Education* (Manila: Central Escolar University, 1981), 119; Harold C. Conklin, Pugguwon Lupaih, and Miklos Pinther, *Ethnographic Atlas of Ifugao: A Study of Environment, Culture, and Society in Northern Luzon* (New York: American Geographical Society, 1960), 12; Lourdes Dulawan, "Ifugao Baki: Rituals for Man

and Rice Culture," *Journal of Northern Luzon* 15, nos. 1–2 (1984–1985): 1–76; Gregorio Lagonsay, *Iluko-English-Tagalog Dictionary* (Quezon City: Phoenix, 1993); Edward P. Dozier, "Religion: Ritual and Beliefs," in *The Kalinga of Northern Luzon, Philippines* (New York: Holt, Rinehart and Winston, 1967), 59; Alicia Magos, *The Enduring Maaram Tradition: An Ethnography of a Kinaray-a Village* (Quezon City: New Day, 1992), xi–xii; Grace Nono, *Song of the Babaylan: Living Voices, Medicines, Spiritualities of Philippine Ritualist-Oralist-Healers* (Quezon City: Institute of Spirituality in Asia, 2013), 106; Grace Nono, *The Shared Voice: Chanted and Spoken Narratives in the Philippines* (Pasig City: ANVIL Publishing and Fundacion Santiago, 2008), 84; F. Landa Jocano, "The Sulod: A Mountain People in Central Panay," *Philippine Studies* 6, no. 4 (1958): 419–21; Diego Bergano, *Vocabulario de la Lengua Pampanga* (Manila: Imprenta de Ramirez y Giraudier, 1860); Robert B. Fox, *Religion and Society among the Tagbanuwa of Palawan Island, Philippines* (Manila: National Museum of the Philippines, 1982), 207; Manolete Mora, "The Sounding Pantheon of Nature: T'boli Instrumental Music in the Making of an Ancestral Symbol," *Acta Musicologica* 59, no. 2 (1987): 190; Virgil Mayor Apostol, *Way of the Ancient Healer: Sacred Teachings from the Philippine Ancestral Traditions* (Berkeley, CA: North Atlantic, 2010), 14–15; Baglyi Arsenio and Glenn Stallsmith, "Preserving Living Traditions in Live Performances: A Traditional Music and Dance Troupe of the Kalanguya of the Northern Philippines," paper presented at the 2nd International Conference on Language Development, Language Revitalization, and Multilingual Education in Ethnolinguistic Communities, Bangkok, Thailand, July 1–3, 2008.

11. From Emma Helen Blair and James Alexander Robertson, eds., *The Philippine Islands, 1493–1898*, 55 vols. [first five volumes were titled *The Philippine Islands, 1493–1803*] (Cleveland, OH: Arthur H. Clark, 1903–1909), see: Miguel de Loarca, "Relation of the Filipinas Islands," 5:131, 133; Juan de Plasencia, "Customs of the Tagalogs," 7:190; Antonio Morga, "Events in the Filipinas Islands," 16:132; Diego Aduarte, "History of the Dominican Province of the Holy Rosary," 30:286; Antonio Pigafetta, "Primo viaggio intorno al mondo," 33:167–71; Francisco Colin, "Native Races and Their Customs," 40:74–6; Domingo Perez, "Relation of the Zambal Indians of Playa Honda, Their Situation and Customs," 47:300–301. (For a list of volume titles and publication dates, see http://philhist.pbworks.com/w/page/16367055/ThePhilippineIslands.) Salazar, "Babaylan in Philippine History," 209–10; Carolyn Brewer, "Baylan, Asog, Transvestism, and Sodomy: Gender, Sexuality and the Sacred in Early Colonial Philippines," *Intersections: Gender, History and Culture in the Asian Context* 2 (1999); Michael G. Peletz, "Transgenderism and Gender Pluralism in Southeast Asia since Early Modern Times," *Current Anthropology* 47, no. 2 (2006): 312–24; Neil C. Garcia, "Male Homosexuality in the Philippines: A Short History," *International Institute for Asian Studies* 35 (2004): 13; Michael L. Tan, "Survival through Pluralism," *Journal of Homosexuality* 40, nos. 3–4 (2001): 127–8; Conklin, Lupaih, and Pinther, *Ethnographic Atlas of Ifugao*, 12; Lourdes Dulawan, "Ifugao Baki," ix; Francis Lambrecht, *The Mayawyaw Ritual* (Washington, DC: Catholic Anthropological Conference, 1932).

12. Salazar, "Babaylan in Philippine History," 219.

13. Dozier, "Religion," 60; José S. Buenconsejo, *Songs and Gifts at the Frontier: Person and Exchange in the Agusan Manobo Possession Ritual, Philippines* (New York: Routledge, 2002), 92–3.

14. On the exclusions of constructions, see Judith Butler, introduction to *Bodies that Matter: On the Discursive Limits of "Sex"* (New York: Routledge, 1999), xx.

15. Petrus de Noxeto, "The Bull Romanus Pontifex (Nicholas V), January 8, 1455," Native Web, http://www.nativeweb.org/pages/legal/indig-romanus-pontifex.html; Robert J. Miller, *Native America, Discovered and Conquered: Thomas Jefferson, Lewis and Clark, and Manifest Destiny* (Westport, CT: Praeger, 2006), 15.

16. Linda Tuhiwai Smith, *Decolonizing Methodologies: Research and Indigenous Peoples* (London: Zed Books, 2004), 42–3.

17. Domenico Pietropaolo, "Alcina in Arcadia," *University of Toronto Quarterly* 72, no. 4 (2003): 864; Brewer, *Shamanism, Catholicism and Gender Relations*, 86.

18. Brewer, *Shamanism, Catholicism and Gender Relations*, 95.

19. Milagros C. Guerrero, "The Babaylan in Colonial Times: Bodies Desecrated/Body Narratives, Metaphors, and Concepts in Philippine Indigenous Religion," in *Gender/Bodies/Religions*, ed. Sylvia Marcos (Mexico City: ALER, 2001), 175–176, citing Gaspar de San Agustín, OSA, *Conquistas de las Islas Filipinas, 1565–1615*, ed. Manuel Merino (Madrid: Consejo Superior de Investigaciones Cientificas Instituto "Enrique Flores," 1975), 660.

20. Aduarte, "Historia," 174.

21. Plasencia, "Customs of the Tagalogs," 196; Richard L. Deats, *Nationalism and Christianity in the Philippines* (Dallas, TX: Southern Methodist University Press, 1967), 16; Brewer, *Shamanism, Catholicism and Gender Relations*, 89.

22. Albert Ernest Jenks, "Religion," *The Bontoc Igorot* (Manila: Bureau of Public Print, 1905), 205.

23. Evelyn Cullamar Tan, *Babaylanism in Negros, 1896–1907* (Quezon City: New Day, 1986), 20, citing US War Department Bureau of Insular Affairs, *The Eighth Annual Report of the Philippine Commission to the Secretary of War, 1907, Part 2* (Washington DC: Government Printing Office, 1908), 310–11.

24. Roy Franklin Barton, *The Religion of the Ifugaos* (Menasha, WI: American Anthropological Association 1946), 203.

25. Gregorio Zaide and Sonia Zaide, *History of the Republic of the Philippines* (Metro Manila: National Bookstore, 1987), 45, 147, 151; Teodoro A. Agoncillo, *History of the Filipino People* (Quezon City: Garotech, 1990), 45, 102–6; Renato Constantino and Letizia Constantino, *The Philippines: A Past Revisited* (Quezon City: Tala, 1975), 85–6, 272–4, 275–9; Onofre D. Corpuz, *The Roots of the Filipino Nation* (Quezon City: Aklahi Foundation, 1989), 1:125–6, 189, 324; 2:502.

26. Constantino and Constantino, *Philippines*, 389; Renato Constantino, "Identity and Consciousness: The Philippine Experience," *Journal of Contemporary Asia* 6, no.1 (1976): 15.

27. See a similar argument in Michel Foucault, "Sciencia Sexualis," in *The History of Sexuality*, vol. 1, *An Introduction*, trans. Robert Hurley (New York: Vintage, 1990), 55.

28. Fe Mangahas, "From Babaylans to Suffragettes: The Status of Filipino Women from Pre-Colonial Times to the Early American Period," in *Kamalayan: Feminist Writings in the Philippines*, ed. Pennie S. Azarcon, 8–20 (Quezon City: Pilipina, 1987), 13.

29. Mangahas, "From Babaylans to Suffragettes," 13, 16–20.

30. Mary John Mananzan, "Religion as a Socializing Force in the 'Woman Question,'" *Review of Women's Studies* 10, no. 1–2 (1999) ["Gender Construction"]: 7, 8.

31. Mary John Mananzan, "The Babaylan in Me," in *Centennial Crossings: Readings on Babaylan Feminism in the Philippines*, ed. Fe B. Mangahas and Jenny R. Llaguno (Quezon City: C & E, 2006), 135.

32. Garcia, "Male Homosexuality in the Philippines," 13; Peletz, "Transgenderism and Gender Pluralism," 312.

33. Garcia, "Male Homosexuality in the Philippines," 13.

34. Meg Wesling, "Agents of Assimilation: Female Authority, Male Domesticity, and the Familial Dramas of Colonial Tutelage," in *Empire's Proxy: American Literature and U.S. Imperialism in the Philippines* (New York: NYU Press, 2011), 106–7.

35. Delia Aguilar, "The Social Construction of the Filipino Woman," *International Journal of Intercultural Relations* 13 (1989): 527–51.

36. Dawn Anne Ottevaere, "The Cost is Sworn to by Women: Gender, Resistance, and Counterinsurgency during the Philippine-American War, 1898–1902" (PhD diss., Michigan State University, 2010), 96.

37. Ofelia Villero, "Religion, Gender and Postcoloniality: The Case of 'Ciudad Mistica de Dios'" (PhD diss., Graduate Theological Union, Berkeley, California, 2010), 63.

38. Bae Manyaguyad Luciana Perez Rico, personal communication, June 19, 2019.

39. Tan, "Survival through Pluralism," 125.

40. Leny Mendoza Strobel, introduction to *Babaylan: Filipinos and the Call of the Indigenous*, ed. Leny Mendoza Strobel (Davao City: Ateneo de Davao University Research and Publications Office, 2010), 29.

41. Strobel, introduction, 27; Leny Mendoza Strobel, *Coming Full Circle: The Process of Decolonization among post-1965 Filipino Americans* (Quezon City: Giraffe, 2001).

42. Strobel, introduction, 46.

43. To date, the Center for Babaylan Studies that Strobel founded has mounted four successful International Babaylan Conferences, in 2010, 2013, 2016, 2019. See Center for Babaylan Studies, https://www.centerforbabaylanstudies.org.

44. Nono, *Song of the Babaylan*, 379.

45. Jane Monnig Atkinson, "Shamanisms Today," *Annual Review of Anthropology* 21 (1992): 310.

46. Atkinson, "Shamanisms Today," 311.

47. Michael Taussig, "Folk Healing and the Structure of Conquest in Southwest Colombia," *Journal of Latin American Lore* 6, no. 2 (1980): 221.

48. Atkinson, "Shamanisms Today," 314, citing D. H. Holmberg, *Order in Paradox: Myth, Ritual and Exchange Among Nepal's Tamang* (Ithaca: Cornell University Press, 1989).

49. Betty Cooper in Terry Macy and Daniel Hart, dir., *White Shamans and Plastic Medicine Men* (Native Voices Public Television, 1996), https://www.youtube.com/watch?v=19JAMhAzXms.

50. Tony Incashola in Macy and Hart, *White Shamans and Plastic Medicine Men*.

51. Incashola in *White Shamans and Plastic Medicine Men*.

52. Andrea Smith, "Queer Theory and Native Studies: The Heteronormativity of Settler Colonialism," *GLQ: A Journal of Lesbian and Gay Studies* 16, nos. 1–2 (2010): 51.

53. Patricia K. Wood, "Aboriginal/Indigenous Citizenship: An Introduction," *Citizenship Studies* 7, no. 4 (2003): 371–8.

54. hooks, "Talking Back," 1, 3.

55. The distinction between descriptive and transformative may not necessarily apply to the experiences of the ritual specialists in the text.

56. Richard King, "Beyond Orientalism? Religion and Comparativism in a Postcolonial Era," in *Orientalism and Religion: Postcolonial Theory, India and the Mythic East*, 187–218 (London: Routledge, 1999), 42–3, 61.

57. King, "Beyond Orientalism?," 42–3, 61.

1. WHO SINGS?

1. Many of the literacy teachers I was traveling with were themselves Indigenous Manobo, helping their kin cope with the rapidly changing times.

2. This two-wheel motorcycle, sometimes with wooden wings to accommodate extra passengers, is a popular mode of transportation in many interior areas of Mindanao.

3. This tod-om was sung by Manobo baylan Lordina "Undin" Potentiano on October 2, 2005, in Barangay Panagangan, La Paz, Agusan del Sur, Caraga region, northeastern Mindanao, southern Philippines. The recording of the tod-om was transcribed in Manobo and translated into kuntoon Manobo, Visayan, and English by Agusan-Manobo pastors Jose and Florencia Havana from October 2 to 4, 2005, and from August 15 to 18, 2012.

The Manobo transcription and English translation of this tod-om were first published in Nono, *Song of the Babaylan*, 169–71.

4. Buenconsejo, *Songs and Gifts at the Frontier*, 264.

5. The panumanan described here took place on October 31, 2005 at the home of Undin's cousin in Barangay Panagangan, La Paz, Agusan del Sur.

6. A fuller transcript of this panumanan may be found in Nono, *Song of the Babaylan*, 146–54.

For the history of kuntoon Manobo, see Jose Havana in Grace Nono, prod., *Kahimunan: Cultural Music of the Manobo, Higaonon, Banwaon of Agusan del Sur* (Quezon City: Tao Foundation for Culture and Arts, 2002), 3.

7. Addressing Sayson.

8. The spirit speaks to the ritual participants.

9. The panumanan is taking place not in Undin's house but in her cousin's, the house of Sayson's father.

10. The abyan thinks that I drink too much (Undin Potenciano).

11. The abyan is also accusing me of not complying with my regular offerings and chastising me for not having a gong of my own (Undin Potenciano).

12. This particular divinatory method is called *beon*. It makes use of a peso coin through which the spirit responds to human questions (Undin Potenciano).

13. To further investigate the situation at hand, the abyan goes to Maibuyan, the city of the dead (Undin Potenciano).

14. Makahagtong is the owner of Maibuyan, the captain of the dead (Undin Potenciano).

15. Addressing the peso coin.

16. What this means is, "Do not tarry in finding out from Maibuyan what will happen" (Robilyn Coguit).

17. Sayson's transgression.

18. A spirit that lives in Inugtuhan, a place between heaven and earth, below Magbabaja's dwelling (Undin Potenciano).

19. Addressing Sayson.

20. Referring to the abyan of Sayson's mother (Robilyn Coguit).

21. If the inflicter makes a demand—such as a *hakyad*, or *kaliga*, or *sugnod* (types of rituals) in exchange for the sick person's recovery—the sick person's family must promise to fulfill it on a designated day, say a week or a month later, depending on when the ritual requirements (including animal offerings) are produced. The fulfilment of this promise is called *limpas buya* (Undin Potenciano).

22. Addressing the ritual participants.

23. See a similar argument in Karen McCarthy Brown, introduction to *Mama Lola: A Vodou Priestess in Brooklyn*, 2nd ed. (Berkeley: University of California Press, 2001), 6.

24. R. C. Lucero and E. A. Manuel, "Agusanon Manobo," in Tiongson, *CCP Encyclopedia of Philippine Art*, 1:40.

25. Ethnolinguist Richard Elkins (1966) coined the term "Proto-Manobo" to designate the stock of aboriginal non-Negritoid people of Mindanao who are spread out across the island speaking different Manobo sublanguages; R. C. Lucero, et al., "Manobo," in Tiongson, *CCP Encyclopedia of Philippine Art*, 2:120; R. C. Lucero and E. A. Manuel, "Agusanon Manobo," in Tiongson, *CCP Encyclopedia of Philippine Art*, 1:40.

26. "Geography of Agusan del Sur," Official Website of the Provincial Government of Agusan del Sur, http://agusandelsur.gov.ph/index/about-pgas/2011-11-17-16-33-44/2011-08-15-05-52-37/geography-demography.

27. Juan Francisco, "On the Date of the Coming of Indian Influences in the Philippines," *Philippine Historical Review* 1, no. 1 (1966): 27; F. Landa Jocano, *Filipino Prehistory: Rediscovering Precolonial Heritage* (Quezon City: Punlad Research House, 1998), 142–5.

28. De Noxeto, "Bull Romanus Pontifex."

29. Miller, *Native America*, 15; Peter Schreurs, MSC, *Caraga Antigua, 1521–1910: The Hispanization and Christianization of Agusan, Surigao and East Davao*, 2nd ed. (Manila: National Historical Institute, 2000), 5.

30. Miller, *Native America*, 10–12.

31. Schreurs, *Caraga Antigua*, 74, 77. On barangay, see Rudy Buhay Rodil, *The Minoritization of the Indigenous Communities of Mindanao and the Sulu Archipelago* (Davao City: Alternate Forum for Research in Mindanao, 1994), 16–17.

32. Schreurs, *Caraga Antigua*, 98, citing Miguel López de Legazpi, "Letter to Felipe II of Spain," in Blair and Robertson, *Philippine Islands*, 2:175.

33. Schreurs, *Caraga Antigua*, 98, 99.

34. Schreurs, *Caraga Antigua*, 118.

35. Schreurs, *Caraga Antigua*, 117, 151.

36. Rodil, *Minoritization*, 19–20.

37. Schreurs, *Caraga Antigua*, 205, 314.

38. Schreurs, *Caraga Antigua*, 312.

39. Schreurs, *Caraga Antigua*, 169, 300, 301.

40. Schreurs, *Caraga Antigua*, 188, 382.

41. Schreurs, *Caraga Antigua*, 389.

42. Schreurs, *Caraga Antigua*, 374.

43. Schreurs, *Caraga Antigua*, 374.

44. Schreurs, *Caraga Antigua*, 373. This was not the first uprising against Spanish domination. Caraga, in cooperation with Sultan Corralat of Jolo, had risen up in revolt in 1631, killing Spaniards and burning churches in the process; Schreurs, *Caraga Antigua*, 107–9, 160–63.

45. Schreurs, *Caraga Antigua*, 373.

46. Rodil, *Minoritization*, 24–5.

47. Rodil, *Minoritization*, 30.

48. Rodil, *Minoritization*, 31.

49. Deats, *Nationalism and Christianity*, 92.

50. Merlyn Guillermo and L. P. Verora, *Protestant Churches and Missions in the Philippines* (Quezon City: World Vision Philippines, 1982), 1–3.

51. On the invention of Native peoples' "cultural backwardness," Willie Jennings, personal communication, December 11, 2018. On missionary strategies to convert the Natives of Mindanao, see John M. Garvan, "Methods Adopted by the Missionaries in the Christianization of the Manobos," in *The Manóbos of Mindanáo* (Washington DC: US Government Printing Office, 1931), 249.

52. Rachelle, Saturday, February 21, 2004 (10:20 p.m.), "Our History," Free Methodist Church (Phils), http://fmc-philippines.blogspot.com/.

53. Florencia Havana, personal communication, March 6, 2020.

54. Following Walter Groesbeck's assignment in Agusan came missionaries Schlosser in 1950; Streutker in 1959; McQuay, Weaver, and Downs in 1965; Bidwell in 1971; Stonehouse in 1972; and Schumacher in 1975 (Florencia Havana, personal communication, August 15–18, 2012).

55. In 1995, the Free Methodist Church in La Paz established a kindergarten and the Light and Life Theological Education (LLTEE; extension from Butuan) (Florencia Havana, personal communication, August 15–18, 2012).

56. Linda Montillo-Burton, "The Impact of Modern Medical Intervention on the Agusan Manobo Medical System of the Philippines," PhD diss., University of Pittsburgh, 1983, i–iii.

57. Florencia Havana, personal communication, June 10, 2005.

58. Buenconsejo, *Songs and Gifts at the Frontier*, 10, 11, 19.
59. Jose Havana in Nono, *Kahimunan*, 3.
60. Nono, *Shared Voice*, 108.
61. On the "embeddedness" of music, see Philip V. Bohlman, "Ontologies of Music," in *Rethinking Music*, ed. Nicholas Cook and Mark Everist (Oxford: Oxford University Press, 1999), 19. See also Philip V. Bohlman, "Musicology as a Political Act," *Journal of Musicology* 11, no. 4 (1993): 420.
62. Bohlman, "Musicology as a Political Act," 420.
63. Ramon Santos, "Philippine Music: The Ethnic Tradition," in Tiongson, *CCP Encyclopedia of Philippine Art*, 6:26–35.
64. Florencia Havana, personal communication, 2013.
65. La Paz Census, 2009.
66. La Paz Census, 2009.
67. Carol Laderman and Penny Esterik, "Introduction: Techniques of Healing in Southeast Asia," *Social Science and Medicine* 27, no. 8 (1988): 747; WHO Unit on Traditional Medicine, *Legal Status of Traditional Medicine and Complementary/Alternative Medicine: A Worldwide Review* (Geneva: World Health Organization, 2001), 165–6.
68. Montillo-Burton, "Impact of Modern Medical Intervention," 329–32.
69. Montillo-Burton, "Impact of Modern Medical Intervention," 329–32.
70. Nono, *Song of the Babaylan*, 167.
71. Nono, *Song of the Babaylan*, 166.
72. Nono, *Song of the Babaylan*, 160.
73. Nono, *Song of the Babaylan*, 160.
74. Nono, *Song of the Babaylan*, 160.
75. Nono, *Song of the Babaylan*, 160.
76. Nono, *Song of the Babaylan*, 160.
77. Nono, *Song of the Babaylan*, 168.
78. Nono, *Song of the Babaylan*, 167.
79. Nono, *Song of the Babaylan*, 167.
80. Nono, *Song of the Babaylan*, 167.
81. Nono, *Song of the Babaylan*, 167.
82. Nono, *Song of the Babaylan*, 167, 168.
83. Nono, *Song of the Babaylan*, 167.
84. Nono, *Song of the Babaylan*, 167.
85. Nono, *Song of the Babaylan*, 168. When Florencia, says "The abyan will never select someone who sings out of tune," what she means is that the abyan tend to choose someone who can sing, not necessarily someone who has accurate pitch. Undin's tod-om and gudgod like many other forms of Asian traditional musics belong to a musical system characterized by unstable pitches where the requirement of pitch accuracy so important in Western music may not apply.
86. The Manobo yagonganon may also recite the panawagtawag or invocation of spirit. It is a skill necessary for a baylan or datu (male chief) or any other leader to be able to seek help from forces greater than one's own to ensure success in any undertaking. A yagonganon may also sing the uyaging or song about history, heroes, wars, victories, tragedies, journeys, or the limbay that is the Higaonon counterpart of the tod-om.—Florencia Havana in Nono, co-prod. *Kahimunan*, 15–22.
87. Nono, *Song of the Babaylan*, 155, 167.
88. Nono, *Song of the Babaylan*, 154.
89. Buenconsejo, *Songs and Gifts at the Frontier*, 360.
90. Judith Becker, *Deep Listeners: Music, Emotion, and Trancing* (Bloomington: Indiana University Press, 2004), 14.

91. Marina Roseman, "'Blowing 'cross the Crest of Mount Galeng': Winds of the Voice, Winds of the Spirits," *Journal of the Royal Anthropological Institute* 13 (2007): S58–S59.

92. Roseman, "Blowing," S58–S59.

93. Anne Karpf, "How We Color Our Voices with Pitch, Volume, and Tempo," in *The Human Voice* (New York: Bloomsbury, 2006), 46.

94. Roland Barthes, "The Grain of the Voice," in *Image-Music-Text* (New York: Hill and Wang, 1977), 181–2.

95. Adriana Cavarero, *For More than One Voice: Toward a Philosophy of Vocal Expression* (Stanford, CA: Stanford University Press, 2005), 3–4.

96. Cavarero, *For More than One Voice*, 3–4.

97. Mladen Dolar, "The Linguistics of the Voice," in *A Voice and Nothing More* (Cambridge, MA: MIT Press, 2006), 22.

98. Steven Connor, "What I Say, Goes," in *Dumbstruck: A Cultural History of Ventriloquism* (New York: Oxford University Press, 2000), 13.

99. Gary Tomlinson, "Voices of the Invisible," in *Metaphysical Song: An Essay on Opera* (Princeton, NJ: Princeton University Press, 1999), 9.

100. Tomlinson, "Voices of the Invisible," 9.

101. Connor, "What I Say, Goes," 13.

102. Andrea Hollingsworth, "Spirit and Voice: Toward a Feminist Pentecostal Pneumatology," *Pneuma* 29, no. 2 (2007): 207–8; J. Martin Daughtry, "Afterword: From Voice to Violence and Back Again," in *Music, Politics, and Violence*, ed. Susan Fast and Kip Pegley (Middletown, CT: Wesleyan University Press, 2012), 248.

103. Nono, *Song of the Babaylan*, 155.

104. "Translation Principles," Summer Institute of Linguistics, https://www.sil.org/translation/translation-principles. The SIL website quotes the Forum of Bible Agencies International (FOBAI): "We affirm the inspiration and authority of the Holy Scriptures and commit ourselves to translate the Scriptures accurately, without loss, change, distortion or embellishment of the meaning of the original text. Accuracy in Bible translation is the faithful communication, as exactly as possible, of that meaning, determined according to sound principles of exegesis" (FOBAI statement #11).

105. On understandings of "language expertise," see David W. Samuels, "Bible Translation and Medicine Man Talk: Missionaries, Indexicality, and the 'Language Expert' on the San Carlos Apache Reservation," *Language in Society* 35 (2006): 531.

106. Nono, *Song of the Babaylan*, 157.

107. On language's extralinguistic features, see Eugene Nida, "Theories of Translation," *TTR: Traduction, Terminologie, Rédaction* 4, no. 1 (1991): 25.

108. Steven Feld et al., "Vocal Anthropology: From the Music of Language to the Language of Song," in *A Companion to Linguistic Anthropology*, ed. Alessandro Duranti (Malden, MA: Blackwell, 2006), 328.

109. Feld et al., "Vocal Anthropology," 322.

110. Ronit Ricci, "On the Untranslatability of 'Translation': Considerations from Java, Indonesia," *Translation Studies* 3, no. 3 (2010): 291–3, 297–8.

111. Of the sociosemiotic perspective of translation, Eugene Nida wrote: "[W]hen people listen to a speaker, they not only take in the verbal message, but on the basis of background information and various extralinguistic (and linguistic) codes, they make judgments about a speaker's sincerity, commitment to truth, breadth of learning, specialized knowledge, ethnic background, concern for other people, and personal attractiveness. In fact, the impact of the verbal message is largely dependent upon judgments based on these extralinguistic codes"; Nida, "Theories of Translation," 26.

112. Nono, *Song of the Babaylan*, 160.

113. Ricci, "On the Untranslatability of 'Translation,'" 296.

114. Vicente L. Rafael, "Untranslatability and the Terms of Reciprocity," in *Contracting Colonialism: Translation and Christian Conversion in Tagalog Society under Early Spanish Rule* (Durham, NC: Duke University Press, 1993), 112–13.

115. Nono, *Song of the Babaylan*, 160.

116. Ana María Ochoa Gautier, "Introduction: The Bar and the Voice in the Lettered City's Geophysical History," in *Aurality: Listening and Knowledge in Nineteenth-Century Colombia* (Durham, NC: Duke University Press, 2014), 4.

117. Deborah Kapchan, "The Aesthetics of the Invisible: Sacred Music in Secular (French) Places," *Drama Review* 57, no. 3 (2013): 139; Kapchan, "The Promise of Sonic Translation: Performing the Festive Sacred in Morocco," *American Anthropologist* 110, no. 4 (2008): 467–83.

118. Kapchan, "Aesthetics of the Invisible," 139; Kapchan, "Promise of Sonic Translation." See also Laderman and Esterik, "Introduction," 749.

119. Julietta Hua writes about the universalism of "rights" but her argument applies well to translation in imperial religious contexts. See Julietta Hua, "Universalism and the Conceptual Limits to Human Rights," in *Trafficking Women's Human Rights* (Minneapolis: University of Minnesota Press, 2010), 13.

120. See a similar argument in Martin F. Manalansan IV, "Speaking in Transit: Queer Language and Translated Lives," in *Global Divas: Filipino Gay Men in the Diaspora* (Durham, NC: Duke University Press, 2003), 47.

121. Such rationalization of interpretive strategies may be tangentially related to Frédérique Apffel-Marglin, "Smallpox in Two Systems of Knowledge," in *Rhythms of Life: Enacting the World with the Goddesses of Orissa* (Oxford: Oxford University Press, 2008), 160–61.

122. Ochoa Gautier, "Introduction," 8, citing Jean Cournut, "De l'écriture à l'inscription ou le scribe de l'inconscient," *Revue Française de Psychanalyse* 38 (1974): 57–74.

123. "Voice exceeds its very inscription"; Ochoa Gautier, "Introduction," 8.

124. F. Landa Jocano, *Folk Medicine in a Philippine Municipality* (Manila: Punlad Research House, 1973), 89.

125. Jocano, *Folk Medicine*, 84–5.

126. Laderman and Esterik, "Introduction," 747.

127. Laderman and Esterik, "Introduction," 747–8.

128. See also Steven M. Friedson, *Remains of Ritual: Northern Gods in a Southern Land* (Chicago: University of Chicago Press, 2008), 3?

129. James Waldram, "The Efficacy of Traditional Medicine: Current Theoretical and Methodological Issues," *Medical Anthropology Quarterly* 14, no. 4 (2000): 617.

130. Friedson, *Remains of Ritual*, 9.

131. Raquel M. Balanay, et al., "Analyzing the Income Effects of Mining with Instrumental Variables for Poverty Reduction Implications in Caraga Region, Philippines," *Journal of International and Global Economic Studies* 7, no. 1 (2014): 20;

Daisy Arago, "No Economic and Job Growth in Mining Industry in the Philippines, Only Plunder Need to Run," *Asia Monitor Resource Center*, April 1, 2012, http://dev.amrc.org.hk/content/no-economic-and-job-growth-mining-industry-philippines-only-plunder-need-run.

132. "Mining Caraga."

133. "Mining Projects in Caraga Generate more than 1B in Taxes," *Mindanao Newsmakers*, July 26, 2011. https://mindanaonewsmakers.wordpress.com/2011/07/26/mining-projects-in-caraga-generate-more-than-1b-taxes/.

134. "14 of RP's poorest towns in Mindanao," *Philstar*, November 24, 2008, https://www.philstar.com/headlines/2008/11/24/417811/14-rps-poorest-towns-mindanao.

135. "What Are the 20 Poorest Provinces in the Philippines?" *ABS-CBN News*, March 24, 2016, https://news.abs-cbn.com/focus/v2/03/24/16/what-are-the-20-poorest-provinces-in-the-philippines; Carolyn Arguillas, "Caraga: Poorest Region No More," *Mindanews*, April 26, 2013, https://www.mindanews.com/governance/2013/04/caraga-poorest-region-no-more/; J. A. Rimando, "11 of 20 Poorest Provinces in South," *Philstar*, December 5, 2011. https://www.philstar.com/nation/2011/12/05/754696/11-20-poorest-provinces-south.

136. Pat Samonte, "Lumads Flee Homes as War Rages in Agsur," *Business Week Mindanao*, August 22, 2014, https://issuu.com/sudaria_publications/docs/caraga_69354d413991a4; Marvyn N. Benaning, "Tribal Group Hits Rights Violations," *Business Mirror*, January 26, 2015, https://businessmirror.com.ph/2015/01/26/tribal-group-hits-rights-violations/; Butch D. Enerio, "NPA Rebels Attack Construction Firm, Burns Equipment," *SunStar Philippines*, March 20, 2015, https://www.sunstar.com.ph/article/188; Omar Ibarra, "AFP Suffers Eight Casualties in NPA Offensives in Agusan del Sur and Norte," National Democratic Front of the Philippines, August 13, 2014, https://ndfp.org/afp-suffers-eight-casualties-in-npa-offensives-in-agusan-del-sur-agusan-del-norte-2/.

137. The traditional housebuilders were Mario Tawede and his son, Robilyn's brother Gomez, Buskad, Dodong, and their leader, Baptist pastor Aylo Tawede.

138. Sacred-secular leaders have been observed in many so-called "traditional" societies in Southeast Asia. See Alfred W. McCoy, "Baylan: Animist Religion and Philippine Peasant Ideology," *Philippine Quarterly of Culture and Society* 10, no. 3 (1982): 145.

139. Willie Jennings, personal communication, December 11, 2018.

2. SHIFTING VOICES AND MALLEABLE BODIES

1. G. S. Casal and D. Javier, "T'boli," in Tiongson, *CCP Encyclopedia of Philippine Art*, 2:394.

2. Nono, *Song of the Babaylan*, 286–7; Nono, *Shared Voice*, 44; Manolete Mora, "Lutes, Gongs, Women and Men: (En)Gendering Instrumental Music in the Philippines," *Ethnomusicology Forum* 17, no. 2 (2008): 230.

3. Mendung possessed a vast oral repertoire that included the T'boli epic *Tudbulul*, the creation song *lingon Sebu*, the healing song *lingon loos*, the short songs *lingon lemnek* including the extemporized *lingon nemo*. Mendung sang in a concert in Australia through the invitation of ethnomusicologist Manolete Mora. She also sang in Manila through my invitation.

4. Manolete Mora, prod., *Utom: Summoning the Spirit: Music in The T'boli Heartland* (Rykodisk/Mickey Hart Series, 1995).

5. Grace Nono, prod., *Mendung Sabal: Tudbulul Lunay Mogul: T'boli Hero of Mogul, the Place of Gongs and Music* (Quezon City: Tao Foundation for Culture and Arts, 2002).

6. Mendung's life and work were cited in the following publications: Manolete Mora, *Myth, Mimesis and Magic in the Music of the T'boli, Philippines* (Quezon City: Ateneo de Manila University Press, 2005), 9–26; Mora, "Lutes, Gongs," 225–47; Nono, *Mendung Sabal: Tudbulul Lunay Mogul*; Nono, *Shared Voice*; Nono, *Song of the Babaylan*.

7. Mendung Sabal won the 2008 Sampung Ulirang Nakatatanda (Outstanding Elderly) award after my nomination.

8. Nono, *Song of the Babaylan*, 287.

9. Nono, *Song of the Babaylan*, 287.

10. Mendung Sabal in Nono, *Song of the Babaylan*, 274–5; Myrna Pula, personal communication, August 3, 2013, and July 18, 2018.

11. See Shelly Errington, "Recasting Sex, Gender, and Power: A Theoretical and Regional Overview," in *Power and Difference: Gender in Island Southeast Asia*, ed. Jane Mon-

nig Atkinson and Shelley Errington (Stanford, CA: Stanford University Press, 1990), 1–58; Christina Blanc-Szanton, "Collision of Cultures: Historical Reformulations of Gender in Lowland Visayas, Philippines," in Monnig and Errington, *Power and Difference*, 345–83; Mary John Mananzan, "Religion as a Socializing Force," 1–15; Fe Mangahas, "The Babaylan Historico-Cultural Context," in *Centennial Crossings: Readings on Babaylan Feminism in the Philippines*, ed. Fe B. Mangahas and Jenny R. Llaguno (Quezon City: C & E, 2006), 21–46.

12. Mangahas, "From Babaylans to Suffragettes," 10; Salazar, "Babaylan in Philippine History," 213–15; Maria Luisa T. Camagay, "Ang Kababaihan sa Pambansang Kamalayan," *Philippine Social Science Review* 52, no. 1–4 (1995): 1–14; Mananzan, "Babaylan in Me," 135; Brewer, "Baylan, Asog."

13. Mangahas, "From Babaylans to Suffragettes," 10; Mangahas, "Babaylan Historico-Cultural Context," 21, 23.

14. Mananzan, "Religion as a Socializing Force," 7.

15. Myrna S. Feliciano, "Law, Gender, and Family in the Philippines," *Law and Society Review* 28, no. 3 (1994): 548–9.

16. Salazar, "Babaylan in Philippine History," 213–15.

17. Brewer, "Baylan, Asog"; Pedro Chirino, *Relación de las Islas Filipinas y de lo que en ellas han trabajado los Padres de la Compañía de Jesús*, trans. Ramon Echevarria (Manila Historical Conservation Society, 1969) (First published Rome: Estevan Paulino, 1604); Francisco Ignacio Alcina, *The Muñoz Text of Alcina's History of the Bisayan Islands (1668): Part 1, Book 3*, trans. Paul S. Lietz (Chicago: Philippine Studies Program, Department of Anthropology, University of Chicago, 1960), 212.

18. Camagay, "Ang Kababaihan," 1–14.

19. Guerrero, "Babaylan in Colonial Times," 176.

20. Luciano P. R. Santiago, "'To Love and to Suffer': The Development of the Religious Congregations for Women in the Philippines during the Spanish Era (1565–1898)," *Philippine Quarterly of Culture and Society* 23, no. 2 (1995): 160.

21. Santiago, "To Love and to Suffer," 160; Luciano Santiago P. R., "The Development of Religious Congregations for Women in the Philippines during the Spanish Period (1565–1898)," *Journal of Sophia Asian Studies* 12 (1994): 52; Guerrero, "Babaylan in Colonial Times," 175–6, 178.

22. Santiago, "To Love and to Suffer," 162–5.

23. Guerrero, "Babaylan in Colonial Times," 178.

24. Fe Mangahas, "Babaylan in Dance Ritual at Spanish Contact: Sacral Vessel of Spirituality and Power," in *Gender/Bodies/Religions*, ed. Sylvia Marcos (Mexico: ALER, 2000), 155.

25. Mangahas, "Babaylan Historico-Cultural Context," 21, 23. The term "feminism" was first used in the Philippines by Concepción Felix and associates with the founding of the Asociación Feminista Filipina in 1905.

26. Mangahas, "Babaylan in Dance Ritual," 155.

27. Mangahas, "From Babaylans to Suffragettes," 16.

28. Mangahas, "From Babaylans to Suffragettes," 16–18; Blanc-Szanton, "Collision of Cultures," 370–371.

29. Camagay, "Ang Kababaihan," 1–14.

30. Salazar, "Babaylan in Philippine History," 221–2.

31. Strobel, introduction, 22–3.

32. Villero, "Religion, Gender and Postcoloniality," 63.

33. Wesling, "Agents of Assimilation," 106–11, 125–6, 133.

34. Center for Babaylan Studies, https://www.centerforbabaylanstudies.org.

35. Errington, "Recasting Sex, Gender, and Power," 1; Blanc-Szanton, "Collision of Cultures," 370–71.

36. Errington, "Recasting Sex, Gender, and Power," 39.

37. Ellen Koskoff, "Gender, Power, and Music," in *The Musical Woman: An International Perspective*, vol. 3, *1986–1990*, ed. Judith Laing Zaimont (Westport, CT: Greenwood, 1991), 771; reprinted in Koskoff, *A Feminist Ethnomusicology: Writings on Music and Gender* (Urbana, Chicago, Springfield: University of Illinois Press, 2014), 79.

38. Koskoff, "Gender, Power, and Music," 772.

39. Koskoff, "Gender, Power, and Music," 772.

40. Koskoff, "Gender, Power, and Music," 772.

41. Koskoff, "Gender, Power, and Music," 771.

42. Mora, "Lutes, Gongs," 226, 233, 245.

43. Mora, "Lutes, Gongs," 228, 233, 237.

44. Mora, "Lutes, Gongs," 232.

45. Mora, "Lutes, Gongs," 225.

46. Mora, "Lutes, Gongs," 239.

47. Mora, "Lutes, Gongs," 244.

48. Mora, "Lutes, Gongs," 244.

49. Myrna Pula, personal communication, August 3, 2013.

50. Errington, "Recasting Sex, Gender, and Power," 1; Blanc-Szanton, "Collision of Cultures," 370–71, 382.

51. By "our," Mora generally meant Westerners or scholars in the Western intellectual tradition; his article published in a UK-based ethnomusicology journal; Mora, "Lutes, Gongs," 226, 245.

52. Errington, "Recasting Sex, Gender, and Power," 5.

53. Mora had previously recorded Mendung's song performance. He had also invited her to perform in Australia. Myrna, on the other hand, had been assisting Mora with his T'boli music research for many years.

54. "Lawang Sebu" was a track in my solo album *Tao Music* (Record Plant, 1992; BMG Pilipinas, 1993). *Lawa* means "lake, pool, lagoon" in the Tagalog language.

55. Davao, also in Mindanao, is located roughly midway between Mendung's and Myrna's home in South Cotabato, and my home in Agusan del Sur.

56. Manolete Mora's recording of T'boli music, which contained a track by Mendung, had not been made publicly available in the Philippines with the exception of personal copies given by Mora to his friends.

57. Myrna Pula and Mendung were accustomed to doing these for researchers they had worked with.

58. Nono, *Mendung Sabal: Tudbulul Lunay Mogul*, 1.

59. Nono, *Mendung Sabal: Tudbulul Lunay Mogul*, 20.

60. Koskoff, *A Feminist Ethnomusicology*, 78.

61. Koskoff, *A Feminist Ethnomusicology*, 78.

62. Nono, *Shared Voice*, 51.

63. Singing for instructional purposes may be related with "illustrative talk." See Steven Feld, "Waterfalls of Song: An Acoustemology of Place Resounding in Bosavi, Papua New Guinea," in *Senses of Place*, ed. Steven Feld and Keith H. Basso (Santa Fe: School of American Research Press, 1996), 128.

64. Nono, *Mendung Sabal: Tudbulul Lunay Mogul*, 21.

65. This T'boli transcription and English translation first appeared in Nono, *Mendung Sabal: Tudbulul Lunay Mogul*, 22–4, and in Nono, *Shared Voice*, 61–3.

66. Dunn and Jones, introduction, 2–3.

67. Ellen Koskoff, "(Left Out in) Left (the Field): The Effects of Post-Postmodern Scholarship on Feminist and Gender Studies in Musicology and Ethnomusicology, 1990–2000," *Women and Music: A Journal of Gender and Culture* 9 (2005): 90–98; Koskoff, *Feminist Ethnomusicology* 159–61.

68. Whenever invited to sing by Father Mansmann, Mendung insisted on doing it outside the church, asserting that the Sebulung (healing ritual), not the Mass, was the T'boli way of praying (Myrna Pula, personal communication, August 3, 2013).

69. Mendung's lifestory as translated by Myrna Pula was cited in Nono, *Song of the Babaylan*, 283–6.

70. Michelle A. Gonzalez, "Our Trinitarian *Imago Dei*," in *Created in God's Image: An Introduction to Feminist Theological Anthropology* (Maryknoll, NY: Orbis, 2007), 141.

71. Myrna Pula, personal communication, August 3, 2013.

72. Myrna Pula, personal communication, August 3, 2013.

73. See Marie Perruchon, "Gender: Complementarity and Competition," in *I Am Tsunki: Gender and Shamanism among the Shuar of Western Amazonia* (Uppsala: Acta Universitatis Upsaliensis, 2003), 297.

74. Miguel López de Legazpi, "Relation of the Filipinas Islands and of the Character and Conditions of Their Inhabitants," in Blair and Robertson, *Philippine Islands*, 3:61.

75. Loarca, "Relation of the Filipinas Islands," 117–19; Francisco de Sande, "Relation of the Filipinas Islands," in Blair and Robertson, *Philippine Islands*, 4:56.

76. Mangahas, "From Babaylans to Suffragettes," 11.

77. Ottevaere, "Cost is Sworn to by Women," 96.

78. Carmen Abubakar, "Advent and Growth of Islam in the Philippines," in *Islam in Southeast Asia: Political, Social and Strategic Challenges for the 21st Century*, ed. K. S. Nathan and Mohammad Hashim Kamali (Singapore: Institute of Southeast Asian Studies, 2005), 47, 51.

79. Abubakar, "Advent and Growth of Islam," 47, 48.

80. Mora, *Myth, Mimesis and Magic*, 12.

81. G. S. Casal and D. Javier, "T'boli," in Tiongson, *CCP Encyclopedia of Philippine Art*, vol. 2 (Manila: Cultural Center of the Philippines, 1994), 394.

82. Mora, *Myth, Mimesis and Magic*, 12.

83. Camillia Fawzi El-Solh and Judy Mabro, *Muslim Women's Choices: Religious Belief and Social Reality* (Oxford: Berg, 1994), 16.

84. El-Solh and Mabro, *Muslim Women's Choices*, 16.

85. El-Solh and Mabro, *Muslim Women's Choices*, 16.

86. Abubakar, "Advent and Growth of Islam," 59.

87. Jocano, *Filipino Prehistory*, 29.

88. Casal and Javier, "T'boli," 394; Rudy Buhay Rodil, *A Story of Mindanao and Sulu in Question and Answer* (Davao City: Mincode, 2003), 36–7.

89. Rodil, *Story of Mindanao and Sulu*, 58–63.

90. Casal and Javier, "T'boli," 394.

91. Casal and Javier, "T'boli," 396.

92. Casal and Javier, "T'boli," 396.

93. Brewer, "Baylan, Asog."

94. Mananzan, "Religion as a Socializing Force."

95. Mananzan, "Religion as a Socializing Force."

96. Dinusha Panditaratne, "Towards Gender Equity in a Developing Asia: Reforming Personal Laws within a Pluralist Framework," *NYU Review of Law and Social Change* 32, no. 83 (2007): 94; Myrna S. Feliciano, "Law, Gender, and the Family in the Philippines," *Law and Society Review* 28, no. 3 (1994): 548.

97. Blanc-Szanton, "Collision of Cultures," 348.
98. Blanc-Szanton, "Collision of Cultures," 348, 351, 370
99. Wesling, "Agents of Assimilation," 125–6.
100. Wesling, "Agents of Assimilation," 111, 125–6.
101. Wesling, "Agents of Assimilation," 125.
102. Wesling, "Agents of Assimilation," 126.
103. Wesling, "Agents of Assimilation," 125, citing Gayatri Spivak.
104. Myrna Pula, personal communication, July 1, 2019.
105. Myrna Pula, personal communication, July 1, 2019.
106. Myrna Pula, personal communication, August 3, 2014.
107. Mora, *Myth, Mimesis and Magic*, 16.
108. Mora, *Myth, Mimesis and Magic*, 16–17.
109. Mora, *Myth, Mimesis and Magic*, 16.
110. Catholics for a Free Choice, *The Holy See and the Convention on the Rights of the Child in the Republic of the Philippines, NGO Report on How the Holy See's Laws Impact the Philippines' Compliance with the Convention* (Quezon City: Likhaan, Child Justice League, Catholics for a Free Choice, 2004), 23, https://resourcecentre.savethechildren.net/sites/default/files/documents/2252.pdf.
111. Myrna Pula, personal communication, August 3, 2014.
112. Catholics for a Free Choice, *Holy See and the Convention on the Rights of the Child*, 23; Robin Hemley, *Invented Eden: The Elusive, Disputed History of the Tasaday* (Lincoln: University of Nebraska Press, 2003), 180.
113. Wesling, "Agents of Assimilation," 133.
114. Martin Amanda, "The T'Boli: Profiles in Transition," *Cultural Survival*, June 1984, http://www.culturalsurvival.org/ourpublications/csq/article/the-tboli-profiles-transition.
115. Joan Carling, ed., *Indigenous Peoples and the Local Government: Building Good Governance in the Philippines* (Baguio City: Cordillera Peoples' Alliance and International Work Group for Indigenous Affairs, 2004), 28.
116. El-Solh and Mabro, *Muslim Women's Choices*, 6, 20.
117. Saba Mahmood, "The Subject of Freedom," in *Politics of Piety: The Islamic Revival and the Feminist Subject* (Princeton, NJ: Princeton University Press, 2005), 6–7.
118. Lila Abu-Lughod, "The Romance of Resistance: Tracing Transformations of Power through Bedouin Women," *American Ethnologist* 17, no. 1 (1990): 47.
119. Lila Abu-Lughod, "Do Muslim Women (Still) Need Saving?" in *Do Muslim Women Need Saving?* (Cambridge, MA: Harvard University Press, 2013), 47.
120. Mahmood, "Subject of Freedom," 6–7.
121. Mahmood, "Subject of Freedom," 6–7.
122. Nono, *Mendung Sabal: Tudbulul Lunay Mogul*, 21.
123. Myrna Pula, personal communication, 2012, 2013, 2015.
124. Myrna Pula in Nono, *Mendung Sabal: Tudbulul Lunay Mogul*, 21.
125. Koskoff, "Gender, Power, and Music."
126. Mahmood, "Subject of Freedom," 20.
127. Manduhai Buyandelger, "Ironies of Gender Neutrality," in *Tragic Spirits: Shamanism, Memory, and Gender in Contemporary Mongolia* (Chicago: University of Chicago Press, 2013), 171.
128. Chandra Talpade Mohanty, "Under Western Eyes: Feminist Scholarship and Colonial Discourses," in *Feminism without Borders: Decolonizing Theory, Practicing Solidarity*, 17–42 (Durham, NC: Duke University Press, 2003), 19.
129. Audre Lorde, "An Open Letter to Mary Daly," in *This Bridge Called My Back: Writings by Radical Women of Color*, ed. Cherrie Moraga and Gloria Anzaldúa (New York: Kitchen Table, 1981), 90–93.

130. Abu-Lughod, "Do Muslim Women (Still) Need Saving?," 40.
131. Abu-Lughod, "Do Muslim Women (Still) Need Saving?," 40.
132. Nono, *Shared Voice*, 43. By "Grace," Mendung was referring to the author.
133. Stephanie Mitchem, "Black Women: Race, Gender and Class," in *Introducing Womanist Theology* (Maryknoll, NY: Orbis, 2002), 4.
134. Devon Abbott Mihesuah, "Feminists, Tribalists or Activists," in *Indigenous American Women: Decolonization, Empowerment, Activism* (Lincoln: University of Nebraska Press, 2003), 160.
135. Mahmood, "Subject of Freedom," 13.
136. Judith Butler, *Gender Trouble: Feminism and the Subversion of Identity*, 2nd ed. (New York: Routledge, 1999), 14–15.
137. Leila Ahmed, conclusion to *Women and Gender in Islam: Historical Roots of a Modern Debate* (New Haven, CT: Yale University Press, 1992), 238.
138. This song about Lemlunay was composed by Mendung Sabal and Myrna Pula.
139. Plasencia, "Customs of the Tagalogs," 7:194; Alcina, *History of the Bisayan Islands*; Boxer codex; Brewer, "Baylan, Asog."
140. Peletz, "Transgenderism and Gender Pluralism," 317, 324.
141. Brewer, *Shamanism, Catholicism and Gender Relations*, 127.
142. Catherine Gueguen, "Sacredness, Death and Landscapes among the Blaan (Mindanao): A Cultural Geography Study," *Philippine Quarterly of Culture and Society* 38, no. 1 (2010): 37–54.
143. Gueguen, "Sacredness, Death and Landscapes," 39–40.
144. Gueguen, "Sacredness, Death and Landscapes," 43, 45.
145. Gueguen, "Sacredness, Death and Landscapes," 39–40.
146. Yadu Karu, "Sitio Atmurok and Their Practice of Customary Law," *Yadu Karu's Blog*, November 14, 2014, https://www.yadukaru.com/2014/11/sitio-atmurok-and-their-practice-of.html.
147. Gueguen, "Sacredness, Death and Landscapes," 37.
148. Gueguen, "Sacredness, Death and Landscapes," 46.
149. Edwin Espejo, "Philippines: Tribal Elder and Son Slain in Bloody Mining Dispute," *Piplinks*, September 5, 2013, http://www.piplinks.org/philippines:-tribal-elder-and-son-slain-bloody-mining-dispute.html; Espejo, "Soldier, Cafgu Man Slain as Tribal Tension Heats Up," *Rappler*, September 13, 2013, https://www.rappler.com/nation/38831-soldier-cafgu-tribal-tension-davao-del-sur.
150. This malem in the Blaan language was sung by Gunintang Freay on July 26, 2019, in Sitio Samlang, Barangay Blaan, Malungon municipality, province of Sarangani. The Blaan transcriptions and Visayan translations were provided by Elia Capeon and the English translation is by Grace Nono.
151. Jose Mencio Molintas, "The Philippine Indigenous Peoples' Struggle for Land and Life: Challenging Legal Texts," *Arizona Journal of International & Comparative Law* 21, no. 1 (2004): 269–306.
152. David Valentine, "'I Went to Bed with My Own Kind Once': The Erasure of Desire in the Name of Identity, *Language and Communication* 23 (2003): 124.
153. Susan Stryker and Aren Z. Aizura. "Introduction: Transgender Studies 2.0," in *The Transgender Studies Reader 2*, ed. Susan Stryker and Aren Z. Aizura (New York: Routledge, 2013), 8.
154. Stryker and Aizura. "Introduction," 8; Valentine, "I Went to Bed with My Own Kind Once," 135.
155. Stryker and Aizura. "Introduction," 8.
156. Stryker and Aizura. "Introduction," 8.
157. Valentine, "'I Went to Bed with My Own Kind Once," 126–7.

158. Valentine, "'I Went to Bed with My Own Kind Once,'" 124.
159. Smith, "Queer Theory and Native Studies," 45.
160. Smith, "Queer Theory and Native Studies," 44–5.
161. Gayle Solomon, "Boys of the Lex: Transgender and Social Construction," in *Assuming a Body: Transgender and Rhetorics of Materiality* (New York: Columbia University Press, 2010), 83; "Definitions Related to Sexual Orientation and Gender Diversity in APA Documents," American Psychological Association, https://www.apa.org/pi/lgbt/resources/sexuality-definitions.pdf.
162. Manalansan, "Speaking in Transit," 47.
163. Beatriz Preciado, "Pharmaco-pornographic Politics: Towards a New Gender Ecology," *parallax* 14, no. 1 (2008): 112. If Preciado asserts technology's ability to construct bodies and subjectivities, this study asserts nonhuman spirits' ability to do the same.
164. Butler, *Gender Trouble*, 13–15.
165. Butler, *Bodies that Matter*, xiv.
166. Mahmood, "Subject of Freedom," 29.
167. Mahmood, "Subject of Freedom," 23.

3. SONG TRAVELS

1. Mamerto "Lagitan" Tindongan, February 22, 2016.
2. These Lawet (baki) chants were performed by Lagitan on February 22, 2016, in New Haven, Connecticut. All Ifugao transcriptions and English translations were provided by Lagitan himself. He and Allen and Aleta Cayong-Abayao, the ritual hosts, tried unsuccessfully to find a recording of these oral performances. Lagitan may have also requested that the ritual not be filmed. This ethnography is a reconstruction of the event, verified for its relative accuracy by Lagitan, Allen, and Aleta.
3. This act of prevention is part of every baki but the liblibayan may also be called to cure stomach pains as a ritual in itself (Lagitan Tindongan, 2015).
4. Tuwali Ifugao Dictionary, "Lagud," accessed January 16, 2021, https://tuwali-ifugao.webonary.org/?s=lagud&search=Search&key=&tax=1&match_whole_words=1&displayAdvancedSearch=0.
5. Thomas Csordas, "Modalities of Transnational Transcendence," *Anthropological Theory* 7 (2007): 260.
6. Antoinette Burton, "Introduction: Traveling Criticism? On the Dynamic Histories of Indigenous Modernity," *Cultural and Social History* 9, no. 4 (2012): 491–6; Wood, "Aboriginal/Indigenous Citizenship," 371–8; Akhil Gupta and James Ferguson, "Beyond 'Culture': Space, Identity, and the Politics of Difference," *Cultural Anthropology* 7, no. 1 (1992): 7; Strobel, introduction, 3, 27–9.
7. The following papers were presented at the Society for Ethnomusicology Conference 2013, Indianapolis, Indiana, November 14–17, 2013: Heidi Aklaseaq Senungetuk, "*Qanukiak Ililuta*: How Shall We Proceed?"; Susan Taffe Reed, "Innovating Tradition: The Spiritual Significance of Powwows in Appalachian Pennsylvania"; Dawn Avery, "Modern/Traditional: What's the Difference? Indigenous Composition, Performance and Methodology."
8. Inderpal Grewal and Caren Kaplan, "Global Identities: Theorizing Transnational Studies of Sexuality," *GLQ: A Journal of Lesbian and Gay Studies* 7, no. 4 (2001): 663–79.
9. Deena Rymhs, "A Different Cosmopolitanism: Indigeneity and Translocality," *Canadian Literature/Littérature Canadienne* 204 (2010): 123, citing Amanda Anderson, "Cosmopolitanism, Universalism, and the Divided Legacies of Modernity," in *Cosmopolitics: Thinking and Feeling Beyond the Nation*, ed. Bruce Robbins and Pheng Cheah (Minneapolis: University of Minnesota Press, 1998), 267.

10. Steven Feld and Keith H. Basso, introduction to *Senses of Place*, ed. Steven Feld and Keith H. Basso (Santa Fe, NM: School of American Research Press, 1996), 4.

11. Arjun Appadurai, "The Production of Locality," in *Modernity at Large: Cultural Dimensions of Globalization* (Minneapolis: University of Minnesota Press, 1996), 179; Aihwa Ong, introduction to *Flexible Citizenship: The Cultural Logics of Transnationality* (Durham, NC: Duke University Press, 1999), 1–26.

12. Provincial Planning and Development Coordinator, *Ifugao Provincial Profile 2000–2010*; Conklin, Lupaih, and Pinther, *Ethnographic Atlas of Ifugao*, 1.

13. William Henry Scott, *The Discovery of the Igorots: Spanish Contacts with the Pagans of Northern Luzon* (Quezon City: New Day, 1974).

14. Scott, *Discovery of the Igorots*.

15. *Ifugao Provincial Profile 2000–2010*; Conklin, Lupaih, and Pinther, *Ethnographic Atlas of Ifugao*, 1.

16. Scott, *Discovery of the Igorots*. The word "Igorot" is derived from the archaic Tagalog word for "mountain people" (formed from the prefix). From the Spanish colonial era to the present, the term has come to collectively refer to the ethnolinguistic groups inhabiting the mountain regions of Northern Luzon that now covers the six provinces of Abra, Apayao, Benguet, Kalinga, Ifugao, Mountain Province, and the city of Baguio, all of which comprise the Cordillera Administrative Region.

17. Fr. Francisco Balacuit and Fr. Vargas Palingping, "Lagawe Catholic Mission, in *Fidelitas: Ten Years Journey, A Souvenir Book on the 10th year anniversary of the Vicariate of Bontoc–Lagawe*, (August 5, 2002), 44.

18. *Ifugao Provincial Profile 2000–2010*.

19. Balacuit and Palingping, "Lagawe Catholic Mission," 44.

20. Stuart Creighton Miller, "Armageddon, 1900," in *Benevolent Assimilation: The American Conquest of the Philippines, 1899–1903* (New Haven, CT: Yale University Press, 1982), 134.

21. Nicholas Roosevelt, *The Philippines: A Treasure and a Problem* (New York: J. H. Sears, 1926).

22. Epifanio San Juan Jr., "U.S. Genocide in the Philippines," The E. San Juan, Jr. Archive, August 31, 2006, http://rizalarchive.blogspot.com/2006/08/us-genocide-in-philippines.html.

23. Sylvester A. Johnson, introduction to *African American Religions, 1500–2000* (Cambridge: Cambridge University Press, 2015), 2.

24. *Ifugao Provincial Profile 2000–2010*.

25. Patricio Guyguyon, "The Story of our BECs in the Vicariate of Bontoc–Lagawe," in *Fidelitas: Ten Years Journey, A Souvenir Book on the 10th year anniversary of the Vicariate of Bontoc–Lagawe*, (August 5, 2002), 4.

26. Balacuit and Palingping, "Lagawe Catholic Mission," 45–6; Guyguyon, "Lamut Catholic Mission," 4.

27. Balacuit and Palingping, "Lagawe Catholic Mission," 46.

28. Pastor Herman Dinumla, personal information, June 2013.

29. Pastor Evangeline Ballangi, personal information, June 2013.

30. Rory Carroll, "Pope Says Sorry for Sins of Church: Sweeping Apology for Attacks on Jews, Women and Minorities, Defies Theologians' Warnings," *The Guardian*, March 13, 2000, https://www.theguardian.com/world/2000/mar/13/catholicism.religion; "Pope John Paul II Offers Aborigines an Apology," *Albawaba News*, November 22, 2001, https://www.albawaba.com/news/pope-john-paul-ii-offers-aborigines-apology; Cass Madden, "Pope Francis Apologizes to Indigenous Peoples for the 'Grave Sins' of the Church during Colonial Era; Yet Doctrine of Discovery Still Stands," *Cultural Survival*, July 25, 2018, https://www.culturalsurvival.org/news/pope-francis-apologizes-indigenous-peoples-grave-sins-church-during-colonial-era-yet-doctrine.

31. Fr. Patricio Guyguyon, "The Story of our BECs in the Vicariate of Bontoc–Lagawe," 6, 7, 8; Fr. Joe Tagupa, SVD, "Banaue Catholic Mission," in *Fidelitas: Ten Years Journey, A Souvenir Book on the 10th year anniversary of the Vicariate of Bontoc–Lagawe*, (August 5, 2002), 52, 53; Ambrocio Dulnuan, personal communication, June 2013.

32. Conklin, Lupaih, and Pinther, *Ethnographic Atlas of Ifugao*, 1; Leah Abayao, "Cultural Resilience and Sustainable Innovation Systems of the Ifugaos in Northern Philippines," paper presented at the International Conference on Innovations and Sustainability Transitions in Asia, University of Malaya, Kuala Lumpur, January 9–11, 2011. See also the Ifugao Provincial Profile 2000–2010.

33. Lambrecht, *Mayawyaw Ritual*; Abayao, "Cultural Resilience."

34. Abayao, "Cultural Resilience."

35. Dulawan, "Ifugao Baki"; Conklin, Lupaih, and Pinther, *Ethnographic Atlas of Ifugao*, 12, 13.

36. This development came about through the cooperation of Ifugao leaders, UNESCO, the National Commission for Culture and Arts, the National Museum, and the National Commission on Tribal Rituals and Practices.

37. See Adam C. Castonguay, Benjamin Burkhard, Felix Müller, Finbarr G. Horgan, and Josef Settele, "Resilience and Adaptability of Rice Terrace Social-Ecological Systems: A Case Study of a Local Community's Perception in Banaue, Philippines, *Ecology and Society* 21, no. 2 (2016): 15; Carl Milos Bulilan, "Experiencing Cultural Heritage and Indigenous Tourism in Banaue," *Philippine Quarterly of Culture and Society* 35 (2007): 100–28. The Banaue rice terraces were in the List of World Heritage in Danger from 2001 to 2011. They have been declared out of danger since 2012.

38. Maria V. Staniukovich, "Factors Affecting Stability/Variability of the Ifugao Hudhud," paper presented at the Peter the Great Museum of Anthropology and Ethnography, St. Petersburg, Russia, 2006.

39. Staniukovich, "Factors Affecting Stability."

40. Abayao, "Cultural Resilience."

41. Abayao, "Cultural Resilience"; Staniukovich, "Factors Affecting Stability"; Roger Blench, *Cultural Bureaucracy and the Manufacture of Ifugao Oral Literature* (Cambridge: Kay Williamson Educational Foundation, 2010).

42. Ifugao Provincial Profile 2000–2010.

43. Francisco, a review of *Ifugao Bibliography*, 1002–1003.

44. Barton, *Religion of the Ifugaos*, 9, 11, 14, 18, 23, 24.

45. Barton, *Religion of the Ifugaos*, 9, 11, 14, 18, 23, 24.

46. Barton, *Religion of the Ifugaos*, 15.

47. Barton, *Religion of the Ifugaos*, 203.

48. Laurel Kendall, *Shamans, Nostalgias, and the IMF: South Korean Popular Religion in Motion* (Honolulu: University of Hawai'i Press, 2009), 29–31.

49. Tisa Wenger, *We Have a Religion: The 1920s Pueblo Indian Dance Controversy and American Religious Freedom* (Chapel Hill: University of North Carolina Press, 2009), 74–5.

50. Conklin, Lupaih, and Pinther, *Ethnographic Atlas of Ifugao*, 12.

51. Lourdes S. Dulawan, "The Ifugaos," *UNITAS* 40, no. 1 (1967): 4, 7.

52. The Ohag is performed within the Chinupchup baki, under the general heading of the Honga (Lagitan Tindongan).

53. The baki performed to register an unborn child to the Ifugao spirit world is called Gutud (Lagitan Tindongan).

54. Paul Alexander Kramer, "Blood Compacts: Spanish Colonialism and the Invention of the Filipino," in *The Blood of Government: Race, Empire, the United States, and the Philippines* (Chapel Hill: University of North Carolina Press, 2006), 36–7.

55. Kramer, "Blood Compacts," 36–7.
56. Kramer, "Blood Compacts," 36–7.
57. Carlos P. Romulo, *Mother America* (Garden City, NY: Doubleday, Doran, 1943), 59.
58. The Peace Corps program run by the United States has represented another transnational presence in Ifugao. See "About." Peace Corps Philippines, "About," accessed January 16, 2021, https://www.peacecorps.gov/philippines/about/#:~:text=In%20October%20 1961%2C%20the%20first,have%20served%20in%20the%20Philippines.&text=Peace%20 Corps%20Response%20Volunteers%20also%20serve%20in%20the%20Philippines.
59. Besides the United States, a number of Ifugao have immigrated to Australia, New Zealand, Japan, Canada, France, England, Italy, Saudi Arabia, Qatar, Iraq, and Israel (Lagitan Tindongan).
60. Mahmood, "Subject of Freedom," 6–7.
61. William Lytle Schurz, "Mexico, Peru, and the Manila Galleon," *Hispanic American Historical Review* 1, no. 4 (1918): 389–402.
62. Eloisa Gomez Borah, "Chronology of Filipinos in America Pre-1898," 1997–2004, https://filipinostudies.files.wordpress.com/2012/01/filamchronology.pdf; Floro Mercene, *Manila Men in the New World: Filipino Migration to Mexico and the Americas from the Sixteenth Century* (Quezon City: University of the Philippines Press, 2007); Carl Nolte, "400th Anniversary of Spanish Shipwreck: Rough First Landing in Bay Area," *SF-Gate*, November 14, 1995, https://www.sfgate.com/news/article/400th-Anniversary-Of -Spanish-Shipwreck-Rough-3019121.php; Laura Westbrook, "Mabuhay Pilipino! (Long Life!): Filipino Culture in Southeast Louisiana," Folklife in Louisiana: Louisiana's Living Traditions, 2008, http://www.louisianafolklife.org/LT/Articles_Essays/pilipino1.html.
63. Noel Teodoro, "Pensionados and Workers: The Filipinos in the United States, 1903–1956," *Asian and Pacific Migration Journal* 8, no. 1–2 (1999): 157–78.
64. Jose Fermin, *1904 World's Fair: The Filipino Experience* (Honolulu: University of Hawai'i Press, 2006); Greg Allen, "'Living Exhibits' at 1904 World's Fair Revisited: Igorot Natives Recall Controversial Display of Their Ancestors," *National Public Radio*, May 31, 2004, http://www.npr.org/templates/story/story.php?storyId=1909651.
65. Paul Kramer, "Making Concessions: Race and Empire Revisited at the Philippine Exposition, St. Louis, 1901–1905," *Radical History Review* 73 (1999): 75–114; Benito M. Vergara, *Displaying Filipinos: Photography and Colonialism in Early 20th Century Philippines* (Quezon City: University of the Philippines Press, 1995).
66. Jack Masson and Donald Guimary, "Asian Labor Contractors in the Alaskan Canned Salmon Industry, 1880–1937," *Labor History* 22, no. 3 (1981): 377–97; Belinda Aquino, "The Filipino Century in Hawaii: Out of the Crucible," *Filipino Centennial Souvenir Program* (Honolulu: Filipino Centennial Celebration Commission, December 10, 2006).
67. Leo Sicat, "I Sacrificed My Five-Year College Education to Become a Steward," in Yen Le Espiritu, *Filipino American Lives* (Philadelphia, PA: Temple University Press, 1995), 105–16.
68. Paul Ong and Tania Azores, "The Migration and Incorporation of Filipino Nurses," in *The New Asian Immigration in Los Angeles and Global Restructuring*, ed. Paul Ong, Edna Bonacich, and Lucie Cheng (Philadelphia, PA: Temple University Press, 1994), 164; Catherine Ceniza Choy, introduction to *Empire of Care: Nursing and Migration in Filipino-American History* (Durham, NC: Duke University Press, 2003), 1.
69. "New Census Data Shows More Than Four Million Filipinos in the US," *Asian Journal Press*, September 15, 2018, https://www.asianjournal.com/usa/dateline-usa/new -census-data-shows-more-than-four-million-filipinos-in-the-us/.
70. Luis H. Francia, *A History of the Philippines: From Indios Bravos to Filipinos* (New York: Overlook, 2010), 170–71.

71. Tom Coy and Don Cox, personal communication, October 12, 2013.

72. Robert L. Daniel, *Athens, Ohio: The Village Years* (Athens: Ohio University Press, 1997), 1–9.

73. Daniel, *Athens, Ohio*, 11.

74. Daniel, *Athens, Ohio*, 11.

75. Daniel, *Athens, Ohio*, 11, 13, 15, 16.

76. Daniel, *Athens, Ohio*, 20–21.

77. Cynthia Tindongan, personal communication, August 13, 2013.

78. Csordas, "Modalities of Transnational Transcendence," 263, citing Eric Wolf, *Europe and the People without History* (Berkeley: University of California Press, 1982).

79. Tom Coy, personal communication, October 12, 2013.

80. Marete Demant Jakobsen, *Shamanism: Traditional and Contemporary Approaches to the Master of Spirits and Healing* (New York: Berghahn, 1999), 157–9, 162; Foundation for Shamanic Studies, "Michael Harner, Founder of The Foundation for Shamanic Studies," https://shamanism.org/fssinfo/index.html.

81. These three Native North American Indian spirits, according to Ramona, were tasked with putting Lagitan in touch with his child self, to be a medicine man and a peacemaker.

82. Crow Swimsaway, and Bekki Shining Bearheart, personal communication, August 2013. See also Crow Swimsaway, introduction to *Circle of Ancestors* (Milverton, UK: Capall Bann, 2009), 16; "European and Eur-Asian Shamanism: an Exploration of our Shamanic Roots," *Out of the Dark*, July 24, 2004, http://www.outofthedark.com/Shamanism/.

83. Sheryl Kay, "The Remedy? A Healing Touch," *Tampa Bay Times*, April 28, 2006, https://www.tampabay.com/archive/2006/04/28/the-remedy-a-healing-touch/.

84. Patricia Minor, personal communication, August 14, 2013.

85. Lagitan graduated valedictorian in elementary school and salutatorian in high school. He held the class presidency from elementary through third-year high school, receiving a leadership award and most medals in his high school graduating class. He further served as scout leader who commanded the higher grades, and as a Banaue youth leader and ROTC (Reserve Officers' Training Corps) Special Force member (Lagitan Tindongan).

86. Suzanne Cusick, personal communication, January 28, 2014.

87. Alcida Ramos, "The Hyperreal Indian," *Critique of Anthropology* 14, no. 2 (1994): 163.

88. Michel Winkelman, "Shamanisms and Survival," *Cultural Survival Quarterly Magazine*, June 2003, https://www.culturalsurvival.org/publications/cultural-survival-quarterly/shamanisms-and-survival.

89. Atkinson, "Shamanisms Today," 309–13; Taussig, "Folk Healing," 221.

90. Tomoko Masuzawa, introduction to *The Invention of World Religions: Or, How European Universalism Was Preserved in the Language of Pluralism* (Chicago: University of Chicago Press, 2005), 4.

91. Johnson, introduction, 2.

92. This was first cited in Grace Nono, "Audible Travels: Oral/Aural Traditional Performances and the Transnational Spread of a Philippine Indigenous Religion," in *Back from the Crocodile's Belly: Philippine Babaylan Studies and the Struggle for Indigenous Memory*, edited by S. Lily Mendoza and Leny Mendoza Strobel (California: Center for Babaylan Studies, 2013), 32.

93. Csordas, "Modalities of Transnational Transcendence," 260.

94. A version of this ethnography was published in the chapter by Nono, "Audible Travels," 35–7.

95. This was a departure from the older way (up to the 1990s) of having the body of the departed don native Ifugao clothing, sit, tied to a chair made of the betel nut trunk,

then placed under an Ifugao house, while continuously being smoked to delay the process of decomposition. One reason for the change was sanitation (Ambrocio Dulnuan, personal communication, February 1, 2013).

96. Tuwali Ifugao Dictionary, "Liwliwa," accessed January 16, 2021, https://www.webonary.org/tuwali-ifugao?s=liwliwa&search=Search&key=&tax=-1&match_whole_words=1&displayAdvancedSearchName=0.

97. Ambrocio Dulnuan, February 1, 2013.

98. Lagitan Tindongan, February 1, 2013.

99. I was also told that even if the family had produced bayah, Huwan, the main celebrant, would not be able to partake of it because his doctor had prohibited him from drinking alcohol.

100. This event took place on August 13, 2013, in Athens, Ohio.

101. This event took place on August 17, 2013, in Logan, Ohio.

102. Whenever Buwaya called on the Halupe outside of the baki or without offerings whenever he worked on recordings, he made it a point to perform the baki with offerings afterward at his home (Lagitan Tindongan).

103. This event took place on June 15, 1913, in Philadelphia, Pennsylvania.

104. Kimberly Boyer, personal communication, August 18, 2013.

105. Kimberly Boyer, personal communication, August 18, 2013.

106. Romulo, *Mother America*, 59.

107. Eliseo Art Silva, personal communication, June 24, 2013.

108. Aida Natividad Rivera, personal communication, July 29, 2013.

109. This event took place on August 18, 2013, in Athens, Ohio.

110. The spirits of the four directions are the spirit of the South: a snake representing the earth and transformation; the spirit of the West: a jaguar or lynx representing water, strength, and flexibility; the spirit of the North: a hummingbird representing air, knowledge, and wisdom; and the spirit of the East: an eagle or condor representing fire and vision (Lagitan Tindongan).

111. These mumbaki ancestors are Bumanghat, Pachinngon, Paiyaya, Mainah, Bistol, Ottengan, and Buwaya (Lagitan Tindongan).

112. This event took place on October 27, 2013, in Los Angeles, California.

113. Janet Scott, personal communication, November 6, 2013.

114. This event took place on October 26, 2013, in Queens, New York.

115. Peter Cohen, "The Orisha Atlantic: Historicizing the Roots of a Global Religion," in *Modalities of Transnational Transcendence: Essays on Religion and Globalization*, ed. Thomas Csordas (Berkeley: University of California Press, 2009), 214.

116. For sacred affect evoked even by recordings, see Kapchan, "Promise of Sonic Translation," 480.

117. Hospicio Dulnuan, personal communication, December 1, 2012; Nono, "Audible Travels," 40.

118. Csordas, "Modalities of Transnational Transcendence," 260–264.

119. Csordas, "Modalities of Transnational Transcendence," 260–264.

120. Jakobsen, *Shamanism*, 162.

121. Jakobsen, *Shamanism*, 162.

122. Senungetuk, "*Qanukiak Ililuta*"; Reed, "Innovating Tradition"; Avery, "Modern/Traditional."

123. Smith, "Queer Theory and Native Studies," 52.

124. Smith, "Queer Theory and Native Studies," 54–55, citing Gayatri Gopinath, *Impossible Desires: Queer Diasporas and South Asian Public Cultures* (Durham, NC: Duke University Press, 2005), 14, 92.

125. Barton, *Religion of the Ifugaos*, 11, 14, 18.

126. Anne McClintock, *Imperial Leather: Race, Gender and Sexuality in the Imperial Contest* (London: Routledge, 1995), 6–7.
127. Jakobsen, *Shamanism*, 179.
128. Brewer, "Baylan, Asog."
129. Jakobsen, *Shamanism*, 164.
130. Emily Thompson, introduction to *The Soundscape of Modernity: Architectural Acoustics and the Culture of Listening in America, 1900–1933* (Cambridge, MA: MIT Press, 2004), 3–4.
131. Suzanne Cusick, personal communication, January 28, 2014.
132. Jakobsen, *Shamanism*, 185.
133. Connor, "What I Say, Goes," 13.
134. Jakobsen, *Shamanism*, 222.
135. Webb Keane, "Religion's Reach," in *Christian Moderns: Freedom and Fetish in the Mission Encounter* (Berkeley and Los Angeles, CA: University of California Press, 2007), 49.
136. Daughtry, "Afterword," 250.
137. This means that deities like the Manahaut are not to be excised from the Ifugao pantheon and social fabric. The Manahaut is not only a deity for war and sorcery but also for one's protection from enemies, a positive function (Lagitan Tindongan).
138. Jakobsen, *Shamanism*, 183, 186, 187.
139. Csordas, "Modalities of Transnational Transcendence," 261, 265.

Glossary

English translations only contain percentages of the full indigenous meanings.
—Agusan-Manobo tribal leader Bae Manyaguyad Luciana Rico

abyan: Visayan: spirit helper, guardian, companion

alim: Ifugao: baki chants

almoos: Blaan: ritual specialist

ambaling lagi: Blaan: female-to-male transgender person

ambaling libun: Blaan: male-to-female transgender person

anislag: Agusan-Manobo: flueggea flexuosa wood

asog: Visayan (archaic): effeminate male ritual specialists

atlatl: Nahualt: spear thrower

Ayag: Ifugao: baki to retrieve lost souls

Babaiyon: Agusan-Manobo: woman leader; also babaihon

Bagor: Ifugao: deities, also maknongan

Baki: Ifugao: ritual

Baltung: Ifugao: call and response chant performed during the baki Ulpi performed after rice planting; baltung is also performed with a different theme during the baki Chinupchup

Bato: Blaan: penis, male genitals

Bayah: Ifugao: rice-wine

Baylan: Agusan-Manobo ritual specialist, one who has a diwata spirit as helper, guardian, companion

Bayoc: Zambal (archaic): effeminate male ritual specialist (Domingo Perez, 1680)

Bayog: Tagalog, Zambal (archaic): effeminate male ritual specialist (Manila Manuscript, 1590; Bolinao Manuscript, 1685)

Bayoguin: Tagalog (archaic): effeminate male (Juan de Placensia, 1589)

beatas: Tagalog: consecrated women, helpers of male priests

benahung: T'boli: an illness or condition caused by the yearnings of the soul

beon: Agusan-Manobo: divinatory method that makes use of a peso coin through which the spirit responds to human questions; also bayaon

betad: T'boli: fine, reparation

boong: Ifugao: beads

boyos: T'boli: spirits with both feminine and masculine genders

buad: Ifugao: chant during the baki

capitanos: Spanish: captains

chin-nadne-nadne: Ifugao: a long, long time ago

Chinupchup: Ifugao: a kind of baki under the general heading of Honga

Choyat: Ifugao: chant during the altar preparation

Chuyu: Ifugao: general term for plate; pamahan is the technical term for the chuyu used to hold the rice wine

d'sol be tonok: T'boli: a healing ritual for a person whose illness is acute

datu: Agusan-Manobo: political leader, chief

demsu: T'boli: offerings to spirits

demsu fankiton: Blaan: water ritual

diwatahan: Agusan-Manobo: person with a spirit helper, guardian, companion; also baylan

diwatas: Agusan-Manobo: general term for spirits, or name of the spirit that enters a baylan, distinguished from other spirits

duwaya: Visayan: the practice of a man taking on several wives; the T'boli term is "demwey"

encomenderos: Spanish: holders of land grants given by the Spanish crown, without the consent of Native peoples

encomienda: Spanish: Native lands granted by the Spanish crown to colonists or adventurers for purposes of tribute and evangelization, without the consent of Native peoples

faglong: Blaan: two-string lute

fais: Blaan: long dagger

gangha: Ifugao: gongs

garu: Blaan: knowledge (spiritual)

gebela: T'boli: fair

gonob: Ifugao: food invocation

gopah: Ifugao: oral chants to deliver blessings

gotad: Ifugao: feast

gudgod: Agusan-Manobo: spirit song that traces the cause and origin of a person's illness, and discovers answers and solutions to questions and problems

hakyad: Agusan-Manobo: a ritual specialist's offering of cooked food to her/his spirit helpers

hapet: Ifugao: voice

hapo: Ifugao: baki invocations

hegelong: T'boli: two-string lute

henghong: Agusan-Manobo: the spirit helper's release from the ritual specialist's body

hewot: T'boli: a singer's introductory call

hilot: Visayan, Tagalog: healing modality through blood vessel, nerve, and musculoskeletal manipulation

hinamar: Ifugao: cooked rice

hongan di page: Ifugao: calendric agricultural rites linked to rice production and consumption

hongan di tagu: Ifugao: rituals for humans associated with health, property, and changes in family and individual status, including death

hungol: T'boli: listening

ihapud: Ifugao: healing rite for someone who was afflicted by the Puchung deity

iklug: Ifugao: eggs

kabobonganan: Agusan-Manobo: mountains

kadangyan: Ifugao: wealthy

kaguluhan: Tagalog: turmoil, unrest

kajo-kajo/*bagnot-bagnot:* Agusan-Manobo: tree and plant medicines

kaliga: Banwaon and Higaonon: a kind of ritual

kanya-kanya: Tagalog: to each his/her own

kawayan buyo: Agusan-Manobo: Schizostachyum lumampao, a species of bamboo

kem libun: T'boli: women, plural for woman

kem logi: T'boli: men, plural for man

kie: Blaan: vagina, female genitals

kinaraan: Visayan: old-time ways

klintang: T'boli: small row of gongs

kolaimni: American (archaic): healing by connecting with the light

kumbing: T'boli: jaw's harp

kuntoon: Agusan-Manobo: now, modern

kuwahil: T'boli: manner of delivering the voice, regardless of the text or tune

kuwahil bot: T'boli: exacting, calculated, highly embellished vocal delivery

kuwahil klolo: T'boli: forceful vocal delivery denoting action

lagi: Blaan: male

laika: Quechua: earth keeper, shaman, medicine person, whose predecessors were persecuted by the Spanish colonizers and branded as witches and sorcerers

lebotu: T'boli: round

lembang: T'boli: large, broad, male, public

lemnek: T'boli: small, tiny, detailed

lemony: T'boli: soft

liblibayan: Ifugao: deities that oversee the wine and the water

libun: T'boli: woman

libun kemukum: T'boli: woman settler of conflicts

lihol: T'boli: voice

limpas buya: Agusan-Manobo: ritual to receive the spirit, to diagnose, to heal; also to fulfill the promise of offerings, that is, in exchange for healing

lingon: T'boli: song

lingon lembang: T'boli: epic song with numerous characters

lingon lemnek: T'boli: short song

lingon loos: T'boli: ritual song for healing

lingon nemo: T'boli: extemporaneous song

lingon Sebu: T'boli: Lake Sebu creation song

linnawa: Ifugao: ancestral spirits

liyah: Ifugao: initiation

logi: T'boli: man

ma'ma'uya: Ifugao: friendly

maayun: Ifugao: slow

magala: Ifugao: fast

magangoh: Ifugao: loud and authoritative

maghihilot: Visayan, Tagalog: healers through blood vessel, nerve, and musculoskeletal manipulation

magin: Blaan: spirit helper, also to magin

maknongan: Ifugao: deity, deities

malem: Blaan: song

malong: Maranao, Maguindanao: tubular cloth wrapper

mamuhatbuhat: Kinamiguin: ritual specialist

mananambe to kajo-kajo/*bagnot-bagnot*: Agusan-Manobo: herbalist

manunuyam Agusan-Manobo: embroiderer

marajow nug sambag tu utow: Agusan-Manobo: someone who gives good counsel, an adviser

maule: Ifugao: gentle or kind

mefeges: T'boli: determined, forceful

megel: T'boli: hard, strong

mo ninum: T'boli: wedding renewal feast and grand healing ceremony

moma: Ifugao: betel quids

mumbaki: Ifugao: ritual specialist

munhapud: Ifugao: diagnost

munpahiya: Ifugao: fearless, arrogant, politician-like

mungopah: Ifugao: chanter of the gopah

munpalukipid: Ifugao: meek

mun-ur-ur-ule: Ifugao: slow singing with prolonged breath

mun-uyad: Ifugao: bonesetter

nawotwot: Ifugao: poor

nungaru: Blaan: person who knows, spirited person

ognangon: Agusan-Manobo: someone who speaks

ohag: Ifugao: chant performed to summon the maknongan to the place of ritual

ongot: Ifugao: coconut shell cups

pa'o: Ifugao: spoon or divination ritual; the mamâo are the mostly women pâo performers

paghilwas: Visayan: articulation

palayah: Ifugao: chant to close the altar

paminog: Agusan-Manobo: listening

panawag-tawag: Agusan-Manobo: invocation of spirit, prayer

panumanan: Agusan-Manobo: ritual observance

paqo: Quechua: holy men and women, healers, mediums, priests, medicine specialists, wise people (shamans)

patakaran: Tagalog, Visayan: rules, regulations, policies

pig-aha dinpuli: Agusan-Manobo: being watched by spirit

pigyunaan: Agusan-Manobo: being entered into by spirit

pinacheng: Ifugao: spirits that inhabit mountains, rivers, trees, and other land and water forms

pinikpikan: Bontoc, Igorot: ritual chicken dish flavored with coagulated chicken blood, burned feathers and skin, and smoked, cured, aged meat

punamhan: Ifugao: wooden ritual box used to connect with the matungūlan group of deities

pun-ngorpan: Ifugao: invocation when an animal is being slaughtered

s'magi: T'boli: gongs

sajow: Agusan-Manobo: dance

sdeme: Blaan: sexual inter

sludoy: T'boli: zither

sogu: T'boli: embellishments

sugnod: Agusan-Manobo: ritual for the souls of the departed

talak k'mawang: T'boli: region between the eight layers of the sky and earth

talak mohin: T'boli: oceans, the place of salty waters

talak tonok: T'boli: earth

talo: Blaan: voice

tang: T'boli: ground (as opposed to figure), drone (as opposed to melody)

tanog: Agusan-Manobo: sound

tau d'mangaw: T'boli: diagnostician who uses finger-span measurements

tau demsu: T'boli: sacrificer

tau gena: T'boli: ancestor

tau k'na: T'boli: dreamer

tau kemukum: T'boli: traditional judge

tau la ton: T'boli: invisible persons

tau lemingon/temutul: T'boli: singer-storyteller

tau m'ton bu: T'boli: a person who sees, ritual specialist

tau mesif: T'boli: embroiderer

tau mewel: T'boli: weaver

tau mulung: T'boli: curer

tau munung: T'boli: spirit helper

tau t'fing: T'boli: the Creator's messengers

tau temool lemilet: T'boli: bead ornaments maker

tau ton: T'boli: visible persons

tawo: Visayan: person

teabobong: Agusan-Manobo: spirit that resides in the mountains and forests

tegbusaw: Agusan-Manobo: war spirits, fierce spirits

tenientes: Spanish: lieutenants

tinandasan: Agusan-Manobo: traditional house

tod-om: Agusan-Manobo: song

tor-ge: Ifugao: women's loin cloth

tua lagi: Blaan: old man

tutul kemo ke taum: T'boli: life story

tuyay: Agusan-Manobo: wood for the trusses of a traditional house

ukol: T'boli: short

uldin: Blaan: sacred law

umagad: Agusan-Manobo: soul, both of the dead and the living

usiba: Agusan-Manobo: play, entertainment

utom: T'boli: figure (as opposed to ground); melody (as opposed to drone)

wonoh Ifugao: men's loin cloth

uloh: Ifugao: blanket

yagong: Agusan-Manobo: voice

yagonganon: Agusan-Manobo: a person who can sing different genres of song

yunaan: Agusan-Manobo: mediumistic trance

Bibliography

ORAL SOURCES
Ballangi, Evangeline
Blagay, Tuning
Bowman, Jen
Boyer, Kimberly
Capeon, Elia Cansing
Capeon, Mining
Cavender, Andree
Coguit, Robilyn Canto, Robilyn
Cox, Don
Coy, Tom
Cusick, Suzanne
Dinumla, Herman
Dulnuan, Ambrocio
Dulnuan, Hospicio
Fikan, Biho
Flang, Mariafe
Freay, Gunintang
Gulae, Jolina "Bie"
Havana, Jose
Havana, Florencia
Jennings, Willie
Kasaw, Danilo
Manguwan, Milin
Minor, Patricia
Nettleship, Martin (Crow Swimsaway)
Potenciano, Lordina "Undin"
Pula, Myrna
Rico, Luciana
Rivera, Aida Natividad
Sabal, Flor
Sabal, Frankie
Sabal, Joanna
Sabal, Manolete
Sabal, Mendung
Sagan, Lucita
Savci, Evren
Scott, Janet
Silva, Eliseo Art
Tawan, Luming
Tawede, Aylo
Tindongan, Cynthia
Tindongan, Mamerto "Lagitan"
Tungay, Mina

BOOKS, ARTICLES, DISSERTATIONS, CONFERENCE PAPERS

Abayao, Leah. "Cultural Resilience and Sustainable Innovation Systems of the Ifugaos in Northern Philippines." Paper presented at the International Conference on Innovations and Sustainability Transitions in Asia, University of Malaya, Kuala Lumpur, January 9–11, 2011.

Abubakar, C., and G. E. P. Cheng. "Tausug." In *CCP Philippine Encyclopedia of Philippine Art*. Vol. 2, *Peoples of the Philippines, Kalinga to Yakan*, edited by Nicanor G. Tiongson, 370–93. Manila: Cultural Center of the Philippines, 1994.

Abubakar, Carmen. "Advent and Growth of Islam in the Philippines." In *Islam in Southeast Asia: Political, Social and Strategic Challenges for the 21st Century*, edited by K. S. Nathan and Mohammad Hashim Kamali, 45–63. Singapore: Institute of Southeast Asian Studies, 2005.

Abu-Lughod, Lila. *Do Muslim Women Need Saving?* Cambridge, MA: Harvard University Press, 2013.

———. "The Romance of Resistance: Tracing Transformations of Power through Bedouin Women." *American Ethnologist* 17, no. 1 (1990): 41–55.

———. "Writing against Culture." In *Recapturing Anthropology: Working in the Present*, edited by Richard G. Fox, 137–62. Santa Fe, NM: School of American Research Press, 1992.

———. *Writing Women's Worlds: Bedouin Stories*. Berkeley: University of California Press, 2008, 1993.

Aduarte, Diego. "History of the Dominican Province of the Holy Rosary." In *The Philippine Islands, 1493–1898*. Vol. 30, *1640*, edited by Emma Helen Blair and James Alexander Robertson, 115–321. Cleveland, OH: Arthur H. Clark, 1905.

Agoncillo, Teodoro A. *History of the Filipino People*. Quezon City: Garotech, 1990.

Aguilar, Delia. "The Social Construction of the Filipino Woman." *International Journal of Intercultural Relations* 13 (1989): 527–551.

Ahmed, Leila. Conclusion to *Women and Gender in Islam: Historical Roots of a Modern Debate*, 235-. New Haven, CT: Yale University Press, 1992.

Alaras, Consolacion R. "Women Spiritual Leaders/Priestesses in Contemporary Times: Bodies Reclaimed, Bodies Enshrined/Body Narratives, Metaphors, and Concepts in Philippine Indigenous Religion." In *Gender/Bodies/Religions*, edited by Sylvia Marcos, 181–91. Mexico City: ALER, 2001.

Alberts, Thomas Karl. "Shamanism." In *Shamanism, Discourse, Modernity*, 45–83. Farnham: Ashgate, 2015.

Alcina, Francisco Ignacio. *The Muñoz Text of Alcina's History of the Bisayan Islands (1668): Part 1, Book 3*. Translated by Paul S. Lietz. Chicago: Philippine Studies Program, Department of Anthropology, University of Chicago, 1960.

Anderson, Amanda. "Cosmopolitanism, Universalism, and the Divided Legacies of Modernity." In *Cosmopolitics: Thinking and Feeling Beyond the Nation*, edited by Bruce Robbins and Pheng Cheah, 265–289. Minneapolis: University of Minnesota Press, 1998.

Apffel-Marglin, Frédérique. "Smallpox in Two Systems of Knowledge." In *Rhythms of Life: Enacting the World with the Goddesses of Orissa*. Oxford: Oxford University Press, 2008.

Apostol, Virgil Mayor. *Way of the Ancient Healer: Sacred Teachings from the Philippine Ancestral Traditions*. Berkeley, CA: North Atlantic, 2010.

Appadurai, Arjun. "The Production of Locality." In *Modernity at Large: Cultural Dimensions of Globalization*, 178–99. Minneapolis: University of Minnesota Press, 1996.

Aquino, Belinda. "The Filipino Century in Hawaii: Out of the Crucible." *Filipino Centennial Souvenir Program*. Honolulu: Filipino Centennial Celebration Commission, December 10, 2006.

Arsenio, Baglyi, and Glenn Stallsmith. "Preserving Living Traditions in Live Performances: A Traditional Music and Dance Troupe of the Kalanguya of the Northern Philippines." Paper presented at the 2nd International Conference on Language Development, Language Revitalization, and Multilingual Education in Ethnolinguistic Communities, Bangkok, Thailand, 2008.

Atkinson, Jane Monnig. "Shamanisms Today." *Annual Review of Anthropology* 21 (1992): 307–30.

Austin, J. L. "Lecture 1." In *How to Do Things with Words*, 1–11. Cambridge, MA: Harvard University Press, 1962.

Avery, Dawn. "Modern/Traditional: What's the Difference? Indigenous Composition, Performance and Methodology." Paper presented at the Society for Ethnomusicology Conference 2013, Indianapolis, Indiana, November 14–17, 2013.

Bada, Teofila G. *A Voice from the Forest: Essays on the Culture and World View of the Manobo of the Agusan River Valley and the Diwata Mountain Range*. Translated and edited by Donna Schumacher and Ron Schumacher. Manila: Summer Institute of Linguistics International, 2011.

Balacuit, Francisco, and Vargas Palingping. "Lagawe Catholic Mission." In *Fidelitas: Ten Years Journey, A Souvenir Book on the 10th year anniversary of the Vicariate of Bontoc–Lagawe*, August 5, 2002.

Balanay, Raquel M., Jose M. Yorobe, Jr., Sheila G. Reyes, Adrilene Mae J. Castaños, Ordem K. Maglente, Jocelyn B. Panduyos, and Charry C. Cuenca. "Analyzing the Income Effects of Mining with Instrumental Variables for Poverty Reduction Implications in Caraga Region, Philippines." *Journal of International and Global Economic Studies* 7, no. 1 (2014): 20–31.

Barthes, Roland. "The Grain of the Voice." In *Image-Music-Text*, 179–89. New York: Hill and Wang, 1977.

Barton, Roy Franklin. *The Religion of the Ifugaos*. Menasha, WI: American Anthropological Association, 1946.

Basa, Charito. "Me, Us and Them: Migrant Women Defining Change." *Development* 49, no. 1 (2006): 120–23.

Battung, Rosario. "Kako and the Women Healers of Capatan." In *Centennial Crossings: Readings on Babaylan Feminism in the Philippines*, edited by Fe B. Mangahas and Jenny R. Llaguno, 93–103. Quezon City: C & E, 2006.

Bauzon, Leslie E., "Modern Millenarianism in the Philippines and the State: Focus on Negros, 1857–1927." Special issue, *Philippine Social Sciences Review* (April 1998): 24–54.

Becker, Judith. *Deep Listeners: Music, Emotion, and Trancing*. Bloomington: Indiana University Press, 2004.

Beltran, Benigno. "The End is Nigh: Militant Millenarianism and Evolutionary Eschatology in the Philippines." In *Old Cultures, Renewed Religions: The Search for Identity in a Changing World*, edited by Leonardo Mercado, 91–116. Manila: Logos, 2001.

Beltran, Myra. "The Dance Artist as Babaylan." In *Centennial Crossings: Readings on Babaylan Feminism in the Philippines*, edited by Fe B. Mangahas and Jenny R. Llaguno, 113–19. Quezon City: C & E, 2006.

Bendix, Regina. "Diverging Paths in the Scientific Search for Authenticity." *Journal of Folklore Research* 29, no. 2 (1992): 103–32.

Bergano, Diego. *Vocabulario de la Lengua Pampanga*. Manila: Imprenta de Ramirez y Giraudier, 1860.

Beyer, H. Otley, and Roy Franklin Burton. "An Ifugao Burial Ceremony." *Philippine Journal of Science* 6, no. 5 (1911): 227–52.

Biehl, João, and Peter Locke. "Introduction: Ethnographic Sensorium." In *Unfinished: The Anthropology of Becoming*, edited by João Biehl and Peter Locke, 1–40. Durham, NC: Duke University Press, 2017.

Blair, Emma Helen, and James Alexander Robertson, eds. *The Philippine Islands, 1493–1898*, 55 vols. Cleveland, OH: Arthur H. Clark, 1903–1909. [First five volumes were titled *The Philippine Islands, 1493–1803*.]

Blanc-Szanton, Cristina. "Collision of Cultures: Historical Reformulations of Gender in the Lowland Visayas, Philippines." In *Power and Difference: Gender in Island Southeast Asia*, edited by Jane Monnig Atkinson and Shelly Errington, 345–84. Stanford, CA: Stanford University Press, 1990.

Blench, Roger. *Cultural Bureaucracy and the Manufacture of Ifugao Oral Literature*. Cambridge: Kay Williamson Educational Foundation, 2010.

Bohlman, Philip V. "Musicology as a Political Act." *Journal of Musicology* 11, no. 4 (1993): 411–36.

Bohlman, Philip V. "Ontologies of Music." In *Rethinking Music*, edited by Nicholas Cook and Mark Everist, 17–34. Oxford: Oxford University Press, 1999.

Boxer codex. Manuscript, ca. 1590. LMC 2444, Lilly Library, Bloomington, Indiana.

Brewer, Carolyn. "Baylan, Asog, Transvestism, and Sodomy: Gender, Sexuality and the Sacred in Early Colonial Philippines." *Intersections: Gender, History and Culture in the Asian Context* 2 (1999). http://intersections.anu.edu.au/issue2/carolyn2.html.

Brewer, Carolyn. *Shamanism, Catholicism and Gender Relations in Colonial Philippines 1521–1685*. Aldershot: Ashgate, 2004.

Brown, Karen McCarthy. *Mama Lola: A Vodou Priestess in Brooklyn*. 2nd ed. Berkeley: University of California Press, 2001.

Buenconsejo, José S. *Songs and Gifts at the Frontier: Person and Exchange in the Agusan Manobo Possession Ritual, Philippines*. New York: Routledge, 2002.

Bulilan, Carl Milos. "Experiencing Cultural Heritage and Indigenous Tourism in Banaue." *Philippine Quarterly of Culture and Society* 35 (2007): 100–128.

Burton, Antoinette. "Introduction: Traveling Criticism? On the Dynamic Histories of Indigenous Modernity." *Cultural and Social History* 9, no. 4 (2012): 491–96.

Butler, Judith. *Bodies that Matter: On the Discursive Limits of "Sex."* New York: Routledge, 1999.

Butler, Judith. *Gender Trouble: Feminism and the Subversion of Identity*. 2nd ed. New York: Routledge, 1999.

Buyandelger, Manduhai. "Ironies of Gender Neutrality." In *Tragic Spirits: Shamanism, Memory, and Gender in Contemporary Mongolia*, 169–201. Chicago: University of Chicago Press, 2013.

Camagay, Maria Luisa T. "Ang Kababaihan sa Pambansang Kamalayan." *Philippine Social Science Review* 52, nos. 1–4 (1995): 1–14.

Carbo, Nick, and Aileen Tabios. Introduction to *Babaylan: An Anthology of Filipina and Filipina American Writers*, edited by Nick Carbo and Aileen Tabios, vii–xii. San Francisco, CA: Aunt Lute, 2000.

Carling, Joan, ed. *Indigenous Peoples and the Local Government: Building Good Governance in the Philippines*. Baguio City: Cordillera Peoples' Alliance and International Work Group for Indigenous Affairs, 2004.

Caronan, Faye. Introduction to *Legitimizing Empire: Filipino American and U.S. Puerto Rican Cultural Critique*, 1–20. Champaign: University of Illinois Press, 2015.

Casal, G. S., and D. Javier. "T'boli." In *CCP Encyclopedia of Philippine Art*. Vol. 2, *Peoples of the Philippines, Kalinga to Yakan*, edited by Nicanor G. Tiongson, 394–411. Manila: Cultural Center of the Philippines, 1994.

Castonguay, Adam C., Benjamin Burkhard, Felix Müller, Finbarr G. Horgan, and Josef Settele. "Resilience and Adaptability of Rice Terrace Social-Ecological Systems: A Case Study of a Local Community's Perception in Banaue, Philippines." *Ecology and Society* 21, no. 2 (2016): 1–14.

Castro, Christi-Anne. "Colonized by Rote: Music Education at the Outset of the U.S. Colonial Era in the Philippines." In *Philippine Modernities Music, Performing Arts, and Language, 1880 to 1941*, edited by José S. Buenconsejo, 111–133. Quezon City: University of the Philippines Press, 2017.

Cavarero, Adriana. *For More than One Voice: Toward a Philosophy of Vocal Expression*. Stanford, CA: Stanford University Press, 2005.

Cawed-Oteyza, Carmencita. "The Culture of the Bontoc Igorots." *Unitas* 38 (1965): 317–77.

Cheng, G. E. P. "Mansaka." In *CCP Encyclopedia of Philippine Art*. Vol. 2, *Peoples of the Philippines, Kalinga to Yakan*, edited by Nicanor G. Tiongson, 148–59. Manila: Cultural Center of the Philippines, 1994.

Chiener, Chou. "Experience and Fieldwork: A Native Researcher's View." *Ethnomusicology* 46, no. 3 (2002): 456–86.

Chirino, Pedro. *Relación de las Islas Filipinas y de lo que en ellas han trabajado los Padres de la Compañía de Jesús*. Translated by Ramon Echevarria. Manila: Historical Conservation Society, 1969. First published Rome: Estevan Paulino, 1604.

Choy, Catherine Ceniza. Introduction to *Empire of Care: Nursing and Migration in Filipino-American History*, 1–14. Durham, NC: Duke University Press, 2003.

Cohen, Peter. "The Orisha Atlantic: Historicizing the Roots of a Global Religion." In *Modalities of Transnational Transcendence: Essays on Religion and Globalization*, edited by Thomas Csordas, 205–29. Berkeley: University of California Press, 2009.

Cole, Fay-Cooper. "The Spirit World." In *The Bukidnon of Mindanao*, 89–96. Chicago: Chicago Natural History Museum, 1956.

———. *The Tinggian Social and Religious and Economic Life of a Philippine Tribe*. Chicago: Field Museum of Natural History, 1922.

———. *The Wild Tribes of Davao District, Mindanao*. Chicago: Field Museum of Natural History, 1913.

Colin, Francisco. "Native Races and Their Customs." In *The Philippine Islands, 1493–1898*. Vol. 40, *1690–1691*, edited by Emma Helen Blair and James Alexander Robertson, 37–98. Cleveland, OH: Arthur H. Clark, 1906.

Colorado, Pamela, and Jane Carroll. "Indigenous Science." *Revision* 18, no. 3 (1996): 6–10.

Conklin, Harold C., Pugguwon Lupaih, and Miklos Pinther. *Ethnographic Atlas of Ifugao: A Study of Environment, Culture, and Society in Northern Luzon*. New York: American Geographical Society, 1960.

Connor, Steven. "What I Say, Goes." In *Dumbstruck: A Cultural History of Ventriloquism*, 3–44. New York: Oxford University Press, 2000.

Consing, M. P. "Ilongot." In *CCP Encyclopedia of Philippine Art*. Vol. 1, *Peoples of the Philippines, Aeta to Jama Mapun*, edited by Nicanor G. Tiongson, 356–65. Manila: Cultural Center of the Philippines, 1994.

Consing, M. P. "Isneg." In *CCP Encyclopedia of Philippine Art*. Vol. 1, *Peoples of the Philippines, Aeta to Jama Mapun*, edited by Nicanor G. Tiongson, 376–87. Manila: Cultural Center of the Philippines, 1994.

Consing, M. P., and R. Matilac. "Cuyunon." In *CCP Encyclopedia of Philippine Art*. Vol. 1, *Peoples of the Philippines, Aeta to Jama Mapun*, edited by Nicanor G. Tiongson, 234–43. Manila: Cultural Center of the Philippines, 1994.

Constantino, Renato. "Identity and Consciousness: The Philippine Experience." *Journal of Contemporary Asia* 6, no. 1 (1976): 5–28.

Constantino, Renato, and Letizia Constantino. *The Philippines: A Past Revisited*. Quezon City: Tala, 1975.

Corpuz, Onofre D. *The Roots of the Filipino Nation*. 2 vols. Quezon City: Aklahi Foundation, Inc., 1989.

Cournut, Jean. "De l'écriture à l'inscription ou *le scribe de l'inconscient*." *Revue Française de Psychanalyse* 38 (1974): 57–74.

Covar, Propero. *Philippine Folk Christianity*. Quezon City: Philippine Social Science Council, 1975.

Csordas, Thomas. "Modalities of Transnational Transcendence." *Anthropological Theory* 7 (2007): 259–72.

Cunningham, Floyd. "Diversities Within Post-War Philippine Protestantism." *The Mediator* 5 (2003): 42–144.

Curfman, Zane. Introduction to *Inka Mountain Magic: A Natural Mystic's Guide to Ascension*, 5–10. Scotts Valley, CA: CreateSpace Independent Publishing Platform, 2011.

Cusick, Suzanne. "Feminist Theory, Music Theory, and the Mind/Body Problem." *Perspectives of New Music* 32, no. 1 (1994): 16–21.

Cutiongco, Maria Eleanor Renee C. "Becoming a Filipino Christian Psychologist: Reclaiming Indigenous Concepts of Faith and Spirituality." Graduate School of Psychology Fuller Theological Seminary, 2009.

Daniel, Robert L. *Athens, Ohio: The Village Years*. Athens: Ohio University Press, 1997.

Datuin, Flaudette May V. "Reclaiming the Southeast Asian Goddess: Examples from Contemporary Art by Women (Philippines, Thailand and Indonesia)." *Image and Gender* 6 (2006): 105–19.

Daughtry, J. Martin. "Afterword: From Voice to Violence and Back Again." In *Music, Politics, and Violence*, edited by Susan Fast and Kip Pegley, 243–63. Middletown, CT: Wesleyan University Press, 2012.

Deats, Richard L. *Nationalism and Christianity in the Philippines*. Dallas, TX: Southern Methodist University Press, 1967.

Decena, Carlos Ulises. "Tacit Subjects." *GLQ: A Journal of Lesbian and Gay Studies* 14, no. 2–3 (2008): 339–59.

De Guia, Katrin. "An Ancient Reed of Wholeness." In *Babaylan: Filipinos and the Call of the Indigenous*, edited by Leny Mendoza Strobel, 109–28. Davao City: Ateneo de Davao University Research and Publications Office, 2010.

De la Costa, Horacio. *Jesuits in the Philippines: From Mission to Province (1581–1768)*. Cambridge, MA: Harvard University Press, 1961.

Demetrio, Francisco R. "Philippine Shamanism and Southeast Asian Parallels." *Asian Studies* 11, no. 2 (1973): 128–54.

Dolar, Mladen. "The Linguistics of the Voice." In *A Voice and Nothing More*, 13–31. Cambridge, MA: MIT Press, 2006.

Dozier, Edward P. "Religion: Ritual and Beliefs." In *The Kalinga of Northern Luzon, Philippines*, 55–66 New York: Holt, Rinehart and Winston, 1967.

Dulawan, Lourdes. "Ifugao Baki: Rituals for Man and Rice Culture." *Journal of Northern Luzon* 15, nos. 1–2 (1984–1985): 1–76.

———. "The Ifugaos." *UNITAS* 40, no. 1 (1967): 4–52.

———. "Singing Hudhud in Ifugao." Paper presented at the Conference on Literature of Voices Epics in the Philippines, Quezon City: Ateneo de Manila, June 29, 2000.

Dulawan, Manuel. *Oral Literature of the Ifugao*. Manila: National Commission for Culture and Arts, 2005.

Dumia, Mariano A. *The Ifugao World*. Quezon City: New Day, 1978.

Dunn, Leslie C., and Nancy A. Jones. Introduction to *Embodied Voices: Representing Female Vocality in Western Culture*, edited by Leslie C. Dunn and Nancy A. Jones, 1–13. Cambridge: Cambridge University Press, 1994.

Earlman, Veit. "But What of the Ethnographic Ear? Anthropology, Sound, and the Senses." In *Hearing Cultures: Essays on Sound, Listening and Modernity*, edited by Veit Earlmann, 1–20. Oxford: Berg, 2005.

Elkins, Richard. "An Extended Proto-Manobo Word List." In *Panagani Language Implementation, and Evaluation: Essay in Honor of Bonifacio P. Sibayan on his Sixty-Seventh Birthday*, edited by A. Gonzalez. Manila: Linguistic Society of the Philippines, 1984.

El-Solh, Camillia Fawzi, and Judy Mabro. *Muslim Women's Choices: Religious Belief and Social Reality*. Oxford: Berg, 1994.

Errington, Shelly. "Recasting Sex, Gender, and Power: A Theoretical and Regional Overview." In *Power and Difference: Gender in Island Southeast Asia*, edited by Jane Monnig Atkinson and Shelley Errington, 1–58. Stanford, CA: Stanford University Press, 1990.

Ezzell, William Edward. "Secular Missionaries: The Early American Teachers in the Philippines." *Proceedings and Papers of the Georgia Association of Historians* 6 (1985): 96–107.

Fabella, Virginia. "Inculturating the Gospel: The Philippine Experience." *The Way* 39, no. 2 (1999): 118–28.

Feld, Steven. "Waterfalls of Song: An Acoustemology of Place Resounding in Bosavi, Papua New Guinea." In *Senses of Place*, edited by Steven Feld and Keith H. Basso, 91–136. Santa Fe, NM: School of American Research Press, 1996.

Feld, Steven, and Keith H. Basso. Introduction to *Senses of Place*, edited by Steven Feld and Keith H. Basso, 3–12. Santa Fe, NM: School of American Research Press, 1996.

Feld, Steven, and Donald Brenneis. "Doing Anthropology in Sound." *American Ethnologist* 31, no. 4 (2004): 461–74.

Feld, Steven, Aaron Fox, Thomas Porcello, and David Samuels. "Vocal Anthropology: From the Music of Language to the Language of Song." In *A Companion to Linguistic Anthropology*, edited by Alessandro Duranti, 321–45. Malden, MA: Blackwell, 2006.

Feliciano, Myrna S. "Law, Gender, and Family in the Philippines." *Law and Society Review* 28, no. 3 (1994): 547–60.

Fermin, Jose. *1904 World's Fair: The Filipino Experience*. Honolulu: University of Hawai'i Press, 2006.

Fernandez, Eleazar. Introduction to *Toward a Theology of Struggle*, 1–5 Ossining, NY: Orbis, 1994.

Figer, Reggy, and Ray Nonnato Leyesa. "Rethinking Identities." *Women in Action* 2 (1998): 57–9.

Foucault, Michel. *The History of Sexuality*. Vol. 1, *An Introduction*. Translated by Robert Hurley. New York: Vintage, 1990.

Fox, Robert B. *Religion and Society among the Tagbanuwa of Palawan Island, Philippines*. Manila: National Museum of the Philippines, 1982.

Francia, Luis H. *A History of the Philippines: From Indios Bravos to Filipinos*. New York: Overlook, 2010.

Francisco, Juan. "On the Date of the Coming of Indian Influences in the Philippines." *Philippine Historical Review* 1, no. 1 (1966): 1–17.

———. Review of *Ifugao Bibliography*, by Harold C. Conklin. *American Anthropologist* 71, no. 5 (1969): 1002–1003.

Friedson, Steven M. *Remains of Ritual: Northern Gods in a Southern Land*. Chicago: University of Chicago Press, 2008.

Funtecha, Henry F., and Ma. Milagros C. Geremia. *The Role of Babaylan Movements in the Nationalist Struggle in Western Visayas.* Ilo-ilo: Center for Western Visayan Studies, 1989.

Garcia, Neil C. "Male Homosexuality in the Philippines: A Short History." *International Institute for Asian Studies* 35 (2004): 13.

Garvan, John M. "Methods Adopted by the Missionaries in the Christianization of the Manobos." In *The Manóbos of Mindanáo*, 249–250. Washington, DC: US Government Printing Office, 1931.

Gaspar de San Agustín, OSA. *Conquistas de las Islas Filipinas, 1565–1615.* Edited by Manuel Merino. Madrid: Consejo Superior de Investigaciones Cientificas Instituto "Enrique Flores," 1975

Gatan, Marino. *Ibanag Indigenous Religious Beliefs: A Study in Culture and Education.* Manila: Central Escolar University, 1981.

Gonzalez, Michelle A. "Our Trinitarian *Imago Dei*." In *Created in God's Image: An Introduction to Feminist Theological Anthropology*, 175–207. Maryknoll, NY: Orbis, 2007.

Gopinath, Gayatri. *Impossible Desires: Queer Diasporas and South Asian Public Cultures.* Durham, NC: Duke University Press, 2005.

Grewal, Inderpal, and Caren Kaplan. "Global Identities: Theorizing Transnational Ideas of Sexuality." *GLQ: A Journal of Lesbian and Gay Studies* 7, no. 4 (2001): 663–79.

Grimes, Ronald L. "Global Spirituality and Ritual." In *Anail De: The Breath of God: Music Ritual and Spirituality*, edited by Helen Phelan, 17–25. Dublin: Veritas, 2001.

Gueguen, Catherine. "Sacredness, Death and Landscapes among the Blaan (Mindanao): A Cultural Geography Study." *Philippine Quarterly of Culture and Society* 38, no. 1 (2010): 37–54.

Guerrero, Milagros C. "The Babaylan in Colonial Times: Bodies Desecrated/Body Narratives, Metaphors, and Concepts in Philippine Indigenous Religion." In *Gender/Bodies/Religions*, edited by Sylvia Marcos, 167–79. Mexico City: ALER, 2001.

Guillermo, Merlyn, and L. P. Verora. *Protestant Churches and Missions in the Philippines.* Quezon City: World Vision Philippines, 1982.

Gupta, Akhil, and James Ferguson. "Beyond 'Culture': Space, Identity, and the Politics of Difference." In *Culture, Power, Place: Explorations in Critical Anthropology*, edited by Akhil Gupta and James Ferguson, 34–51. Durham: Duke University Press, 1997.

———. "Culture, Power, Place: Ethnography at the End of an Era." In *Culture, Power, Place: Explorations in Critical Anthropology*, edited by Akhil Gupta and James Ferguson, 1–29. Durham, NC: Duke University Press, 1997.

Guyguyon, Patricio. "The Story of our BECs in the Vicariate of Bontoc–Lagawe." In *Fidelitas: Ten Years Journey, A Souvenir Book on the 10th year anniversary of the Vicariate of Bontoc–Lagawe*, August 5, 2002.

Haraway, Donna. "Situated Knowledges: The Science Question in Feminism and the Privilege of Partial Perspective." *Feminist Studies* 14, no. 3 (1988): 575–599.

Harvey, Graham. General introduction to *Shamanism: A Reader*, edited by Graham Harvey, 1–24. New York: Routledge, 2003.

Hefti, Anny Misa. "Globalization and Migration: Activist Responses." *Canadian Women's Studies/Les Cahiers De La Femme* 22, no. 3–4 (2003): 200–202.

Hemley, Robin. *Invented Eden: The Elusive, Disputed History of the Tasaday.* Lincoln: University of Nebraska Press, 2003.

Herndorn, Marcia, and Norma McLeod. "Sound, Meaning and Diversity." In *Music as Culture*, 1–24. Richmond, CA: MRI, 1990.

Hila, Antonio. *Musika: An Essay on Philippine Music*. Manila: Cultural Center of the Philippines, 1989.
Hollingsworth, Andrea. "Spirit and Voice: Toward a Feminist Pentecostal Pneumatology." *Pneuma* 29, no. 2 (2007): 189–213.
hooks, bell. "Talking Back." In *Talking Back: Thinking Feminist, Thinking Black*. Boston, MA: South End, 1989.
Hopkins, Dwight N., Lois Ann Lorentzen, Eduardo Mendieta, and David Batstone. Introduction to *Religions/Globalizations: Theories and Cases*, 1–4. Durham, NC: Duke University Press, 2001.
Hornedo, F. H., and E. Maranan. "Ivatan." In *CCP Encyclopedia of Philippine Art*. Vol. 1, *Peoples of the Philippines, Aeta to Jama Mapun*, edited by Nicanor G. Tiongson, 396–495. Manila: Cultural Center of the Philippines, 1994.
Hua, Julietta. "Universalism and the Conceptual Limits to Human Rights." In *Trafficking Women's Human Rights*, 1–26. Minneapolis: University of Minnesota Press, 2010.
Provincial Planning and Development Coordinator. *Ifugao Provincial Profile 2000–2010*.
Ileto, Reynaldo Clemena. *Pasyon and Revolution: Popular Movements in the Philippines 1840–1910*. Quezon City: Ateneo de Manila University Press, 1979.
Innes, Robert Alexander. "Introduction: Native Studies and Native Cultural Preservation, Revitalization and Persistence." *American Indian Culture and Research Journal* 34, no. 2 (2010): 1–9.
Irving, D. R. M. "The Hispanization of Filipino Music." In *Colonial Counterpoint: Music in Early Modern Manila*, 99–133. Oxford: Oxford University Press, 2010.
Jakobsen, Marete Demant. *Shamanism: Traditional and Contemporary Approaches to the Master of Spirits and Healing*. New York and Oxford: Berghahn Books, 1999.
Javier, D. V., M. P. Consing, C. Hila, W. R. Torralba, R. P. Santos, E. A. Manuel. "Gaddang." In *CCP Encyclopedia of Philippine Art*. Vol. 1, *Peoples of the Philippines, Aeta to Jama Mapun*, edited by Nicanor G. Tiongson, 244–259. Manila: Cultural Center of the Philippines, 1994.
Jenks, Albert Ernest. *The Bontoc Igorot*. Manila: Bureau of Public Print, 1905.
Jocano, F. Landa. "Concepts of Health and Illness." In *Folk Medicine in a Philippine Municipality*, 79–92. Manila: Punlad Research House, 1973.
Jocano, F. Landa. *Filipino Prehistory: Rediscovering Precolonial Heritage*. Quezon City: Punlad Research House, 1998.
———. *Folk Medicine in a Philippine Municipality*. Manila: Punlad Research House, 1973.
———. "The Sulod: A Mountain People in Central Panay." *Philippine Studies* 6, no. 4 (1958): 401–436.
John Paul II. *Redemptoris Missio*. Encyclical Letter. Vatican website. December 7, 1990. http://w2.vatican.va/content/john-paul-ii/en/encyclicals/documents/hf_jp-ii_enc_07121990_redemptoris-missio.html.
Johnson, Sylvester A. Introduction to *African American Religions, 1500–2000*, 1–9. Cambridge: Cambridge University Press, 2015.
Juergensmeyer, Mark. Introduction to *Global Religions: An Introduction*, edited by Mark Juergensmeyer, 3–16. Oxford: Oxford University Press, 2003.
Kapchan, Deborah. "The Aesthetics of the Invisible: Sacred Music in Secular (French) Places." *Drama Review* 57, no. 3 (2013): 132–47.
———. "The Promise of Sonic Translation: Performing the Festive Sacred in Morocco." *American Anthropologist* 110, no. 4 (2008): 467–83.
Karpf, Anne. "How We Color Our Voices with Pitch, Volume, and Tempo." In *The Human Voice*, 33–47. New York: Bloomsbury, 2006.

Keane, Webb. "Religion's Reach." In *Christian Moderns: Freedom and Fetish in the Mission Encounter*, 37–58. Berkeley: University of California Press, 2007.
Kendall, Laurel. *Shamans, Nostalgias, and the IMF: South Korean Popular Religion in Motion*. Honolulu: University of Hawai'i Press, 2009.
King, Richard. "Beyond Orientalism? Religion and Comparativism in a Postcolonial Era." In *Orientalism and Religion: Postcolonial Theory, India and the Mythic East*, 187–218. London: Routledge, 1999.
Knoper, Mark J. "Ilonggo Religious Beliefs and Practices: A Case of Christian Conversion." PhD diss., Trinity International University, Deerfield, Illinois, May 2003.
Koskoff, Ellen. "Both In and Between: Women's Musical Roles in Ritual Life." *Concilium* 222 (1989): 97–110.
———. *A Feminist Ethnomusicology: Writings on Music and Gender*. Urbana-Champaign: University of Illinois Press, 2014.
———. "Gender, Power, and Music." In *The Musical Woman: An International Perspective*. Vol. 3, *1986–1990*, edited by Judith Laing Zaimont, 769–88. Westport, CT: Greenwood, 1991.
———. "(Left Out in) Left (the Field): The Effects of Post-Postmodern Scholarship on Feminist and Gender Studies in Musicology and Ethnomusicology, 1990–2000." *Women and Music: A Journal of Gender and Culture* 9 (2005): 90–98.
———. "When Women Play: The Relationship between Musical Instruments and Gender Style." *Canadian University Music Review* 16, no. 1 (1995): 114–127.
Kramer, Paul. "Making Concessions: Race and Empire Revisited at the Philippine Exposition, St. Louis, 1901–1905." *Radical History Review* 73 (1999): 75–114.
Kramer, Paul Alexander. "Blood Compacts: Spanish Colonialism and the Invention of the Filipino." In *The Blood of Government: Race, Empire, the United States, and the Philippines*, 35–86. Chapel Hill: University of North Carolina Press, 2006.
Kwiatkowski, Lynn M. "Ifugao." In *Encyclopedia of Sex and Gender: Men and Women in the World's Cultures*. Dordrecht: Springer Science and Business Media, 2003.
Laderman, Carol, and Penny Esterik. "Introduction: Techniques of Healing in Southeast Asia." *Social Science and Medicine* 27, no. 8 (1988): 747–50.
Lagonsay, Gregorio. *Iluko-English-Tagalog Dictionary*. Quezon City: Phoenix 1993.
Lambrecht, Francis. *The Mayawyaw Ritual*. Washington, DC: Catholic Anthropological Conference, 1932.
———. "The Missionary as Anthropologist: Religious Belief among the Ifugao." *Philippine Studies* 5, no. 3 (1957): 271–86.
La Paz, Agusan del Sur 2009 Census.
Lapiz, Ed. *Paano Maging Pilipinong Kristiano: Becoming Filipino Christian*. Makati City: Kaloob, 1997.
———. *Pagpapahiyang: Redeeming Culture and Indigenizing Christianity*. Makati City: Kaloob, 2000.
Legazpi, Miguel López de. "Letter to Felipe II of Spain." In *The Philippine Islands, 1493–1803*. Vol. 2, *1521–1569*, edited by Emma Helen Blair and James Alexander Robertson, 174–82. Cleveland, OH: Arthur H. Clark, 1903.
———. "Relation of the Filipinas Islands and of the Character and Conditions of Their Inhabitants." In *The Philippine Islands, 1493–1803*. Vol. 3, *1569–1576*, edited by Emma Helen Blair and James Alexander Robertson, 54–61. Cleveland, OH: Arthur H. Clark, 1903.
Loarca, Miguel de. "Relation of the Filipinas Islands." In *The Philippine Islands, 1493–1803*. Vol. 5, *1582–1583*, edited by Emma Helen Blair and James Alexander Robertson, 34–187. Cleveland, OH: Arthur H. Clark, 1903.

Lorde, Audre. "An Open Letter to Mary Daly." In *This Bridge Called My Back: Writings by Radical Women of Color*, edited by Cherrie Moraga and Gloria Anzaldúa, 90–93. New York: Kitchen Table, 1981.
Lucero, R. C., et al. "Manobo," in *CCP Encyclopedia of Philippine Art*. Vol. 2, *Peoples of the Philippines, Kalinga to Yakan*, edited by Nicanor G. Tiongson, 120–47. Manila: Cultural Center of the Philippines, 1994.
Lucero, R. C. "Livunganen-Arumanen Manobo." In *CCP Encyclopedia of Philippine Art*. Vol. 2, *Peoples of the Philippines, Kalinga to Yakan*, edited by Nicanor G. Tiongson, 68–75. Manila: Cultural Center of the Philippines, 1994.
Lucero, R. C., D. G. Fernandez, E. A. Manuel, R. Obusan, F. N. Zialcita. "Ilonggo." In *CCP Encyclopedia of Philippine Art*. Vol. 1, *Peoples of the Philippines, Aeta to Jama Mapun*, edited by Nicanor G. Tiongson, 334–55. Manila: Cultural Center of the Philippines, 1994.
Lucero, R. C., and C. Hila. "Samal." In *CCP Encyclopedia of Philippine Art*. Vol. 2, *Peoples of the Philippines, Kalinga to Yakan*, edited by Nicanor G. Tiongson, 264–81. Manila: Cultural Center of the Philippines, 1994.
Lucero, R. C., and E. A. Manuel. "Agusanon Manobo." In *CCP Encyclopedia of Philippine Art*. Vol. 1, *Peoples of the Philippines, Aeta to Jama Mapun*, edited by Nicanor G. Tiongson, 40–55. Manila: Cultural Center of the Philippines, 1994.
———. "Capiznon." In *CCP Encyclopedia of Philippine Art*. Vol. 1, *Peoples of the Philippines, Aeta to Jama Mapun*, edited by Nicanor G. Tiongson, 192–205. Manila: Cultural Center of the Philippines, 1994.
———. "Ibaloy." In *CCP Encyclopedia of Philippine Art*. Vol. 1, *Peoples of the Philippines, Aeta to Jama Mapun*, edited by Nicanor G. Tiongson, 260–71. Manila: Cultural Center of the Philippines, 1994.
Macdonald, Nicole Revel. "Palawan." In *CCP Encyclopedia of Philippine Art*. Vol. 2, *Peoples of the Philippines, Kalinga to Yakan*, edited by Nicanor G. Tiongson, 182–97. Manila: Cultural Center of the Philippines, 1994.
Maceda, Jose, Corazon Dioquino, and Ramon Santos. "Philippine Music." In *CCP Encyclopedia of Philippine Art*. Vol. 6, *Music*, edited by Nicanor G. Tiongson, 18–25. Manila: Cultural Center of the Philippines, 1994.
Madale, Nagasura, and G. E. P. Cheng. "Maranao." In *CCP Encyclopedia of Philippine Art*. Vol. 2, *Peoples of the Philippines, Kalinga to Yakan*, edited by Nicanor G. Tiongson, 160–81. Manila: Cultural Center of the Philippines, 1994.
Magos, Alicia. "The Concept of Mari-it (Dangerous Zones) in Panaynon Worldview and Its Impact on Sustainable Human Development." *SEAMEO Jasper Fellowship Monograph Series* 5–8 (2000): 9–40.
———. *The Enduring Maaram Tradition: An Ethnography of a Kinaray-a Village*. Quezon City: New Day, 1992.
Mahmood, Saba. "The Subject of Freedom." In *Politics of Piety: The Islamic Revival and the Feminist Subject*, 1–39. Princeton, NJ: Princeton University Press, 2005.
Majul, Cesar Adib. "Islamic and Arab Cultural Influences in the South of the Philippines." *Journal of Southeast Asian History* 7, no. 2 (1966): 61–73.
Manalansan, Martin F., IV. "Speaking in Transit: Queer Language and Translated Lives." In *Global Divas: Filipino Gay Men in the Diaspora*, 45–61. Durham, NC: Duke University Press, 2003.
Mananzan, Mary John. "The Babaylan in Me." In *Centennial Crossings: Readings on Babaylan Feminism in the Philippines*, edited by Fe B. Mangahas and Jenny R. Llaguno, 135–46. Quezon City: C & E, 2006.
———. "Religion as a Socializing Force in the 'Women Question.'" *Review of Women's Studies* 9, no. 1 and 2 (1999) ["Gender Construction"]: 1–15.

———. *Woman, Religion and Spirituality in Asia*. Pasig: ANVIL, 2004.
Mangahas, Fe. "The Babaylan Historico-Cultural Context." In *Centennial Crossings: Readings on Babaylan Feminism in the Philippines*, edited by Fe B. Mangahas and Jenny R. Llaguno, 21–46. Quezon City: C & E, 2006.
———. "Babaylan in Dance Ritual at Spanish Contact: Sacral Vessel of Spirituality and Power." In *Gender/Bodies/Religions*, edited by Sylvia Marcos, 155–79. Mexico City: ALER, 2000.
———. "From Babaylan to Suffragettes: The Status of Filipino Women from Pre-Colonial Times to the Early American Period." In *Kamalayan: Feminist Writings in the Philippines*, edited by Pennie S. Azarcon, 8–20. Quezon City: Pilipina, 1987.
Mangahas, Fe B. "Pag-uugnay at Pagtatawid: Connecting and Crossing/Interview with Marianita Beatriz 'Girlie' C. Villariba." In *Centennial Crossings: Readings on Babaylan Feminism in the Philippines*, edited by Fe B. Mangahas and Jenny R. Llaguno, 159–70. Quezon City: C & E, 2006.
Manuel, E. Arsenio. *Agyu: Epic of Mindanao*. Manila: University of Santo Tomas, 1969.
Maquiso, Elena. "A Study of Indigenous Hymns in the Evangelical Church in the Philippines: Implications for Christian Education." PhD diss., Hartford Seminary Foundation, 1966.
Maranan, E. "Batak." In *CCP Encyclopedia of Philippine Art*. Vol. 1, *Peoples of the Philippines, Aeta to Jama Mapun*, edited by Nicanor G. Tiongson, 96–105. Manila: Cultural Center of the Philippines, 1994.
———. "Kankanay." In *CCP Encyclopedia of Philippine Art*. Vol. 2, *Peoples of the Philippines, Kalinga to Yakan*, edited by Nicanor G. Tiongson, 38–51. Manila: Cultural Center of the Philippines, 1994.
———. "Subanon." In *CCP Encyclopedia of Philippine Art*. Vol. 2, *Peoples of the Philippines, Kalinga to Yakan*, edited by Nicanor G. Tiongson, 282–95. Manila: Cultural Center of the Philippines, 1994.
———. "Tiruray." In *CCP Encyclopedia of Philippine Art*. Vol. 2, *Peoples of the Philippines, Kalinga to Yakan*, edited by Nicanor G. Tiongson, 426–39. Manila: Cultural Center of the Philippines, 1994.
Maranan, E., F. Prudente, and Sr. Obusan, "Bilaan." *CCP Encyclopedia of Philippine Art*. Vol. 1, *Peoples of the Philippines, Aeta to Jama Mapun*, edited by Nicanor G. Tiongson, 130–41. Manila: Cultural Center of the Philippines, 1994.
Maranan, Edgar B., and Nicole Revel-Macdonald. *Kudaman: Isang Epikong Palawan na Inawit ni Usuy*. Quezon City: Ateneo de Manila University Press, 1991.
Marcos, Sylvia, ed. *Women and Indigenous Religions*. Santa Barbara, CA: Praeger, 2010.
Marcus, George E. "Ethnography In/Of the World System: The Emergence of Multisited Ethnography." *Annual Review of Anthropology* 24 (1995): 95–117.
Martinez, Theresa A. "The Double-Consciousness of Du Bois and the 'Mestiza Consciousness' of Anzaldúa." *Race, Gender and Class* 9, no. 4 (2002): 158–76.
Masson, Jack, and Donald Guimary. "Asian Labor Contractors in the Alaskan Canned Salmon Industry, 1880–1937." *Labor History* 22, no. 3 (1981): 377–97.
Masuzawa, Tomoko. Introduction to *The Invention of World Religions: Or, How European Universalism Was Preserved in the Language of Pluralism*, 1–35. Chicago: University of Chicago Press, 2005.
Matory, J. Lorand. "The Many Who Dance in Me: Afro-Atlantic Ontology and the Problem with 'Transnationalism." In *Modalities of Transnational Transcendence: Essays on Religion and Globalization*, edited by Thomas Csordas, 231–62. Berkeley: University of California Press, 2009.
McClary, Susan. "*Feminine Endings* in Retrospect." In *Feminine Endings: Music, Gender, and Sexuality*, ix–xx. Rev. ed. Minneapolis: University of Minnesota Press, 2002.

McClintock, Anne. *Imperial Leather: Race, Gender and Sexuality in the Imperial Contest.* London: Routledge, 1995.
McCoy, Alfred W. "Baylan: Animist Religion and Philippine Peasant Ideology." *Philippine Quarterly of Culture and Society* 10, no. 3 (1982): 141–94.
——. "Sugar Barons: Formation of a Native Planter Class in Colonial Philippines." *Journal of Peasant Studies* 19, no. 3–4 (1992): 106–141.
Mendoza-Guazon, Maria Paz. *The Development and Progress of the Filipino Women.* 2nd ed. Manila: Government of the Philippine Islands Department of the Interior, Office of the Public Welfare Commissioner, 1951.
Mendoza, S. Lily. "Bearing the Babaylan Body Memory, Colonial Wounding, and Return to Indigenous Wildness." In *Back from the Crocodile's Belly: Philippine Babaylan Studies and the Struggle for Indigenous Memory*, edited by S. Lily Mendoza and Leny Mendoza Strobel, 243–56. Sunnyvale, CA: Center for Babaylan Studies, 2013.
Mercado, Leonardo. *Pagans to Partners: The Change in Catholic Attitudes towards Traditional Religion.* Manila: Logos, 2000.
Mercene, Floro. *Manila Men in the New World: Filipino Migration to Mexico and the Americas from the Sixteenth Century.* Quezon City: University of the Philippines Press, 2007.
Miclat-Cacayan, Agnes. "Babaylan: She Dances in Wholeness." In *Centennial Crossings: Readings on Babaylan Feminism in the Philippines*, edited by Fe B. Mangahas and Jenny R. Llaguno, 49–72. Quezon City: C & E, 2006.
Mihesuah, Devon Abbott. "Feminists, Tribalists or Activists." In *Indigenous American Women: Decolonization, Empowerment, Activism*, 159–71. Lincoln: University of Nebraska Press, 2003.
Miller, Robert J. *Native America, Discovered and Conquered: Thomas Jefferson, Lewis and Clark, and Manifest Destiny.* Westport, CT: Praeger, 2006.
Miller, Stuart Creighton. "Armageddon, 1900." In *Benevolent Assimilation: The American Conquest of the Philippines 1899–1903*, 129–49. New Haven, CT: Yale University Press, 1982.
Mitchem, Stephanie. "Black Women: Race, Gender and Class." In *Introducing Womanist Theology*, 3–24. Maryknoll, NY: Orbis, 2002.
Mohanty, Chandra Talpade. "Under Western Eyes: Feminist Scholarship and Colonial Discourses." In *Feminism without Borders: Decolonizing Theory, Practicing Solidarity*, 17–42. Durham, NC: Duke University Press, 2003.
Mojares, R., and M. P. Monsing. "Cebuano." In *CCP Encyclopedia of Philippine Art.* Vol. 1, *Peoples of the Philippines, Aeta to Jama Mapun*, edited by Nicanor G. Tiongson, 206–233. Manila: Cultural Center of the Philippines, 1994.
Molintas, Jose Mencio. "The Philippine Indigenous Peoples' Struggle for Land and Life: Challenging Legal Texts." *Arizona Journal of International & Comparative Law* 21, no. 1 (2004): 269–306. Montillo-Burton, Linda. "The Impact of Modern Medical Intervention on the Agusan Manobo Medical System of the Philippines." PhD diss., University of Pittsburgh, 1983.
Mora, Manolete. "Lutes, Gongs, Women and Men: (En)Gendering Instrumental Music in the Philippines." *Ethnomusicology Forum* 17, no. 2 (2008): 225–47.
——. *Myth, Mimesis and Magic in the Music of the T'boli, Philippines.* Quezon City: Ateneo de Manila University Press, 2005.
——. "The Sounding Pantheon of Nature: T'boli Instrumental Music in the Making of an Ancestral Symbol." *Acta Musicologica* 59, no. 2 (1987): 187–212.
Morga, Antonio. "Events in the Filipinas Islands." In *The Philippine Islands, 1493–1898.* Vol. 16, *1609*, edited by Emma Helen Blair and James Alexander Robertson, 25–209. Cleveland, OH: Arthur H. Clark, 1904.

Moses, Bernard. *Spain's Declining Power in South America, 1730–1806*. Berkeley: University of California Press, 1919.
Muyco, Maria Christine. "As Healers Dance: A Processual View of Panay Bukidnon's Babaylan in Motion." In *Back from the Crocodile's Belly: Philippine Babaylan Studies and the Struggle for Indigenous Memory*, edited by S. Lily Mendoza and Leny Mendoza Strobel, 107–124. Sunnyvale CA: Center for Babaylan Studies, 2013.
Nakpil, Carmen Guerrero. "The Filipino Woman." *Philippines Quarterly* 1, no. 4 (1952): 8–10.
Nelmida, P., M. Nelmida, D. Javier, and N. Tiongson. "Pangasinan." In *CCP Encyclopedia of Philippine Art*. Vol. 2, *Peoples of the Philippines, Kalinga to Yakan*, edited by Nicanor G. Tiongson, 224–243. Manila: Cultural Center of the Philippines, 1994.
Nida, Eugene. "Theories of Translation." *TTR: Traduction, Terminologie, Rédaction* 4, no. 1 (1991): 19–32.
Nono, Grace. "Audible Travels: Oral/Aural Performances and the Global Dispersal of a Philippine Indigenous Religion." In *Back from the Crocodile's Belly: Philippine Babaylan Studies and the Struggle for Indigenous Memory*, edited by S. Lily Mendoza and Leny Mendoza Strobel, 29–43. Sunnyvale, CA: Center for Babaylan Studies, 2013.
Nono, Grace, ed. *Kahimunan: Cultural Music of the Manobo, Higaonon and Banwaon of Agusan del Sur*. Quezon City: Tao Foundation for Culture and Arts, 2002.
Nono, Grace, prod. *Mendung Sabal: Tudbulul Lunay Mogul: T'boli Hero of Lunay, The Place of Gongs and Music*. Quezon City: Tao Foundation for Culture and Arts, 2002.
Nono, Grace. *The Shared Voice: Chanted and Spoken Narratives from the Philippines*. Pasig City: ANVIL and Fundacion Santiago, 2008.
Nono, Grace. *Song of the Babaylan: Living Voices, Medicines, Spiritualities of Philippine Ritualist-Oralist-Healers*. Quezon City: Institute of Spirituality in Asia, 2013.
Obusan, Teresita. Foreword to *Pamamaraan: Indigenous Knowledge and Evolving Research Paradigms*, edited by Teresita Obusan, ix–xi. Quezon City: University of the Philippines Asian Center, 1994.
Ochoa Gautier, Ana María. "Introduction: The Bar and the Voice in the Lettered City's Geophysical History." In *Aurality: Listening and Knowledge in Nineteenth-Century Colombia*, 1–29. Durham, NC: Duke University Press, 2014.
Ong, Aihwa. Introduction to *Flexible Citizenship: The Cultural Logics of Transnationality*, 1–26. Durham, NC: Duke University Press, 1999.
Ong, Paul, and Tania Azores. "The Migration and Incorporation of Filipino Nurses." In *The New Asian Immigration in Los Angeles and Global Restructuring*, edited by Paul Ong, Edna Bonacich, and Lucie Cheng, 164–95. Philadelphia, PA: Temple University Press, 1994.
Ong, Walter. *Orality and Literacy: The Technologizing of the Word*. New York: Methuen, 1982.
Opiniano, Jeremaiah M. "Statistics on Filipinos' International Migration: Issues and Steps Towards Harmonizing Data." Paper presented at the 19th National Convention on Statistics (NCS), Mandaluyong City, Metro Manila, Philippines, October 1–2, 2007.
Orbeta, Jr., Aniceto and Michael Abrigo. "Philippine International Labour Migration in the Past 30 Years: Trends and Prospects." Paper presented at the International Labor Organization Meeting, Bangkok, Thailand, May 18–20, 2009.
Ottevaere, Dawn Anne. "The Cost is Sworn to by Women: Gender, Resistance, and Counterinsurgency during the Philippine-American War, 1898–1902." PhD diss., Michigan State University, 2010.
Padilla, Malu. "Women Changing our Lives, Making History: Migration Experiences of Babaylan Philippine Women's Network in Europe." In *In de Olde Worlde: Views of*

Filipino Migrants in Europe, edited by Filomenita Mongaya Hoegsholm, 75–101. Quezon City: Philippine Social Science Center, 2007.
Panditaratne, Dinusha. "Towards Gender Equity in a Developing Asia: Reforming Personal Laws within a Pluralist Framework." *NYU Review of Law and Social Change* 32, no. 83 (2007): 83–129.
Peletz, Michael G. "Transgenderism and Gender Pluralism in Southeast Asia since Early Modern Times." *Current Anthropology* 47, no. 2 (2006): 309–340.
Pe-Pua, Rogelia, and Elizabeth Protacio-Marcelino. "Sikolohiyang Pilipino (Filipino Psychology): A Legacy of Virgilio G. Enriquez." *Asian Journal of Social Psychology* 3 (2000): 49–71.
Perez, Domingo. "Relation of the Zambal Indians of Playa Honda, Their Situation and Customs." In *The Philippine Islands, 1493–1898*. Vol. 47, *1728–1759*, edited by Emma Helen Blair and James Alexander Robertson, 289–332. Cleveland, OH: Arthur H. Clark, 1903–1909.
Perruchon, Marie. "Gender: Complementarity and Competition." In *I Am Tsunki: Gender and Shamanism among the Shuar of Western Amazonia*, 271–313. Uppsala: Uppsala Press, 2003.
Phelan, John Leddy. *The Hispanization of the Philippines: Spanish Aims and Filipino Responses 1565–1700*. Madison: University of Wisconsin Press, 1967.
Pietropaolo, Domenico. "Alcina in Arcadia." *University of Toronto Quarterly* 72, no. 4 (2003): 858–69.
Pigafetta, Antonio. "Primo viaggio intorno al mondo." In *The Philippine Islands, 1493–1898*, Vol. 33, *1519–1522*, edited by Emma Helen Blair and James Alexander Robertson, 26–272. Cleveland, OH: Arthur H. Clark, 1906.
Plasencia, Juan de. "Customs of the Tagalogs." In *The Philippine Islands, 1493–1589*. Vol. 7, *1588–1591*, edited by Emma Helen Blair and James Alexander Robertson, 173–97. Cleveland, OH: Arthur H. Clark, 1903.
Preciado, Beatriz. "Pharmaco-pornographic Politics: Towards a New Gender Ecology." *parallax* 14, no. 1 (2008): 105–17.
Quijano, Anibal. "Coloniality of Power and Eurocentrism in Latin America." *International Sociology* 15, no. 2 (2000): 215–32.
Rafael, Vicente L. "Untranslatability and the Terms of Reciprocity." In *Contracting Colonialism: Translation and Christian Conversion in Tagalog Society under Early Spanish Rule*, 110–35. Durham, NC: Duke University Press, 1993.
Ramos, Alcida Rita. "The Hyperreal Indian." *Critique of Anthropology* 14, no. 2 (1994): 153–71.
Reed, Susan Taffe. "Innovating Tradition: The Spiritual Significance of Powwows in Appalachian Pennsylvania." Paper presented at the Society for Ethnomusicology Conference 2013, Indianapolis, Indiana, November 14–17, 2013.
Ricci, Ronit. "On the Untranslatability of 'Translation': Considerations from Java, Indonesia." *Translation Studies* 3, no. 3 (2010): 287–301.
Robbins, Joel. "The Trans- in Transnational." In *Modalities of Transnational Transcendence: Essays on Religion and Globalization*, edited by Thomas Csordas, 55–77. Berkeley: University of California Press, 2009.
Rodil, Rudy Buhay. *The Minoritization of the Indigenous Communities of Mindanao and the Sulu Archipelago*. Davao City: Alternate Forum for Research in Mindanao, 1994.
Rodil, Rudy Buhay. *A Story of Mindanao and Sulu in Question and Answer*. Davao City: Mincode, 2003.
Romulo, Carlos P. *Mother America*. Garden City, NY: Doubleday, Doran, 1943.
Roosevelt, Nicholas. *The Philippines: A Treasure and a Problem*. New York: J. H. Sears, 1926.

Rosaldo, Renato. "The Erosion of Classic Norms." In *Culture and Truth: The Remaking of Social Analyses*, 25–45. 2nd ed. Boston, MA: Beacon: 1993.

Roseman, Marina. "'Blowing 'cross the Crest of Mount Galeng': Winds of the Voice, Winds of the Spirits." *Journal of the Royal Anthropological Institute* 13 (2007): S55–S69.

Rudolph, Susanne Hoeber. "Religion, States, and Transnational Civil Society." In *Transnational Religion, the State, and Global Civil Society*, edited by Susanne Hoeber Rudolph and James P. Piscatori, 1–24. Boulder, CO: Westview, 1997.

Rymhs, Deena. "A Different Cosmopolitanism: Indigeneity and Translocality." *Canadian Literature/Littérature Canadienne* 204 (2010): 123–125.

Said, Edward. Introduction to *Orientalism*, 1–28. New York: Vintage, 1979.

Salazar, Vicente. "Historia de la Provincia del Santissimo Rosario de Philipinas, China, y Tunking,del Sagrado Orden de Predicadores 1683." In *Documentary Sources of Philippine History* 5, edited and translated by Gregorio Zaide, 125–33. Manila: Manila Book Store, 1990.

Salazar, Zeus. "The Babaylan in Philippine History." In *Women's Role in Philippine History: Selected Essays*. 2nd ed. Translated by Proserpina Domingo-Tapales, 209–222. Quezon City: University of the Philippines University Center for Women's Studies, 2001.

Samuels, David W. "Bible Translation and Medicine Man Talk: Missionaries, Indexicality, and the 'Language Expert' on the San Carlos Apache Reservation." *Language in Society* 35 (2006): 529–57.

San Antonio, Juan Francisco de. *Chronicas de la Apostoloca Provincia de S. Gregorio de Religiosos Descalzos de n. s. p. San Francisco en las Islas Philipinas, China, Japon*. Vol. 2. Manila, 1738.

Sande, Francisco de. "Relation of the Filipinas Islands." In *The Philippine Islands, 1493–1803*. Vol. 4, *1576–1582*, edited by Emma Helen Blair and James Alexander Robertson, 21–118. Cleveland, OH: Arthur H. Clark, 1903.

San Nicolas, Andrés de. "Early Recollect Missions in the Philippines: General History of the Discalced Augustinian Fathers." In *The Philippine Islands, 1493–1898*, Vol. 21, *1624*, edited by Emma Helen Blair and James Alexander Robertson, 111–317. Cleveland, OH: Arthur H. Clark, 1905.

Sa-onoy, Modesto. *A History of Negros Occidental*. Bacolod City: Today, 1992.

Santiago, Luciano P. R. "The Development of Religious Congregations for Women in the Philippines during the Spanish Period (1565–1898)." *Journal of Sophia Asian Studies* 12 (1994): 49–71.

Santiago, Luciano P. R. "'To Love and to Suffer': The Development of the Religious Congregations for Women in the Philippines during the Spanish Era (1565–1898)." *Philippine Quarterly of Culture and Society* 23, no. 2 (1995): 151–95.

Santos, Ramon. "Philippine Music: The Ethnic Tradition." In *CCP Encyclopedia of Philippine Art*. Vol. 6, *Music*, edited by Nicanor G. Tiongson, 26–35. Manila: Cultural Center of the Philippines, 1994.

Saway-Llesis, Irene. "Experiences in Ulaging Documentation and Research (Talaandig-Bukidnon)." In *Literature of Voice: Epics of the Philippines*, edited by Nicole Revel, 85–93. Quezon City: Ateneo de Manila University, 2005.

Schiller, Nina Glick, Linda Basch, and Cristina Blanc-Szanton. "Towards a Definition of Transnationalism: Introductory Remarks and Research Questions." *Annals of the New York Academy of Sciences* 645 (1992): 1–24.

Schreurs, Peter, MSC. *Caraga Antigua, 1521–1910: The Hispanization and Christianization of Agusan, Surigao and East Davao*. Cebu City: University of San Carlos, 1989.

Schurz, William Lytle. "Mexico, Peru, and the Manila Galleon." *Hispanic American Historical Review* 1, no. 4 (1918): 389–402.

Schwenken, Helen. "'Domestic Slavery' Versus 'Workers Rights': Political Mobilizations of Migrant Domestic Workers in the European Union." Paper presented at the Center for Comparative Immigration Studies, University of California, San Diego, 2005.

Scott, James C. Preface to *Domination and the Arts of Resistance: Hidden Transcripts*, ix–xiii. New Haven, CT: Yale University Press, 1990.

Scott, William Henry. *Barangay: Sixteenth-Century Philippine Culture and Society*. Manila: Ateneo de Manila University Press, 1994.

———. "Class Structure in the Unhispanized Philippines." In *Cracks in the Parchment Curtain*. Quezon City: New Day, 1985.

———. *The Discovery of the Igorots: Spanish Contacts with the Pagans of Northern Luzon*. Quezon City: New Day, 1974.

Senungetuk, Heidi Aklaseaq. "*Qanukiak Ililuta*: How Shall We Proceed?" Paper presented at the Society for Ethnomusicology Conference 2013, Indianapolis, Indiana, November 14–17, 2013.

Seyfert, Robert. "Beyond Personal Feelings and Collective Emotions: Toward a Theory of Social Affect." *Theory Culture Society* 29, no. 6 (2012): 27–46.

Sicat, Leo. "I Sacrificed My Five-Year College Education to Become a Steward." In Yen Le Espiritu, *Filipino American Lives*, 105–16. Philadelphia, PA: Temple University Press, 1995.

Smith, Andrea. "Indigenous Feminism without Apology." In *Unsettling Ourselves: Reflections and Resources for Deconstructing Colonial Mentality*, 158–60. Dakota: Unsettling Minnesota Collective, 2009. https://unsettlingminnesota.files.wordpress.com/2009/11/um_sourcebook_jan10_revision.pdf.

———. "Queer Theory and Native Studies: The Heteronormativity of Settler Colonialism." *GLQ: A Journal of Lesbian and Gay Studies* 16, no. 1–2 (2010): 41–68.

Smith, Linda Tuhiwai. *Decolonizing Methodologies: Research and Indigenous Peoples*. London: Zed Books, 2004.

Solomon, Gayle. "Boys of the Lex: Transgender and Social Construction." In *Assuming a Body: Transgender and Rhetorics of Materiality*, 69–94. New York: Columbia University Press, 2010.

Spivak, Gayatri Chakravorty. "The Politics of Translation." In *Outside the Teaching Machine*, 179–200. New York: Routledge, 1993.

Staniukovich, Maria V. "Factors Affecting Stability/Variability of the Ifugao Hudhud." Paper presented at the Peter the Great Museum of Anthropology and Ethnography, St. Petersburg, Russia, 2006.

Stoler, Ann Laura. "Colonial Archives and the Arts of Governance." *Archival Science* 2 (2002): 87–109.

Stowasser, Barbara Freyer. "Liberated Equal or Protected Dependent? Contemporary Paradigms on Women's Status in Islam." *Arab Studies Quarterly* 9, no. 3 (1987): 260–83.

Strobel, Leny Mendoza. *Coming Full Circle: The Process of Decolonization among post-1965 Filipino Americans*. Quezon City: Giraffe, 2001.

———. Introduction to *Babaylan: Filipinos and the Call of the Indigenous*, edited by Leny Mendoza Strobel, 1–58. Davao City: Ateneo de Davao University Research and Publications Office, 2010.

Stryker, Susan, and Aren Z. Aizura. "Introduction: Transgender Studies 2.0." In *The Transgender Studies Reader 2*, edited by Susan Stryker and Aren Z. Aizura, 1–12. New York: Routledge, 2013.

Sturtevant, David. *Popular Uprisings in the Philippines 1840–1940*. Ithaca: Cornell University Press, 1976.

Sugbo, V., and G. Zafra. "Waray." In *CPP Encyclopedia of Philippine Art.* Vol. 2, *Peoples of the Philippines, Kalinga to Yakan,* edited by Nicanor G. Tiongson, 440–63. Manila: Cultural Center of the Philippines, 1994.
Swimsaway, Crow. Introduction to *Circle of Ancestors.* Milverton, UK: Capall Bann, 2009.
Tagupa, Joe, SVD. "Banaue Catholic Mission." In *Fidelitas: Ten Years Journey, A Souvenir Book on the 10th Year Anniversary of the Vicariate of Bontoc–Lagawe,* August 5, 2002.
Tan, Evelyn Cullamar. *Babaylanism in Negros, 1896–1907.* Quezon City: New Day, 1986.
Tan, Michael L. "Survival through Pluralism." *Journal of Homosexuality* 40, no. 3–4 (2001): 117–42.
Tadiar, Neferti Xina M. "Filipinas 'Living in a Time of War." In *Pinay Power: Peminist Critical Theory,* edited by Melinda L. de Jesús, 374–84. New York: Routledge, 2005.
Taray, Leonila L. "Understanding Ancestor Reverence in the Benguet Tradition." *Asia-Pacific Social Science Review* 8, no. 1 (2008): 61–72.
Taussig, Michael. "Cane Toads, An Unnatural History." In *The Nervous System,* 79–82. New York: Routledge, 1992.
———. "Folk Healing the Structure of Conquest in Southwest Columbia." *Journal of Latin American Lore* 6, no. 2 (1980): 217–78.
Taussig, Michael M. "The Nervous System: Homesickness and Dada." *Kroeber Anthropological Society Papers* 69–70 (1989): 32–61.
Taylor, Diana. "Acts of Transfer." In *The Archive and the Repertoire: Performing Cultural Memory in the Americas,* 1–52. Durham, NC: Duke University Press, 2003.
Teodoro, Noel. "Pensionados and Workers: The Filipinos in the United States, 1903–1956." *Asian and Pacific Migration Journal* 8, no. 1–2 (1999): 157–78.
Thompson, Emily. Introduction to *The Soundscape of Modernity: Architectural Acoustics and the Culture of Listening in America, 1900–1933,* 1–12. Cambridge, MA: MIT Press, 2004.
Tiongson, Nicanor G., ed. *CCP Encyclopedia of Philippine Art.* 12 vols. Manila: Cultural Center of the Philippines, 1994.
Tomlinson, Gary. *The Singing of the New World: Indigenous Voice in the Era of European Contact.* Cambridge: Cambridge University Press, 2007.
———. "Voices of the Invisible." In *Metaphysical Song: An Essay on Opera,* 3–6. Princeton, NJ: Princeton University Press, 1999.
Trabich, Leah. "Native American Genocide still Haunts the United States." *The End to Intolerance* 5 (1997).
Tsing, Anna Lowenhaupt. Introduction to *Friction: An Ethnography of Global Connection,* 1–18. Princeton, NJ: Princeton University Press, 2005.
US War Department Bureau of Insular Affairs. *The Eighth Annual Report of the Philippine Commission to the Secretary of War, 1907, Part 2.* Washington, DC: Government Printing Office, 1908.
Valentine, David. "'I Went to Bed with My Own Kind Once': The Erasure of Desire in the Name of Identity." *Language and Communication* 23 (2003): 123–38.
Vergara, Benito M. *Displaying Filipinos: Photography and Colonialism in Early 20th Century Philippines.* Quezon City: University of the Philippines Press, 1995.
Villero, Ofelia. "Religion, Gender and Postcoloniality: The Case of 'Ciudad Mistica de Dios.'" PhD diss., Graduate Theological Union, Berkeley, California, 2010.
Villoldo, Alberto. "Introduction: The Way of the Earthkeepers." In *The Four Insights: Wisdom, Power, and Grace of the Earthkeepers.* Carlsbad: CA: Hay House, 2006.
Waldram, James. "The Efficacy of Traditional Medicine: Current Theoretical and Methodological Issues." *Medical Anthropology Quarterly* 14, no. 4 (2000): 603–25.
Wallace, Ben J. *Shifting Cultivation and Plow Agriculture in Two Pagan Gaddang Settlements.* Manila: National Institute of Science and Technology, 1970.

Wenger, Tisa. Introduction to *Religious Freedom: The Contested History of an American Ideal*, 1–14. Chapel Hill: University of North Carolina Press, 2017.

———. *We Have a Religion: The 1920s Pueblo Indian Dance Controversy and American Religious Freedom*. Chapel Hill: University of North Carolina Press, 2009.

Wernstedt, Frederick L., and J. E. Spencer. "Southern Country: Mindanao and Sulu." In *The Philippine Island World: A Physical, Cultural and Regional Geography*, 502–97. Berkeley: University of California Press, 1967.

Wesling, Meg, "Agents of Assimilation: Female Authority, Male Domesticity, and the Familial Dramas of Colonial Tutelage." In *Empire's Proxy: American Literature and U.S. Imperialism in the Philippines*, 104–38. New York: NYU Press, 2011.

WHO Unit on Traditional Medicine. *Legal Status of Traditional Medicine and Complementary/Alternative Medicine: A Worldwide Review*. Geneva: World Health Organization, 2001.

Willcox, Cornelis De Witt. *The Head Hunters of Northern Luzon From Ifugao to Kalinga: A Ride Through the Mountains of Northern Luzon With an Appendix on the Independence of the Philippines*. Kansas City, MO: Franklin Hudson, 1912.

Wolf, Eric. *Europe and the People Without History*. Berkeley: University of California Press, 1982.

Wood, Patricia K. "Aboriginal/Indigenous Citizenship: An Introduction." *Citizenship Studies* 7, no. 4 (2003): 371–78.

Zaide, Gregorio, and Sonia Zaide, *History of the Republic of the Philippines*. Metro Manila: National Bookstore, 1987.

ONLINE ARTICLES, WEBSITES, BLOGS

Allen, Greg. "'Living Exhibits' at 1904 World's Fair Revisited: Igorot Natives Recall Controversial Display of Their Ancestors." *National Public Radio*, May 31, 2004. http://www.npr.org/templates/story/story.php?storyId=1909651.

Amanda, Martin. "The T'Boli: Profiles in Transition." *Cultural Survival*, June 1984. http://www.culturalsurvival.org/ourpublications/csq/article/the-tboli-profiles-transition.

American Psychological Association. "Definitions Related to Sexual Orientation and Gender Diversity in APA Documents." Accessed January 16, 2021. https://www.apa.org/pi/lgbt/resources/sexuality-definitions.pdf.

Arago, Daisy. "No Economic and Job Growth in Mining Industry in the Philippines, Only Plunder Need to Run." *Asia Monitor Resource Center*, April 1, 2012. https://www.amrc.org.hk/content/no-economic-and-job-growth-mining-industry-philippines-only-plunder-need-run.

Arguillas, Carolyn. "Caraga: Poorest Region No More." *Minda News*, April 26, 2013. https://www.mindanews.com/governance/2013/04/caraga-poorest-region-no-more/.

Benaning, Marvyn N. "Tribal Group Hits Rights Violations." *Business Mirror*, January 26, 2015. https://businessmirror.com.ph/2015/01/26/tribal-group-hits-rights-violations/.

Borah, Eloisa Gomez. "Chronology of Filipinos in America Pre-America Pre-1898." 1997–2004. https://filipinostudies.files.wordpress.com/2012/01/filamchronology.pdf.

Cabiling, Bebot. "Mining Projects in Caraga Generate more than 1B in Taxes." *Mindanao Newsmakers*, July 26, 2011. https://mindanaonewsmakers.wordpress.com/2011/07/26/mining-projects-in-caraga-generate-more-than-1b-taxes/.

CARAGA Watch, "Mining Caraga," October 2009.

Carroll, Rory. "Pope says Sorry for Sins of Church: Sweeping Apology for Attacks on Jews, Women and Minorities, Defies Theologians' Warnings." *The Guardian*, March 13, 2000. https://www.theguardian.com/world/2000/mar/13/catholicism.religion.

Catholics for a Free Choice. *The Holy See and the Convention on the Rights of the Child in the Republic of the Philippines: NGO Report on How the Holy See's Laws Impact the*

Philippines' Compliance with the Convention. Quezon City: LIKHAAN, Child Justice League, Catholics for a Free Choice, 2004. https://resourcecentre.savethechildren.net/sites/default/files/documents/2252.pdf.

Center for Babaylan Studies. https://www.centerforbabaylanstudies.org/.

Crow Swimsaway, Ph.D. Accessed September 20, 2013. http://crowswimsaway.org/.

De Noxeto, Petrus. "The Bull Romanus Pontifex (Nicholas V), January 8, 1455." Native Web, http://www.nativeweb.org/pages/legal/indig-romanus-pontifex.html.

Encyclopedia Britanica Online. "Patria Potestas." Accessed January 16, 2021. http://www.britannica.com/EBchecked/topic/446579/patria-potestas.

Enerio, Butch D. "NPA Rebels Attack Construction Firm, Burns Equipment." *SunStar Philippines*, March 20, 2015. https://www.sunstar.com.ph/article/188.

Espejo, Edwin. "Philippines: Tribal Elder and Son Slain in Bloody Mining Dispute." *Piplinks*, September 5, 2013. http://www.piplinks.org/philippines:-tribal-elder-and-son-slain-bloody-mining-dispute.html.

———. "Soldier, Cafgu Man Slain as Tribal Tension Heats Up." *Rappler*, September 13, 2013. https://www.rappler.com/nation/38831-soldier-cafgu-tribal-tension-davao-del-sur.

"European and Eur-Asian Shamanism: An Exploration of our Shamanic Roots." *Out of the Dark*, July 24, 2004. http://www.outofthedark.com/Shamanism/.

Filipino-American Women's Network. "Spirit, Leadership, Success." Accessed January 16, 2021. http://fawn2005.com/about.html#theme.

Foundation for Shamanic Studies. "Michael Harner, Founder of The Foundation for Shamanic Studies." Accessed January 16, 2021. https://shamanism.org/fssinfo/index.html.

Free Methodist Church (Phils). http://fmc-philippines.blogspot.com/.

Goaynon, Jomorito, Eliza Rose Pangilinan, and Datu Bagal Mauro Mansilyohan. "Banwaon Datus: Mining Interest Leads to Human Rights Violations." *Piplinks*. February 2, 2015. http://www.piplinks.org/banwaon-datus:-mining-interest-leads-human-rights-violations.html.

Ibarra, Omar. "AFP Suffers Eight Casualties in NPA Offensives in Agusan del Sur and Norte." National Democratic Front of the Philippines, August 13, 2014. https://ndfp.org/afp-suffers-eight-casualties-in-npa-offensives-in-agusan-del-sur-agusan-del-norte-2/.

Karu, Yadu. "Sitio Atmurok and Their Practice of Customary Law." *Yadu Karu's Blog.* https://www.yadukaru.com/2014/11/sitio-atmurok-and-their-practice-of.html.

Kay, Sheryl. "The Remedy? A Healing Touch." *Tampa Bay Times*, April 28, 2006. https://www.tampabay.com/archive/2006/04/28/the-remedy-a-healing-touch/.

Limos, Mario Alvaro. "The Fall of the Babaylan: How the Most Powerful Class of Filipinos Came to an End." *Esquire Magazine*, March 18, 2019. https://www.esquiremag.ph/long-reads/features/the-fall-of-the-babaylan-a2017-20190318.

Madden, Cass. "Pope Francis Apologizes to Indigenous Peoples for the 'Grave Sins' of the Church during Colonial Era; Yet Doctrine of Discovery Still Stands." *Cultural Survival*, July 15, 2015. https://www.culturalsurvival.org/news/pope-francis-apologizes-indigenous-peoples-grave-sins-church-during-colonial-era-yet-doctrine.

"New Census Data Shows More Than Four Million Filipinos in the US." *Asian Journal Press*, September 15, 2018. https://www.asianjournal.com/usa/dateline-usa/new-census-data-shows-more-than-four-million-filipinos-in-the-us/.

1904 World's Fair: Looking Back at Looking Forward. "Constructing the Fair." Accessed January 16, 2021. https://mohistory.org/exhibitsLegacy/Fair/WF/HTML/About/.

Nolte, Carl. "400th Anniversary of Spanish Shipwreck: Rough First Landing in Bay Area." *SFGate*, November 14, 1995. https://www.sfgate.com/news/article/400th-Anniversary-Of-Spanish-Shipwreck-Rough-3019121.php.

Peace Corps Philippines. "About." Accessed January 16, 2021. https://www.peacecorps.gov/philippines/about/#:~:text=In%20October%201961%2C%20the%20first,have%20served%20in%20the%20Philippines.&text=Peace%20Corps%20Response%20Volunteers%20also%20serve%20in%20the%20Philippines.

"Pope John Paul II Offers Aborigines an Apology." *Albawaba News*, November 22, 2001. https://www.albawaba.com/news/pope-john-paul-ii-offers-aborigines-apology.

Province of South Cotabato Official Website. Accessed July 7, 2013. https://southcotabato.gov.ph/.

Provincial Government of Agusan del Sur. "Geography of Agusan del Sur." July 2, 2012. http://agusandelsur.gov.ph/index/about-pgas/2011-11-17-16-33-44/2011-08-15-05-52-37/geography-demography.

Rimando, J. A. "11 of 20 Poorest Provinces in South." *Philstar*, December 5, 2011. https://www.philstar.com/nation/2011/12/05/754696/11-20-poorest-provinces-south.

Rusling, General James. "Interview with President William McKinley." *Christian Advocate*, January 22, 1903. http://historymatters.gmu.edu/blackboard/mckinley.html.

Samonte, Pat. "Lumads Flee Homes as War Rages in Agsur." *Business Week Mindanao*, August 22, 2014. https://issuu.com/sudaria_publications/docs/caraga_69354d413991a4.

San Juan, Epifanio, Jr. "U.S. Genocide in the Philippines." *The Epifanio San Juan, Jr. Archive*, August 31, 2006. https://rizalarchive.blogspot.com/2006/08/us-genocide-in-philippines.html.

Summer Institute of Linguistics. "Translation Principles." https://www.sil.org/translation/translation-principles.

Tuwali Ifugao Dictionary. "Lagud." Accessed January 16, 2021. https://tuwali-ifugao.webonary.org/?s=lagud&search=Search&key=&tax=1&match_whole_words=1&displayAdvancedSearch=0.

———. "Liwliwa." Accessed January 16, 2021. https://www.webonary.org/tuwali-ifugao?s=liwliwa&search=Search&key=&tax=-1&match_whole_words=1&displayAdvancedSearchName=0.

University of the Philippines Diliman Babaylan. "UP Babaylan." http://angupbabaylan.blogspot.com/2009/08/our-history_31.html.

US Legal. "Pater Familias Law and legal Definition. Accessed January 21, 2021. http://definitions.uslegal.com/p/pater-familias/.

Westbrook, Laura. "Mabuhay Pilipino! (Long Life!): Filipino Culture in Southeast Louisiana." Louisiana's Living Traditions: Articles and Essays, 2008. http://www.louisianafolklife.org/LT/Articles_Essays/pilipino1.html.

"What Are the 20 Poorest Provinces in the Philippines?" *ABS-CBN News*, March 24, 2016. https://news.abs-cbn.com/focus/v2/03/24/16/what-are-the-20-poorest-provinces-in-the-philippines.

Winkelman, Michel. "Shamanisms and Survival." *Cultural Survival Quarterly Magazine*, June 2003. https://www.culturalsurvival.org/publications/cultural-survival-quarterly/shamanisms-and-survival.

FILM AND AUDIO RECORDINGS

Macy, Terry and Daniel Hart, dir. *White Shamans and Plastic Medicine Men*. Native Voice Public Television, 1996. https://www.youtube.com/watch?v=19JAMhAzXms.

Mora, Manolete, prod. *Utom: Summoning the Spirit: Music in The T'boli Heartland*. Rykodisc/Mickey Hart Series,1995.

Nono, Grace, co-prod. *Kahimunan: Cultural Music of the Manobo, Higaonon and Banwaon of Agusan del Sur*. Quezon City: Tao Foundation for Culture and Arts, 2002.

Nono, Grace, co-prod. *Mendung Sabal: Tudbulul Lunay Mogul: T'boli Hero of Lunay, The Place of Gongs and Music*. Quezon City: Tao Foundation for Culture and Arts, 2002.

Nono, Grace, prod. "Lawang Sebu." In *Tao Music*. Quezon City: BMG Records (Pilipinas), Inc., 1993.
Nono, Grace, co-prod. *The Shared Voice: Chanted and Spoken Narratives from the Philippines*. Pasig City: ANVIL and Fundacion Santiago, 2008.
Nono, Grace, co-prod. *Song of the Babaylan: Living Voices, Medicines, Spiritualities of Philippine Ritualist-Oralist-Healers*. Quezon City: Institute of Spirituality in Asia, 2013.

Index

Page numbers followed by letter *f* refer to figures.

Abubakar, Carmen, 96
Abu-Lughod, Lila, 101–2, 105
abyan (spirit helper, companion, in Visayan), 15; acquiring, 41; and *baylan,* intermingling of voices of, 43–46, 63; and Christian ideas, 50–51, 60; direct communication with, 59–60; experience of being sung through by, 42–43; good vs. bad, 30, 60–61; *gudgod* sung by, 22–23, 26–27, 42; and healing, 27–30, 38; language used by, 47; ontology of, 46; relationship between humans and, 39; sacred mountains protected by, 54; sensing of, 45; summoning of, 46; Undin's reliance on, 19, 20, 21; voices of, 42, 47–48, 49
Aduarte, Diego, 5
Afable, Patricia, 128
Aguilar, Delia, 95
Agusan del Sur, 11*f,* 31*f,* 32; missionaries in, 33, 34; subdivision of, 32; wealth/poverty/violence in, 53
Agusan-Manobo people, 30; ancestral land of, 31*f,* 32; Christianity and, 35, 56–57; colonization and, 32–34, 61–62; language of, 35. See also *baylan*
Ahmed, Leila, 108
almoos (Blaan ritual specialist), 3, 111, 114
ambaling lagi (female-to-male transgender persons, in Blaan), 111–20
ambaling libun (male-to-female transgender persons, in Blaan), 115, 119
American colonization, 5, 33–34, 134; and Blaan identity, 110; and gender relations, 97; resistance to, 68
Anggodon (mumbaki), 135
animal sacrifice: in *baki* (Ifugao ritual), 126, 128, 147, 150, 156, 157; and chicken bile reading, 150, 167, 167*f*; as optional, 147, 173–74; as dramatized at Philadelphia mural unveiling, 160, 161; in *tinandasan* (Manobo traditional house) construction ritual, 56
anthropology: on Native ritual specialists, 5, 137–38; studies of Ifugao people, 5, 137–39; unequal power relations in, 127–28

audio recording: of *baki* ritual, 138, 139, 152, 168–69; of gudgod, 42; of *tau m'ton* songs, 74, 75
Ayag (soul-retrieval ritual, Ifugao), 145, 164–65

babaiyon (woman leader), training as, 59
babaylan: alleged disappearance of, 1, 6, 15; at Bunawan intertribal gathering, 55–58, 57*f*; discourses about, 4–9; of elite vs. real Filipino, 6–7, 68–70; primary vs. secondary, 7–8, 9; as protofeminists, framing of, 2, 6, 15, 67–70, 87, 105, 109, 121; twenty-first century, 1–2; use of term, 3, 4; written vs. oral accounts of, 10
babaylanismo, 68
Bahug (mumbaki), 135
baki (Ifugao ritual): abbreviated, 173; animal sacrifice in, 126, 128, 147, 150, 156, 157; anthropologists' approach to, 137; after Buwaya's death, 154, 155–57; community division over, 153, 154; curses in, 147, 158, 175; deities' names recited at, 159; hybridization of, 169–71; impact of Christianization on, 135, 139, 140; *liyah* (initiation) into, 149–50, 168, 169; location of, importance of, 152; mastery of, path to, 149–52, 169; Native class hierarchies and, 138; and neoshamanism, 175; performance in the United States, 123–30, 131*f,* 172–73; recording technology and, 139, 152, 168–69; and relational voice, 174–75; "silent," 172; terrace farming and, 136; trance possession during, 126, 174–75; translocality of, 152, 167; U.S.-Ifugao exchanges and, 168–69
Ballangi, Evangeline, 135
Banaue rice terraces, 136, 143
Barthes, Roland, 44
Barton, Roy Franklin, 5, 137, 171
baylan (Agusan-Manobo ritual specialist), 3; and *abyan,* intermingling of voices of, 43–46, 63; author's encounters with, 14, 15–16; characteristics of, 41; and Christians, listening between, 57–58; continued

231

baylan (*Continued*)
patronage of, 35; conversion to Christianity, 15, 34–35; educated Manobos' attitudes toward, 35; experience of being sung through by *abyan*, 42–43; female, marginalization of, 54–56; healing by, 27–30, 37, 38, 48, 52–53, 54; and *henghong* (heaving sound signifying the spirit helper's release from the ritual specialist's body), 27, 46; listening during *gudgod,* 45, 49; as maternal nurse (midwife), 40, 41, 48; missionaries' position on, 50–51; obligations of, 41; *panumanan* ritual performed by, 21–30; path to becoming, 39–41; poverty of, 54; pre-colonization, 32, 33; reliance on *abyan* (spirit helper), 19, 20, 21; respect for, 41; self-introduction through song *(tod-om),* 16–20

Blaan people, 110; *almoos* (ritual specialists) of, 3, 111, 114; arranged marriage among, 112; dispossession of, 110; history of, 110; sex designations among, 115; transgender persons among, 111–20. See also *nugaru*

Black Womanists, 106

Blagay, Tuning, 91

Blanc-Szanton, Cristina, 68, 97

body: of *abyan,* 46; malleable, 64; permeable, 44–45, 174

Bowers, George, 5

Bowman, Jen, 163

Boyer, Kimberly, 160–61

boyos (mixed gender persons, in T'boli), 66–67, 119

Brewer, Carolyn, 5, 67, 96–97

Buenconsejo, José, 20, 43

Bunawan, 31*f,* 32; intertribal gathering in, 55–58, 57*f;* Protestant missionaries in, 34

Butler, Judith, 107, 120

Butuan, 31*f;* Protestant missionaries in, 34; Spanish conquest of, 32–33

Buyanderger, Manduhai, 105

Calvino, Italo, 44

Camagay, Maria Luisa, 68

Candelario, Huwan, 135, 155, 155*f,* 176; Lawet performed by, 156–57

Capeon, Elia Cansing, 109, 110, 113, 115, 116

Capeon, Mining, 114–15, 121

capitalism: and gender relations, 70, 99–100; and land as commodity, 99

Caraga region, 31*f,* 32; natural resources of, 53; poverty and violence in, 53

Casal, G. S., 96

Catholicism: and gender ideology, 96–97; Spanish colonization and, 33; tolerance of Indigenous traditions, 60, 98, 135

Cavarero, Adriana, 44

Cavender, Andree, 162

Cayong-Abayao, Aleta and Allen, 125, 127

chicken bile reading, 150, 167, 167*f,* 174

Christianity: and Agusan-Manobo identity, 56–57; and Blaan identity, 110; conversion of *baylan* to, 15, 34–35; and diminishing power of *abyan,* 39; and gender ideology, 96–98; and Ifugao identity, 134–35, 139, 140; and Indigenous traditions, reconciliation of, 60, 61, 62; missionaries and spread of, 33, 34; and persecution of Native ritual specialists, 1, 5; and T'boli identity, 96–98; and translations of Native rituals, 49

class status: and *baki* (Ifugao ritual), 138; increasing divisions based on, 51, 55, 77, 78, 100; of Native ritual specialists, 3–4, 7, 8, 69, 77, 131, 138; race/gender and, intersecting oppressions of, 106–7, 144

Coguit, Ebeng, 21*f,* 55

Coguit, Robilyn, 10, 21*f;* on *abyan* (spirit helpers), 30, 41, 54, 60–61; *abyan* of, communication with, 59–60; *baylan* lineage of, 16, 34; at Bunawan intertribal gathering, 55–58, 57*f;* Christianity and Indigenous traditions reconciled by, 60, 61, 62; on education, impact of, 36; as embroiderer, 1, 58, 59; grandfather of, 34, 45, 61; at International Women's Month celebrations in Manila, 1–2; in Manila, 58–59; training as *babaiyon* (woman leader), 59; on *yagong* (voice), 42

colonization/colonialism: discourses associated with, 4; feminism and, 7, 69, 97; and feminization, 171–72; impact on Agusan-Manobo people, 31–34, 61–62; impact on Blaan people, 110; impact on Ifugao people, 133–34, 140; impact on T'boli people, 90–91, 93, 96–98, 99, 106; renaming as strategy of, 139; voice transformed by, 2. *See also* American colonization; resistance; Spanish colonization

Compton, Ramona, 145–46

Conklin, Bruce, 125, 127, 128

Conklin, Harold, 123, 127; *baki* ritual after death of, 123–30; Ifugao research assistant of, 123, 127, 138–39; Lagitan's feelings toward, 127–28; on *mumbaki* (Ifugao ritual specialist), 137–38

Connor, Steven, 44–45

Cooper, Betty, 9

INDEX   233

Covid-19 pandemic, 176
Cox, Don, 145
Coy, Tom, 145, 171
curses: in *baki* (Ifugao ritual), 147, 158, 175; punishment for, 61

Datu Tagleong (Agusan-Manobo supreme chief and *baylan*), 34, 45, 61
Daughtry, Martin, 174–75
demsu fankiton (water ritual, Blaan), 116
Dinumla, Herman, 135
diwateros/diwathan (people entered into by *abyan*), 41, 45, 46
Doctrine of Discovery, 4, 32
Dolar, Mladen, 44
Dulawan, Lourdes, 138
Dulnuan, Hospicio, 153, 160, 168, 169
duwaya practice (polygyny), among T'boli, 92–94, 96, 103

education: impact on Native peoples, 35, 36, 91–92, 93, 98; missionaries and, 98, 134
El-Solh, Camillia Fawzi, 95, 96, 100
Engels, Frederick, 70
Errington, Shelley, 70, 73
Esterik, Penny, 52

false consciousness, 101–2
Farley, Margaret, 87
Fee, Mary, 97
Feliciano, Myrna, 67
feminism: and colonialism, 7, 69, 97; on gender complementarity, 87; and voice, reclamation of term, 2; Western, critique of, 105; white, vs. Black Womanists, 106; white, vs. Native American perspective, 106–7; women babaylan associated with, 2, 6, 15, 67–70, 87, 105, 109, 121
feminization, colonization and, 171–72
Fikan, Biho, 90, 101
Filipino(s): colonial division into "civilized" and "wild," 34; discrimination against Igorots, 140, 161; immigration to Americas, 141–42; origins of term, 139
Flang, Mariafe, 90, 91, 92, 100
Freay, Gunintang, 64, 113, 117f; challenges experienced by, 118; different sense of identity and freedom, 121; lifestory of, 114–15; *malem* (song) of, 111, 113–14, 116; voice of, compared to Mendung's voice, 116–18; and water ritual, 116
Free Methodism, in Agusan, 34
Friedson, Steven, 53

Garza, Mechi, 146
gender: collapsing into continuum of sonic relations, 63; equality of, babaylan as symbol of, 2, 6, 7; fluid, of spirit helper, impact on ritual specialist, 112, 119; of Native ritual specialists, 3, 148–49; private property and stratification of, 70; as relational, 107, 120, 148–49; of T'boli *boyos*, 66–67; voices denoting, in *Tudbulul* epic, 63, 71–73, 107. *See also* gender complementarity; gender ideologies; transgenderism; women
gender complementarity, among T'boli, 67, 71; and inequality, 83, 86–87, 90–94; Mendung and, 107; questioning of, 73; *Tudbulul* epic on, 83
gender ideologies: capitalism and, 70, 99–100; Christianity and, 96–98; definition of, 74; Islam and, 95, 108; oral performances as codifications of, 74; Spanish colonization and, 96–97; T'boli, 77, 79, 81, 88–94, 106; in *Tudbulul* epic, 76–81, 83–84, 95, 100, 102
gonob (food invocation, in Ifugao), 128–29
Gonzalez, Michelle, 87
gopah (oral chants, in Ifugao), 165–66
Groesbeck, Walter and Gertrude, 34
gudgod (spirit song that traces the cause and origin of a person's illness and discovers answers and solutions to questions and problems), 22–23, 26–27, 42; *baylan's* experience of, 42–43; as condition of voice, 45; as embodied technology, 52; missionary perspective on, 35, 51; voices of *abyan* in, 42, 47–48
Guerrero, Milagros, 68
Gulae, Bie, 64, 110–13, 117f; challenges experienced by, 118; different sense of identity and freedom, 121; lifestory of, 111–13; *magin* (spirit helper) of, 111, 112–13; *malem* (song) of, 111, 116; on *nugaru* vocation and transgenderism, 115; and water ritual, 116

Halupe (Ifogan deities), 159, 160
hapet (voice, in Ifugao): evolution of, 148, 166; relationality of, 174–75
Harner, Michael, 146
Havana, Florencia, 10, 15, 21f; on *abyan* (spirit helpers), 30, 39; on *baylan,* respect for, 41; on conversion of *baylan* to Christianity, 34; interpretation of Undin's *gudgod,* 48; and Manobo language teaching, 35, 36; missionary view of, 50–51; translations by, 47, 49–50

Havana, Jose, 10, 15, 21*f*; as *baylan,* 15, 38; on *baylan-abyan* relationship, 46; on conversion of *baylan* to Christianity, 34; on experience of being sung through by *abyan,* 42–43, 45; interpretation of Undin's *gudgod,* 48; missionary bias of, 50–51; participation in *panumanan,* 22, 24, 26, 27; translations by, 22, 47, 49–50

healing: *baylan* (Agusan-Manobo ritual specialist) and, 27–30, 37, 38, 48, 52–53, 54; blending of traditions in, 146, 162–65, 170, 173, 176; *mumbaki* (Ifugao ritual specialist) and, 162–65; neo-shamanism and, 146; *nungaru* (Blaan persons who know) and, 111; relational voice and, 52–53, 58; shamanism associated with, 8; *tau m'ton bu* (T'boli ritual specialist) and, 86

health care system, inadequacy of, and *baylan*'s role, 37, 38, 41

henghong (heaving sound signifying the spirit helper's release from the ritual specialist's body), 27, 46

hilot (healer through blood vessel, nerve, and musculoskeletal manipulation), 37, 41

Hinogwakan (Ifugao deity), 126, 155, 156–57

hooks, bell, 2, 12

house(s): of Blaan *nungaru* (persons who know), 121; Ifugao traditional, building in the United States, 167; Manobo traditional *(tinandasan),* construction ritual for, 55, 56–57

Hudhud (Ifugao chant), 136

hungol (listening, in T'boli), to *Tudbulul* epic, 71–73

hybridized traditions: Catholic missionaries and, 98; healing, 146, 162–65, 170, 173, 176; transnational *mumbaki* and, 162, 163, 169–71

Ifugao, 123; anthropological studies of, 5, 137; Christianization and, 134–35, 139, 140; colonization and, 133–34, 140; global tourism and, 136, 139; and Native Americans, shared histories of, 142, 145, 146, 154; pantheon of spirits/deities, 126, 135, 137; province of, 11*f,* 132, 133*f*; relations with other tribes, 132–33; rice terracing traditions of, 136, 143; ritual specialists among, 3; woodworking tradition of, 139. *See also baki; mumbaki*

Ifugao Center for Living Culture, 176

Igorots (Igorrotes), 133, 140; vs. Filipinos, 140, 161; at St. Louis World Fair, 141

Inajow (spirit), 28, 29, 48, 52
Incashola, Tony, 9
International Women's Month celebrations, 1
Islam: arrival in Philippines, 95–96; and gender ideologies, 95, 108

Jakobsen, Marete, 169, 172, 173, 174
Javier, D., 96
Jenks, Albert Ernest, 5
Jesuits, in Agusan, 33
Jocano, F. Landa, 52
Johnson, Sylvester, 134

kahimunan (Agusan-Manobo ritual, assembly, feast), 41
Kapchan, Deborah, 51
Kasaw, Danilo, 90, 101
Kawig, Ungoy "Mafok," 98
kinaraan (Visayan settler songs), 42
Kindipan (mumbaki), 168
kolaimni (healing method), 146, 163, 170
Koskoff, Ellen, 74, 83, 104
Kramer, Paul Alexander, 140

Laderman, Carol, 52
Lagitan. *See* Tindongan, Mamerto "Lagitan"
lands, ancestral: of Agusan-Manobo people, 31*f,* 32; of Blaan people, loss of, 110; colonization and, 34; discursive confinement of ritual specialists to, 9, 12; rich mineral deposits of, 53, 54; as spirit helpers' dwellings, 54; of T'boli people, loss of, 99, 106

language(s): linguistic and extralinguistic aspects of, 52; non-Indigenous, continued dominance of, 35; reduction of music to, protests against, 49

La Paz, 31*f,* 32; education in, 58–59; encounter with baylan in, 15–16; health care system in, inadequacy of, 37, 41; pastors in, 15; poverty in, 53

Lawet (Ifugao ritual): after Buwaya's burial, 154, 155–57; after Conklin's death, 123–30, 131*f,* 157

Legazpi, Miguel López de, 33, 94

Lemlunay (place of justice, fairness, peace, contentment, and celebration, in T'boli), 66, 82, 108

lihol (voice, in T'boli), 63; gender shifts in, 63; Mendung's, 75

limpas buya (Agusan-Manobo ritual to receive the spirit, to diagnose, to heal; also to fulfill the promise of offerings, that is, in exchange for healing), 30, 53

lingon (song, in T'boli), 63
listening: by *baylan,* during *gudgod,* 45, 49; between pastors and *baylan,* 57–58; different modes of, 48–49; during *gudgod,* discrepancies in, 47–51; as site of ambiguity/multiplicity, 51; sustained dialogue and, 177; to *Tudbulul* epic, gender distinction in, 71–73; to voices of Native ritual specialists, 14
liwliwa chanting session, Ifugao, 153–54
liyah (initiation), into *baki* priesthood, 149–50, 168, 169
Loarca, Miguel de, 94
Lorde, Audre, 105

Mabro, Judy, 95, 96, 100
Mabungot (Ifogan deities), 159, 160
magin (also *to magin,* spirit helper, in Blaan), 111; Bie's, 111, 112–13; gender of, impact on *nungaru,* 112, 119
Maguindanao: acceptance of American sovereignty, 96; relations with T'boli, 95; ritual specialists among, 3
Mahmood, Saba, 101, 102, 104, 122
Maibuyan (city of the dead, in Manobo), 48, 49
maknongan (Ifugao deities/spirits), 126, 135, 137; mobility/translocality of, 152; silent calls to, 173; summoning of, 126, 138, 141, 147, 151, 155
malem (song, in Blaan), 111, 113–14
Mananzan, Mary John, 6, 67, 97
Mangahas, Fe, 6, 67, 68, 95
Manguwan, Milin, 90, 100, 102
Manobo: increasing abandonment of ancestral ways, 39; kuntoon language of, 15, 35; pre-colonization, 32–33; ritual specialists among, 3, 14; and traditional healers, decision to consult, 37–38. *See also* Agusan-Manobo people
Mansmann, Rex, 98
marriage: arranged, among Blaan, 112, 118; arranged, among T'boli, 78, 80–81, 83, 84–85, 86, 88, 94, 103; to multiple wives (*duwaya* practice), among T'boli, 92–94, 96, 103
Marx, Karl, 70
McClintock, Anne, 171
midwife, *baylan* as, 40, 41
Mihesuah, Devon Abbott, 106–7
Mikdong (spirit), 47–48, 52
Minor, Patricia, 146, 147–48
missionaries: and Blaan identity, 110; Catholic, Spanish colonization and, 33; and Ifugao people, 134–35; medical missions by, 38; Protestant, American colonization and, 34; in T'boli lands, 98
Mohanty, Chandra, 105
Montillo-Burton, Linda, 37–38
Mora, Manolete, 64, 71, 73, 95, 98
Moro sultanates, American colonization and, 33, 96, 134
mumbaki (Ifugao ritual specialist), 3; anthropologists on, 5, 137–38; ethnography of two generations of, 12, 151; healing by, 162–65; path to becoming, 138–39, 141; physical mobility of, 131; and possession trance, 126, 174–75; relational mobility of, 131–32; transnational, 123, 128, 132, 166; voice of, 126. *See also* Tindongan, Mamerto "Lagitan"
mungopah (gopah chanter), Ifugao, 165
music: reduction to language, protests against, 49; T'boli, patterns of gender difference in, 71; Western, vs. Philippine Indigenous traditions, 36. *See also* song(s)

Native Americans: and Ifugao, shared histories of, 142, 145, 146, 154; and neo-shamanism, 145–46; racist vs. sexist oppression of, 106–7; rituals of, blending with Ifugao rituals, 163, 171
Native ritual specialists, Filipino. *See* ritual specialists
neo-shamanism: abbreviated ritual in, 173; *baki* (Ifugao ritual) and, 175; critiques of, 149; as highly individualized process, 169; Lagitan and, 145–49, 169, 172, 173, 174; Native Americans and, 145–46; silence in, 172
Nolan, George, 98
Nono, Grace: dissertation defense of, 128; engagement with Native ritual specialists, 10, 14, 15–16; and Lagitan, 128, 153; launch of book by, 163–64, 165; mother of, 14–15, 35
nungaru (persons who know, in Blaan), 12, 63–64, 111; different sense of identity and freedom, 121; female-to-male transgender, 12, 63–64, 109, 115; gendered voices of, 116–18; healing practice of, 111; introduction to, 109; *magin*'s gender and, 112, 119

Ofong, Diwa, 92
ohag (chant, in Ifugao), 138
Oknabanon (spirit), 22, 47, 48, 49–50, 52
Ottengan (mumbaki), 138

Pagaddut, Jose "Nabbud," 155, 156, 176
paghilwas (articulation), 22; discrepancies in, 47, 49–51

palayah (chant to close the altar), Ifugao, 129–30
paminog (listening), during *gudgod*, 45; discrepancies in, 47–51
Panditaratne, Dinusha, 97
panumanan (Agusan-Manobo ritual observance), 21–30, 40*f*; missionary perspective on, 35
pa'o (Ifugao female priesthood), 172
Papa Isio (Visayan babaylan and anticolonial resistance leader), 6
Paris, Treaty of (1898), 34
patriarchal norms: Catholicism and, 97; internalization of, 101; Western influences and, 70
Pensionado Act, 141
Perez, Hiram, 120
Philip II (King of Spain), 33, 139
Philippine-American War, 134, 141; memorial to honor martyrs of, 160
Philippine Revolution, 33, 134
Philippines: independence of, 142; map of, 11*f*
Piang, Datu, 96
pig-aha dinpuli (being watched by spirit), 43, 44, 59
pigyunaan (being entered into by spirit), 43
Placensia, Juan de, 5
Pondog, Lita, 21*f*
possession trance: Agusan-Manobo *baylan* and, 43, 44; Ifugao *mumbaki* and, 126, 174–75
Potenciano, Lordina "Undin," 10, 15, 21*f*; on *abyan*, diminishing power of, 39; on *abyan* as person, 46; *abyan* of, different voices of, 42, 47–48; at Bunawan intertribal gathering, 55, 56; composure of, 15; death of, 61; evolution as singer, 42; hardship experienced by, 20, 21; healing by, 27–30, 48, 53; as maternal nurse (midwife), 40, 41, 48; negotiation with neocolonial realities in rituals of, 61–62; *panumanan* ritual performed by, 21–30, 40*f*; path to baylanhood, 39–41; reliance on *abyan* (spirit helper), 19, 20, 21; self-introduction through song *(tod-om)*, 16–20; *tinandasan* construction ritual performed by, 56–57; as *yagong*anon, 42
poverty: of *baylan*, 54; of Indigenous Peoples, 53
prayers, as therapeutic instruments, 52
Preciado, Beatriz, 120
private property: and gender stratification, 70; introduction of idea of, 33, 34
Protestant missionaries: American colonization and, 34; and gender relations, 97
Puchung (Ifugao guardian deities), 158, 159

Pugong (mumbaki), 135
Pula, Myrna, 12, 64, 66, 103*f*; author's acquaintance with, 73–74; commentary on *Tudbulul* epic, 74, 80, 82, 95, 101, 103–4; on education, 92; on gender complementarity/inequality, 87, 88–89, 94, 96; lifestory of, 88–89, 93; as Mendung's interpreter, 75, 105–6; on Mendung's *Tudbulul* performance, 71; at mission school, 98; on T'boli dispossession, 99; on T'boli women working overseas, 91; and transgender ritual specialists, introduction to, 109, 110

Q'ero tradition, 146, 147, 148, 163, 175
Quintilian, 44

Rafael, Vicente, 51
Ramos, Alcida, 149
recording technology: and *baki* ritual, 139, 152, 168–69; of gudgod, 42; and *tau m'ton* songs, 74, 75
reiki, 147
relational gender, 107, 120, 148–49
relational listening, 58
relational mobility, of Native ritual specialists, 131–32
relational voice, 45; *baki* (Ifugao ritual) and, 174–75; and gender shifts, 63; and healing, 52–53, 58; negotiation between ritual specialist and spirit helper and, 116–18
resistance, to colonization: Agusan-Manobo and, 33; babaylan as symbol of, 5, 6–7, 68, 69; Ifugao and, 134
Rico, Luciana, 201
rice terraces, Ifugao, 136, 143
ritual specialists, Native: age of, 3; and ancestral lands, discursive confinement to, 12; anthropologists on, 5, 137–38; author's engagement with, 10; beneficent roles of, 1; class status of, 3–4, 7, 8, 69, 77, 131, 138; composure of, 15; discursive erasure of, 1, 5–6, 7; gender of, 3; hegemonic constructions about, 4–7, 122, 177; loss of individual identity and freedom, 121; as oral singers and speakers, 2; physical mobility of, 131; psychological state associated with, 8; relational mobility of, 131–32; subjection to spirit, 122; terms for, 3; younger generation of, 121. *See also* babaylan; women, ritual specialists
Rivera, Aida Navidad, 162
Rodil, Rudy Buhay, 34
Romulo, Carlos P., 161
Roseman, Marina, 44

INDEX

Ross, Susan, 87
Ruether, Rosemary Radford, 87

Sabal, Datu, 66, 77, 85–86, 92, 104
Sabal, Flor, 93
Sabal, Frankie, 91, 92, 93
Sabal, Joanna, 93
Sabal, Manolete, 92
Sabal, Mendung, 12, 63, 72*f*; author's acquaintance with, 73–74; gendered voice of, 63, 71–73, 107; healing practice of, 86; initiation into *tau m'ton bu* vocation, 64–66; interpreter of, 75, 105–6; on Lemlunay (place of justice), 66, 82, 108; multiple roles of, 64; physical appearance of, 64; recording of songs of, 74, 75; on singing process, 74; status of, 77, 92, 104; *tau munung* (spirit helpers) of, 66, 74, 75; *Tudbulul* performance by, 63, 71–73, 74, 75–83, 102, 104, 107; *tutul kemo ke taum* (lifestory) of, 84–86; voice of, compared to Gunintang's voice, 116–18; and women's rights, support for, 104
Sagan, Lucita, 91
Salazar, Zeus, 67, 69
Sande, Francisco de, 94
Santa Cruz mission, 98
Santos, Ramon, 36
Scott, William Henry, 133
Sebu, Lake, 64, 65*f*
sexuality, and ritual specialization, 109
shamanism: as mental state, 8; Western discourses on, 8–9. *See also* neo-shamanism
Sheppard, Susan, 146
Shining Bearheart, Bekki, 146
silent *baki*, 172–73
Silva, Eliseo Art, 159–62
Smith, Andrea, 120, 170
song(s): internal commingling of voices in, 43–46, 63; *kinaraan*, 42; *lingon*, 63; *malem*, 111, 113–14; and Monobo language teaching, 35, 36; self-introduction through, 16–20, 111; *tod-om*, 16–20, 42; writing down, advantages and disadvantages of, 36. *See also gudgod* (spirit song)
soul-retrieval ceremony: Ifugao *(Ayag)*, 145, 164–65; neo-shamanic, 145–46
sound: importance in ritual, 173; and voice, relationship of, 42, 43–44
South Cotabato, 11*f*, 64, 65*f*
Spanish colonization: and gender ideology, 96–97; and Ifugao people, 133–34; and persecution of Native ritual specialists, 4–5, 68; resistance to, women ritual specialists and, 5, 6–7, 68

spirits: Native North American, 146; Native ritual specialists' subjection to, 122; T'boli pantheon of, 66–67. *See also abayan; magin; maknongan; tau munung*
Stanyukovich, Maria, 136
St. Louis World Fair, Igorots at, 141
Strobel, Leny Mendoza, 7–8
Swimsaway, Crow, 146

Taft, William Howard, 134
Tagleong (Agusan-Manobo supreme chief and *baylan*), 34, 45, 61
Talking Back (hooks), 2, 12
talo (voice, in Blaan), 111, 116
tanog (sound, in Manobo), and *yagong* (voice), relationship of, 42, 43–44
Tapnajanon (spirit), 48
tau m'ton bu (T'boli ritual specialist), 12, 64; gender shifts in voice of, 63; initiation of, 64–66; multiple roles of, 64; women, limitations placed on, 89. *See also* Sabal, Mendung
tau munung (spirit helper, in T'boli), 63; Mendung's, 66, 74, 75; summoning of, 75
Tawan, Luming, 92, 101
Tawede, Aylo and Julia, 55, 56, 57*f*
T'boli people, 103*f*; arranged marriage among, 78, 80–81, 83, 84–85, 86, 88, 94, 103; Christian influences on, 96–98; dispossession of, 99, 106; *duwaya* practice (polygyny) among, 92–94, 96, 103; gender complementarity/plurality among, 67, 71, 73, 83, 86–87; gender ideology of, 77, 79, 81, 88–94, 106; homeland of, 64, 65*f*; impact of education on, 91–92, 93, 98; impact of Visayan settlers on, 90–91, 93; loss of ancestral lands, 99; Muslim neighbors of, influence of, 95–96; pantheon of spirits, 66–67; ritual specialists among, 3, 12, 64; tourism boom and, 99. *See also tau m'ton bu; Tudbulul* epic; women, T'boli
tinandasan (Manobo traditional house), 55; construction ritual for, 56–57
Tindongan, Amihan, 159, 162, 167, 167*f*
Tindongan, Bruno "Buwaya," 12, 140, 151*f*, 173; as Conklin's Ifugao language teacher and informant, 123, 127, 138–39, 140–41; exchange of knowledge with son, 151; and Lagitan's initiation into *baki* priesthood, 149–50; Lawet performed after burial of, 154, 155–57; path to becoming *mumbaki*, 138–39, 141; photographic memory of, 152; wake and funeral for, 153–54, 155*f*, 174

238   INDEX

Tindongan, Cynthia (White), 140, 144
Tindongan, Joannah, 140
Tindongan, Malaya, 173
Tindongan, Mamerto "Lagitan," 12; activities in Ohio, 157–59; on anthropology, unequal power relations in, 127–28; author's introduction to, 153; *baki* ritual performed by, 123–30, 131*f*, 157; blending of traditions in ritual practice of, 162, 163, 169–71; experience of mobility, 132; at father's wake and funeral, 153–54, 155*f*; feelings of alienation, 143; gender identity of, changes in, 148–49, 171–72; *gonob* (food invocation) by, 128–29; healing methods of, 146, 162–65, 170, 173, 176; and Ifugao Center for Living Culture, 176; illness of, 143–44, 175, 176; immigration to the United States, 140, 143–44; and individualized process of *baki* mastery, 169; lifestory of, 139–41, 143, 171; *liyah* (initiation) into *baki* priesthood, 149–50, 168, 169; modifications of traditional Ifugao rituals, 158, 159, 166, 172–75; and neo-shamanism, 145–49, 169, 172, 173, 174; *palayah* (chant to close the altar) by, 129–30; path to *baki* mastery, 149–52; physical appearance of, 150, 153, 172; public performances by, 159–62, 163, 165, 166; Q'ero tradition and, 146, 147, 148, 163, 175; ritual modalities used by, 152–53; silent *baki* of, 172–73; soul-retrieval ceremony by, 163–65; spirit helpers of, 146, 163; as transnational *mumbaki*, 123, 128, 132; visits to Ifugao, 168; voice *(hapet)* of, evolution of, 148, 166; wood sculpture of, 165
Tindongan, Pedro, 150, 155, 156, 157, 168
Tindongan, Torin, 167
tod-om (song): crossing over to *gudgod* (spirit song), 22–23; effect of attracting spirits' attention, 46; as sung by *yagong*anon, 42; Undin's, 16–20
Tomlinson, Gary, 44
Tordesillas, Treaty of, 32
tourism: in Ifugao lands, 136, 139; in T'boli lands, 99
trade, pre-colonization, 32–33
transgenderism, ritual: Blaan *nungaru* and, 12, 63–64, 109, 115; discourses on, 3, 6, 109, 118
transgender persons: *boyos,* among T'boli, 66–67, 119; female-to-male *(ambaling lagi),* among Blaan, 111–20; *magin* (spirit helper) and, 112, 119; male-to-female *(ambaling libun),* among Blaan, 115, 119

Tudbulul epic: Biho's performance of, 90; composition of, 75; and *duwaya* practice, 93–94; gendered voices in performance of, 63, 71–73, 107; gender relations in, 76–81, 83–84, 95, 100, 102; importance to T'boli people, 74, 100–101, 106; Mendung's lifestory compared to, 86; Mendung's performance of, 63, 71–73, 74, 75–83, 102, 104, 107; Milin's performance of, 100, 102; Myrna's commentary on, 74, 80, 82, 95, 101, 103–4; renditions of, 102; T'boli women's experience and understandings of, 100–104, 106
Tungay, Mina, 90–91, 92

Undin. *See* Potenciano, Lordina "Undin"
United States: annexation of Philippine islands by, 5, 33–34, 134; *baki* ritual in, 123–30, 131*f*, 172–73; Filipino immigration to, 141–42; Lagitan's immigration to, 140, 143–44; resistance to occupation by, 68; transnational *mumbaki* in, 123, 128. *See also* American colonization
usiba (Agusan-Monobo entertainment), 36

Valentine, David, 119
Villero, Ofelia, 7, 69
violence, against women, 80, 83, 101, 103
Visayan settlers: impact on T'boli society, 90–91, 93; ritual specialists among, 3; songs of *(kinaraan),* 42
voice(s): of *abyan* (spirit helper), 42, 47–48, 49; of *baylan* (Agusan-Manobo ritual specialist), 22, 23, 25, 51, 52; Blaan term for, 111; chorus of, 178; and cultural reinforcement, 2; embodies singularity of, Western perspective on, 44, 45; gendered, in *Tudbulul* epic performance, 63, 71–73, 107; gendered, Blaan transgender *nungaru* and, 116–18; *gudgod* (spirit song) as condition of, 45; Ifugao term for, 148, 166; internal commingling of, in song, 43–46, 63; Manobo term for, 42; Mendung's, compared to Gunintang's, 116–18; of *mumbaki* (Ifugao ritual specialist), 126; Native, colonization and transformation of, 2; of Native ritual specialists, listening to, 14; overlapping selves projected through, 174–75; permeable, conceptions of, 45; T'boli term for, 63; term reclaimed by feminists, 2. *See also* relational voice

Wenger, Tisa, 137
Wesling, Meg, 97, 98

Western influence: vs. Indigenous healing practices, 38–39; in music, vs. Philippine Indigenous traditions, 36; and patriarchal/patrilineal arrangements, 70
White, Cynthia, 140, 144
Williams, Delores, 106
witches, babaylan equated with, 1, 2, 4–5
women: depiction in *Tudbulul* epic, 76–81, 83–84; education and, 92; high status in precolonial time, claims regarding, 67–68, 94–95; power of, babaylan as symbol of, 2, 6, 7, 67, 68–69; Third World, discursive colonization of, 105; violence against, 80, 83, 101, 103
women, ritual specialists, 3; charges of witchcraft against, 1, 2, 4–5; marginalization of, 54–55; persecution by colonizers, 4–5; as protofeminists, portrayal of, 2, 6, 15, 67–70, 87, 105, 109, 121; and resistance against colonizers, 5, 6–7, 68
women, T'boli, 103*f*; arranged marriages of, 78, 80–81, 83, 84–85, 86, 88, 94, 103; capitalism and, 99; limitations on, 89; responses to *Tudbulul* epic, 100–104, 106; status of, 77, 79, 100; work overseas, 91, 99–100
World Health Organization, on Indigenous practices, 37
World Wildlife Fund, 143

yagong (voice, in Manobo): of *baylan*, changes during ritual, 22, 23, 25; commingling with *abyan*'s voice(s), 43–46, 63; effect of attracting spirits' attention, 46; and *tanog* (sound), 42, 43–44; use of term, 42
*yagong*anon, 42
yuna (possession trance), 43, 44